Anti-money Laundering and C

Anti-money Laundering and Counter-terrorism Financing Law and Policy

Nijhoff Law Specials

VOLUME 97

The titles published in this series are listed at *brill.com/nlsp*

Anti-money Laundering and Counter-terrorism Financing Law and Policy

Showcasing Australia

By

Anne Imobersteg Harvey

BRILL
NIJHOFF

LEIDEN | BOSTON

The Library of Congress Cataloging-in-Publication Data is available online at http://catalog.loc.gov

Typeface for the Latin, Greek, and Cyrillic scripts: "Brill". See and download: brill.com/brill-typeface.

ISSN 0924-4549
ISBN 978-90-04-35909-3 (hardback)
ISBN 978-90-04-35910-9 (e-book)

This book is printed on acid-free paper and produced in a sustainable manner.

Contents

Tables

Abbreviations and Acronyms

AMLD	Directive of the European Parliament and of the Council amending Directive on the prevention of the use of the financial system for the purposes of money laundering or terrorist financing, 2015
ACC	Australian Crime Commission
ACC Act	*Australian Crime Commission Act 2002* (Cth)
ACT	Australian Capital Territory
ADJR Act	*Administrative Decisions (Judicial Review) Act 1977* (Cth)
AFP	Australian Federal Police
AML/CTF	Anti-money laundering and counter-terrorism financing
AML/CTF Act	*Anti-Money Laundering and Counter-Terrorism Financing Act* 2006 (Cth)
AUD	Australian dollar
AUSTRAC	Australian Transaction Reports and Analysis Centre
CBA	Commonwealth Bank of Australia
CBM-BNI	Cross-border movements of bearer negotiable instruments
CBM-PC	Cross-border movements of physical currency
CDD	Customer due diligence
CDPP	Commonwealth Director of Public Prosecutions
CEO	Chief Executive Officer
CFSP	Common Foreign and Security Policy
CFI	Court of First Instance of CJEU
CJEU	Court of Justice of the European Union
CFT	Countering the financing of terrorism (FATF and UN terminology)
CTF	Counter-terrorism financing (Australian terminology)
COE	Council of Europe, Strasbourg
CFD	Council Framework Decision
CODE	*Criminal Code* (Cth)
CODEXTER	CoE Committee of experts on terrorism
COTUNA	*Charter of the United Nations Act 1945* (Cth)
DTA	*Drug Trafficking Act 1994* (Cth)
ECHR	European Convention for the Protection of Human Rights and Fundamental Freedoms

ECtHR	European Court of Human Rights, Strasbourg
ECJ	European Court of Justice, Luxembourg
ECOSOC	United Nations Economic and Social Council
EP	European Parliament
EU	European Union
EUR	Euro
European Charter	*Charter of Fundamental Rights of the European Union*
European Council	Heads of State or Government of the EU Member States, together with its President and the President of the Commission
FBI	USA Federal Bureau of Investigation
FinCEN	Financial Crimes Enforcement Network (USA)
FTRA	*Financial Transaction Reports Act 1988*
GBP	British pound (currency)
HCA	High Court of Australia
HRC	UN Human Rights Committee
ICCPR	International Covenant on Civil and Political Rights
IFTIS	International funds transfer instructions
IMF	International Monetary Fund
INSLM	Independent National Security Legislation Monitor
ISIL	Islamic State in Iraq and the Levant
KYC	*know-your-customer*
FATF	Financial Action Task Force
LCA	Law Council of Australia
Merida Convention	UN *Convention against Corruption* (UNCAC), 2349 UNTS 41
ML/TF	Money laundering and terrorism financing
NSW	New South Wales
NT	Northern Territory
OECD	Organisation for Economic Co-operation and Development
OLAF	European Anti-Fraud Office (Office européen de lutte anti-fraude)
OJ	Official Journal of the EU
Palermo Convention	UN *Convention against Transnational Organised Crime* (UNTOC), 2000, 225 UNTS 20
POAC	Proscribed Organisations Appeal Commission is the specialist body set up by the UK Parliament to hear and determine appeals brought against decisions proscribing, or refusing to lift the proscription

	of, organisations regarded as terrorist by the Home Secretary
PNR	Passenger Name Record
POAC	Proscribed Organisations Appeal Commission (UK)
POCA	*Proceeds of Crime Act* (Cth)
RBA	Risk-based approach
Rec	Recommendation
RICO	*Racketeer Influenced and Corrupt Organizations Act* (US)
QLD	Queensland
SA	South Australia
SBA	Swiss Bankers Association
SCAG	Standing Committee of Attorneys General
SLCALC	Senate Legal and Constitutional Affairs Legislation Committee
SLRC	Security Legislation Review Committee
SMR	Suspicious Matter Report
SOCA	Serious Organised Crime Agency, UK
STR	Suspicious Transaction Report
Strasbourg Convention	Council of Europe *Convention on Laundering, Search, Seizure and Confiscation of the Proceeds from Crime*, 1990, ETS n°141
STC-LCA	Senate Standing Committee on Legal and Constitutional Affairs
TRACFIN	Traitement du Renseignement et Action contre les Circuits Financiers clandestins (French Financial Intelligence Unit)
The Code	*Criminal Code Act 1995* (Cth)
TTR	Threshold Transactions Report
UK	United Kingdom
UN	United Nations Organisation
UNCFT	*International Convention for the Suppression of the Financing of Terrorism*, 1999, 2178 UNTS 197
UNODC	United Nations Office on Drugs and Crime
UNSC	United Nations Security Council
UNSCR	United Nations Security Council Resolution
UNTOC	UN *Convention against Transnational Organised Crime*, 2000 (Palermo Convention)
US, USA	United States of America
USC	*United States Code* (US criminal code)
USD	United States dollar

VC	Virtual currencies
VCPPS	VC payment products and services
Vienna Convention	UN *Convention against Illicit Traffic in Narcotic Drugs and Psychotropic Substances*, 1988, 1582 UNTS 95
WA	Western Australia
WMD	Weapons of mass destruction
WW II	World War II

CHAPTER 1

Introduction

> When a moral panic is created, as was the case after the Royal Commissions of the late 1970s and early 1980s, when the end of civilisations as we know it seems nigh, when a social object, like the elimination of organised crime or drug-trafficking seems worthy enough, the pressure to create legislation that allow fewer rights to individuals is intense and often proves irresistible.[1]
>
> ARIE FREIBERG

∴

Confronted with major societal changes, including ideological challenges, governments have shown a tendency to rely on criminal law to solve emerging problems. Drug consumption, drug trafficking, and money laundering have given rise to an arsenal of new laws. Ideologies which do not support the political regime are ostracised and their supporters blacklisted, sometimes on the basis of mere suspicions or hearsay. This latter trend is not limited to totalitarian regimes. In recent years, democratic societies have been drawn to use criminal law as a tool of social control and have broadened the scope of preventative measures in the face of increased danger.

There is more to anti-money laundering (AML) and counter-terrorism financing (CTF) legislation than meets the eye: the nature of criminal law is changing; offences are drafted to tackle conduct further upstream than ordinary criminal law permits; there is an erosion of fundamental rights and freedoms; the role of private sector in law enforcement tasks is rising, judicial review of official agencies is reduced, while laws are passed without proper parliamentary scrutiny. In short, AML/CTF legislation has triggered a radical mutation in criminal law and in the way institutions operate. It is submitted that these changes were neither foreseen nor intended. How did they happen? Arguably, this transformation could be seen as collateral damage in the "war against crime". In every conflict, there comes a time when the situation needs to be appraised. Are the instruments of the warfare adequate? Are smart sanctions really reaching

---

1 Freiberg (1992), p. 69.

 | DOI:10.1163/9789004359109_002

the intended targets? Is the collateral damage outweighing the gains? What are the expected outcomes of that "war"? AML/CTF legislation has not sparked much debate, either in the media or in the Parliament, when it was passed mainly with bi-partisan support, nor after the Panama Papers affair where 11,5 million documents were leaked from law firm Mossack Fonseca revealing that 1,200 Australians might have evaded taxes,[2] or even after the terrorist attacks that Australia suffered. The Commonwealth Bank of Australia (CBA) scandal, and the major breaches to the AML/CTF regime it revealed, will hopefully lead to a renewed interest in the examination of the basis, mechanisms, and scope of the legislation, as well as in an appraisal of its long-term effects.

Australian AML/CTF legislation can be considered a showcase of the efforts that have been deployed to counter the perceived very serious threats to both the domestic and international community. More importantly, it contains arguably the seeds of the subsequent transformation of the nature of criminal law. The present in-depth study of its development, provisions and caselaw contributes to an assessment of AML/CTF legislation and a reflection on the way forward, as well its impact on democracy.

1.1 From Organised Crime to Money Laundering

The adoption of anti-money laundering legislation is intrinsically linked to the rise of organised crime. Similarly, the counter-terrorism financing laws are linked to the rise of new forms of terrorist activities. Given the transnational character of organised crime and terrorism, an overview of the international legal framework is outlined in Chapter 2, providing the international context in which Australia's AML/CTF stands. The first steps towards a weakening of national parliament prerogatives can be traced in the initiatives taken by the key international players, such as the UN Security Council, the G-7, the Financial Action Task Force (FATF) as well as the private sector, in the legislative process.

Legislating against organised crime may be an elusive task. Organised crime is a very vague and flexible concept,[3] which is more of a sociological or criminological categorisation than an actual crime.[4] It covers a complex and diverse reality, capturing both legitimate[5] and illegitimate businesses. Organised

2 Kahdem (2017).

3 Manacorda (2002), p. 235.

4 Bassiouni (1990), p. 18; Meagher (1983), p. 77. Morrison (2002).

5 Graycar, Grabosky, Tailby, Keelty (2001), pp. 1, 2.

crime developed considerably last century with the increased prevalence of drug trafficking. In today's terminology, it seeks to capture activities of criminal organisations that emerged with drug trafficking and expanded with globalisation, mainly in the areas of trafficking of human beings and corruption.[6] Its effect has been felt worldwide and organised crime has been described in terms of global harm, danger to democracy and economic development, as well as a threat to national security, rather than only as harm to the individual.[7]

In many parts of the world, such as the EU, it is the liberalisation of border controls that is seen as having led to an increase of both legitimate and illegitimate movements of persons and services. In Australia, it is the deregulation of the financial industry which is considered as having provided new opportunities for money launderers.[8] However, there is no suggestion to return to the *status quo ante*. The free movement of goods and services, including financial services, is considered part and parcel of the globalisation of the economy. Nonetheless, as a consequence of the rise of organised crime, funds transfers have come under greater scrutiny and new barriers have been set up worldwide to control the movement of persons and assets both tangible and intangible.

Given the global menace, a worldwide concerted response was required. However, defining organised crime is a very arduous task, and even more so in an international community with different legal traditions and conflicting economic interests. Rather than tackling the problem through ordinary offences and traditional methods of law enforcement, which were seen as not being very effective against this new type of crime, the international community developed two strategies. The first one sought to deprive criminal organisations of the financial benefit of their activities. The profit that these organisations make is perceived as being both the motive behind the crime and the means for the organisations to expand and corrupt others. In order to facilitate the seizure and confiscation of assets belonging to criminal organisations, the offence of money laundering was introduced at the international level with the 1988 UN *Convention against Illicit Traffic in Narcotic Drugs and Psychotropic Substances* (1988 UN Drug Convention or Vienna Convention). It was thought that if heads of criminal organisations could not be prosecuted for their involvement in illegal trafficking, corruption and murders, they could at least be charged for tax offences, as Al Capone had been.[9] The efficiency attributed to

6 Bassiouni, Vetere (1998), p. xxv. UNODC (2010), p. 29; Bottomley, Bronitt (2012), p. 397.

7 Shelley (1995), p. 464.

8 Costigan (1986), pp. 200–204; Sherman (1991), p. 30; Briggs (2010), p. 3.

9 Bernasconi (1988), p. 31; Schloenhardt (2009), p. 35; Vlcek (2008), p. 24.

legislation against money laundering has led the UN to include a specific provision in its 2000 *Convention against Transnational Organised Crime*. Hence, money laundering may be considered as the first generation of legislative measures against organised crime.

The second strategy adopted aimed at tackling not just the individual involved, but the organisations themselves. Criminal law, which had been mainly concerned with individual misconduct and guilt,[10] was found to be ill-equipped to effectively address the new form of criminality. Since the chain of command between the head of the organisation and the perpetrator of a specific crime is often unknown, the prosecution is faced with considerable difficulties when trying to prove the exact involvement of each participant in the commission of the crime, even though the criminal activities of the organisation and the association of one person with the group are established. Also, incitement, like the accessory offences before or after the fact, is limited to one event. Furthermore, secondary offences such as accessory offences, only capture those who did not commit the main offence, whereas from the perspective of a criminal organisation, the perpetrator who acts under orders, though he commits the offence, does not play a more significant role than another accessory.[11] Means were developed to address organised crime without having to prove a participation in a specific offence. The offences criminalising the membership and various forms of support of a criminal organisation can therefore be considered as the second generation of offences against organised crime.

To operationalise these strategies, States have used their prerogative to legislate in criminal matters. However, in Australia, the Commonwealth has, according to its Constitution, only a subsidiary competence in criminal law, related to the heads of power in the Constitution, the plenary competence resting with the states and territories.[12] There is therefore a mosaic of criminal laws in Australia, and a considerable potential overlap between federal, State and Territory legislation.[13]

Federal criminal offences are defined according to the *Commonwealth Criminal Code 1995* (Cth) (the Code) which follows its own case law. The Code

10 Weigend (1996), p. 555.

11 Meagher (1983), p. 62.

12 New South Wales (NSW), Queensland (QLD), Tasmania (TAS), Victoria (VIC), Western Australia (WA), Australian Capital Territory (ACT) and Northern Territory (NT).

13 When a law of a State is inconsistent with a law of the Commonwealth, the latter prevails, and the former is invalidated, to the extent of the inconsistency. S 109, Australian Constitution. The unifying factor is the case law of the High Court of Australia (HCA), which is the ultimate appellate court for all Australian jurisdictions (federal, state and territories).

deals exclusively with offences against Commonwealth legislation. It does not however contain an exhaustive list of offences against federal law since a number of offences can still to be found in other Commonwealth laws, such as the *Financial Management and Accountability Act 1997*. In Australia, the Code contains general principles of criminal responsibility for Commonwealth offences. These principles apply not only to those offences enacted in the Code but to all other Commonwealth offences, defined in any federal law, committed on and after 15 December 2001.[14]

Australia has responded to the rise of organised crime by relying on the constitutional heads of power pertaining to taxation, external affairs, international trade and commerce to create new federal offences.[15] For instance, the Commonwealth uses its legislative power to legislate on money laundering based on its power to legislate on taxation. Federal legislation on drug trafficking and trade in persons is based on its competence to legislate for external affairs and trade.[16] The external affairs power has been read expansively to support legislation against crimes against humanity and war crimes, as well as any criminal sanctions against violations of international treaties to which Australia is a party.[17]

The legal basis to support specific Commonwealth legislation against organised crime has been debated. Australia is a party to the UN *Convention against Transnational Organised Crime* (UNTOC). The Federal parliament is therefore authorised to enact laws to prohibit various forms of participation in a criminal organisation, as defined in the convention.[18] Given that the offences under UNTOC are all transnational in nature, UNTOC cannot be considered a sufficient basis for legislation to deal with organised crime offences which have only a domestic character.[19] Hence, only criminal offences that have a transnational character should come under the Code, leaving most of the activities of a criminal organisation conducted in Australia to fall under relevant state and territory legislation. For instance, Commonwealth legislation applies to international trafficking for the sex trade.[20] However if the person has not been coerced to come to Australia, or is an Australian citizen, or if the person is forced into the sex trade after having entered legally or even

14 Odgers (2010), p. 1.
15 S 51, Australian Constitution.
16 Bronitt (2010), p. 51.
17 Hanks, Keyzer, Clarke (2004), pp. 170, 171.
18 AGD (2008), p. 4.
19 Saul (2008), p. 4.
20 S 271.5, *Criminal Code* (Cth).

after having migrated illegally to Australia, then state or territory legislation applies. Nevertheless, even though Commonwealth legislation against organised crime should be restricted to Commonwealth offences, the meaning of an Australian offence under Division 390 [Criminal associations and organisations], introduced into the Code in 2010, has been extended to include offences against a law of the Commonwealth, a state or territory. This extension is constitutionally permitted because of the Constitution power of federal parliament to legislate to give effect to international treaties such as UNTOC.

1.2 From Anti-money Laundering to Counter-terrorism Financing

Australia was a forerunner of the fight against money laundering when it introduced its *Proceeds of Crime Act 1987* (Cth) (POCA). In Chapter 3, the various elements of the Code's dealing with property offences are analysed in detail and contrasted with the international treaties' money laundering provisions, exposing the eminently preventative character of Australia's legislation and its aversion to risk-taking. The large use of recklessness and negligence as fault elements compounds the offences' breadth. They are sanctioned with very high penalties which are equivalent to those of the most serious crimes against bodily harm.

In the 1990s, Australia lost momentum and failed to update its legislation to keep pace with the international developments. The Commonwealth had no anti-terrorism legislation in place to respond to the events that unfolded in September 2001. In face of the perceived urgency to pass new legislation, Australia adopted the *Suppression of the Financing of Terrorism Act* 2002 along with other anti-terror laws. The latter led to the enactment of specific laws against organised crime (*Crimes Legislation Amendment (Serious and Organised Crime) Act (No.2) 2010*). In the following years, the ill-preparedness of the original legislation was demonstrated by the numerous amendments, over 50, which were hastily passed.[21]

21 The initial package of Acts introduced in 2002 were the *Security Legislation Amendment (Terrorism) Act* (No.2); the *Suppressing of the Financing of Terrorism Act*, the *Criminal Code Amendment (Suppression of Terrorist Bombings) Act*; the *Border Security Legislation Amendment Act* and the *Telecommunications Interception Legislation Amendment Act*. The Australian Security Intelligence Organisation Legislation Amendment (Terrorism) Bill 2002 ("the ASIO Bill"), though submitted in 2002, was substantially amended and passed in 2003. The ASIO Act was subsequently amended several times. The *Criminal Code Amendment (Terrorist Organisation Act) 2002* was introduced and passed in 2002. The provisions of the *Criminal Code* regarding terrorist organisations were amended

Terrorism has been a concern for the international community for the most part of the 20th century. The first attempt to deal with terrorism was in the 1930s, when the League of Nations drafted a convention, which never came into force. It presented a dilemma that still exists today. For centuries, democratic societies have protected exiled political opponents and those seeking self-determination, granting them asylum. The international community could not reconcile what they considered the fundamental right to rise against oppression and the right of asylum with the need to sanction acts of terrorism.[22] Hence, criminal offenses inspired by political motives could warrant the suspension of extradition proceedings. Over the years, the political exception to extradition has tentatively been limited more and more to non-criminal acts.

Since there was no consensus on a definition of terrorism, the international community resorted to criminalising particular acts of terrorism, such as hijacking of aircraft, to ensure that there would be no impediment to international mutual assistance and that most offenders would be prosecuted. Thirteen international conventions against various acts of terrorism were adopted between 1963 and 2005. However, even under those conventions, political exceptions often prevail.

Until the later part of the 20th century, threats to institutions and democracy were usually identified at times of uprising, or *coups d'état*. Domestic legislation already provides for measures through state of emergency regulations in case of attacks on the state institutions. However, such emergency measures are only meant to be temporary, while the political rhetoric on organised crime and terrorism is about tackling a long-lasting menace.[23] Hence political authorities called for new laws and police powers that would not infringe on human rights.[24] The consensus was that to defend human rights and democracy, the new measures had to respect those human rights and the legal order that supported a democratic society.[25]

While comprehensive international legislation against terrorism was at a stalemate, (since 1996, an UN Ad Hoc Committee has been working on a draft of

several times in the following years, allowing *inter alia* the introduction of a new offence of "association with a terrorist organisation" with the *Crimes Legislation Amendment (Serious and Organised Crime) Act (No.2)* 2010. Williams (2011), p. 1142.

22 See Van Den Wijngaert (1980).

23 Costa (2009).

24 UNODC (2003a), point 74; UN (2005), point 46.

25 EU Council Resolution of 21 December 1998 on the prevention of organised crime with reference to the establishment of a comprehensive strategy for combating it, OJC 408, 29/12/1998, pp. 1–4. Annan (2006).

an international convention against terrorism), the international community was nevertheless able to adopt in 1999 the *Convention for the Suppression of Terrorist Financing* to supplement related existing international instruments. It is worth noting that the international community adopted provisions against money laundering in the absence of a definition of organised crime and long before criminal organisations were defined, even at national level. Similarly, measures against the financing of terrorism have been adopted despite the lack of an internationally agreed definition of terrorism.

Building on the money laundering strategy against organised crime, the UN Security Council ordered, in the wake of the terrorist attacks of September 2001, a number of specific measures to be taken against the financing of terrorism, against terrorists and in favour of interstate cooperation.[26] Prompted by the Security Council stance, the FATF swiftly issued several Special Recommendations on Terrorist Financing which are mainly a repeat of some of its previous Recommendations on Money Laundering.[27] Chapter 4 offers a detailed outline of the essence of the FATF special recommendations on terrorism financing and assesses them against AML recommendations. Despite the political rhetoric, their added value is not as significant as we were led to believe.

Australia was not a signatory to the 1999 *Convention for the Suppression of Terrorist Financing* when the terrorist attacks took place in the USA on 11 September 2001. Australia became a signatory on 15 October 2001, and a party to the treaty on 26 September 2002. The Australian definition of CTF offences is different from those of the international treaties, notably because its definition of terrorism is different, but also because the mental element is not the same, following there in the footprint of AML legislation. Australian CTF legislation's emphasis on organisations to counter terrorism financing needs to be questioned given the recent terrorist attacks carried out by home-grown terrorists.

In a similar manner to that for organised crime, the Commonwealth's competence to legislate in terrorism matters was based on a mosaic of heads of power. To strengthen its legislative competence, the Commonwealth also sought an agreement by which the states and territories referred their power to

---

26 UNSCR 1373 (2001).

27 The FATF Eight Special Recommendations (SR) regarding the financing of terrorism, issued on 31 October 2001 are regarded as complementary to the Forty Recommendations. In 2003, the FATF updated all the Recommendations allegedly to create a comprehensive framework of measures to prevent and combat money laundering and terrorist financing. The latest version (2012) integrates the SR into the Forty Recommendations.

legislate to the Commonwealth in matters pertaining to terrorism. This Agreement was signed on 5 April 2002.[28]

Though Australia was ill-prepared to legislate on the new forms of terrorism, the Code's provisions on *dealing with money and property* fitted well into the new context. Australia's AML legislation criminalises conduct (dealing) when money or property is proceeds of crime, or at risk of becoming an instrument of crime, independently of its origin being legitimate or criminal. The Australian offence, which is not built upon the original idea of money laundering which is exclusively concerned with proceeds of a criminal activity, fits therefore very well in the new legal CTF landscape which aims at preventing funds of whatever origin, whether legitimate or criminal, from being used to finance a terrorist act. Consequently, Australia's CTF legislation bears many similarities with AML legislation and is intertwined with it. It is drafted in similar terms and is characterised by the same breadth with an extensive use of recklessness as a fault element as demonstrated in Chapter 4.

Hence, Australian AML/CTF legislation illustrates the preventative character of legislation against organised crime and terrorism by sanctioning conduct which only entails a risk of a potential danger. In addition, given the breadth Australian legislation, a large margin of appreciation is bestowed on law enforcement agencies in deciding what to investigate and what to ignore. The strict legal criteria under legislation have been relaxed, with the effect that even a strong suspicion would be enough to warrant being put on a list of terrorism financiers. Although there is a clear need to act preventively against terrorism, the breadth of Australian legislation is such that it does not offer sufficient guarantee of targeting the right individuals, wasting law enforcement agencies precious time and resources, as well as threatening fundamental rights.

1.3 Protecting Fundamental Rights

There is a consensus within the international community that organised crime and terrorism threaten our way of life, freedoms, security, democracy and human rights. Upon its introduction, AML/CTF legislation has been justified in order to protect the rule of law and human rights. National criminal codes, constitutions and legal traditions, all safeguard in one way or another fundamental principles, which can be appraised against the benchmark of international treaties, and domestic human rights legislation.

28 See Terrorism (Commonwealth Powers) Bill 2002.

The Commonwealth of Australia has no Bill of Rights or Human Right Act that would complement it. The deliberate omission from the Australian Constitution reflects a belief that individual rights are on the whole best left to the protection of the common law and the supremacy of the Parliament.[29] It is therefore incumbent on the Courts to ensure that fundamental rights and the rule of law are respected. However, Dawson J's reasoning applies to common law and may not offer sufficient guarantee under the Code, as evidenced by terrorism legislation. For instance, Division 115 (Harming Australians), adopted in response to the terrorist attacks that happened in Bali in 2002, has been made retroactive.[30] Other provisions, such as control orders and proscription regulations, have reduced judicial review. Even though Australia is party to the *International Covenant on Civil and Political Rights* (ICCPR), to the *Convention against Torture and Other Cruel, Inhuman or Degrading Treatment or Punishment* (UNCAT)[31] and other international treaties, these are not directly enforceable. Chapter 5 details Australia's prescriptive regimes of terrorist organisations under the *Charter of the United Nations Act 1945* (Cth) (COTUNA) and the Code and assesses their implementation in regard to international requirements and practice. The difficulties of implementing CTF legislation, in particular UNSCRs 1267 and 1317, in accordance with the principles enshrined in international instruments on fundamental freedoms and human rights are explained through the study of international court cases. The discussion leads to an understanding of the role that human rights can play in safeguarding the democratic order that organised crime and terrorism legislation is meant to protect. Suggestions are offered on how to interpret Australia's current legislation in accordance with internationally held fundamental rights. Given the impact of AML/CTF provisions on property rights and terrorism legislation on other human rights, fundamental rights and freedoms would be better protected in Australia if a Bill of Rights reflecting the principles laid down in the ICCPR or the *European Convention for the Protection of Human Rights and Fundamental Freedoms* (ECHR) were adopted, and the judiciary were to interpret the Code according to the Bill of Rights.[32]

---

29 Dawson J in *Kruger v Commonwealth* (the *Stolen Generation* case) (1997) 190 CLR 1 [61].

30 Bronitt (2010), pp. 52, 53.

31 *Convention against Torture and Other Cruel, Inhuman or Degrading Treatment or Punishment* (UNCAT), 4 February 1985, 1465 UNTS 85.

32 The Government's Framework fails to implement the key recommendation of the National Human Rights Consultation Report (which was supported by over 87% of a record

1.4 Increased International Cooperation

To counter the transnational character of organised crime and modern terrorism and ensure that criminals do not go unpunished, a coordinated response is required at three levels: the prohibited conduct must be defined at international level; national legislation must be adopted in accordance with international definitions, and international cooperation should be reinforced.

The international concern over organised crime, and more particularly over drug trafficking, has coincided with more coordinated action on the international level. Not only has the 1988 UN Drug Convention been ratified by most of the world States, but practical steps have been taken for its implementation on national, regional and international levels, which is quite unique. Close working relationships have been developed between various agencies, whether national authorities, regional or international institutions, to coordinate, update and optimise their efforts in the legislative and procedural fields, and in investigation methods. This was only made possible by the perceived nature of the threat originating in organised crime which, as Tom Sherman, AO, former Chairman of the National Crime Authority and former Chairman of the FATF, put it, "has a corrosive effect on society and political institutions, and if unchecked risks challenging the state itself".[33] Similarly, the threat of terrorism galvanised international cooperation only because its most spectacular manifestation – the destruction of the New York World Trade Centre twin towers – was perceived as the epitome of the destructive threat to democratic values and societies. Condemning these attacks, the UN Security Council issued a resolution (UNSCR 1373) calling for all member States to ratify without delay the *Convention for the Suppression of Terrorist Financing* and to increase their cooperation.

To contribute to the international efforts and improve its cooperation in criminal matters, Australia had modernised its legislation on mutual assistance and extradition. The *Mutual Assistance in Criminal Matters Act* was

---

35,000 submissions) that Australia enact a federal Human Rights Act (see NHRC (2009) Rec. 18), Instead, in 2010 the Attorney-General issued the Australia's Human Rights Framework which requires that each new Bill introduced into Parliament be accompanied by a statement of compatibility with Australia's international human rights obligations and establishes a new Parliamentary Joint Committee on Human Rights to provide greater scrutiny of legislation for compliance with international human rights obligations. Though a positive step, it does not however compensate for the absence of a Bill of Rights.

33 Sherman (1993), p. 16.

adopted in 1987. The *Extradition Act* 1988 replaced the outdated provisions of *Extradition Act* 1966.[34] With the entry into force of the *Extradition and Mutual Assistance in Criminal Matters Legislation Amendment Act* 2012, further improvements were introduced to streamline and accelerate procedures and increase international cooperation. For instance, the range of extraditable offences has been extended and the rights of appeal have been restricted to the Federal Court of Australia. In addition, the competence of the Attorney-General Department has been extended. In particular, the grounds for the Attorney-General to refuse mutual assistance or extradition requests have been clarified and enlarged, thereby extending the protection against torture, in line with the requirements of UNCAT. In addition, Australia has excluded the use of the political offence exception for cases of terrorism, genocide or war crimes or a crime against humanity, as defined by Australian law. The exceptions to the definition of the political exceptions are now generally contained in regulations, rather than in the Act, so that they can be speedily modified, without parliamentary approval, and be kept up-to-date with the international developments. Furthermore, Australia is now competent to prosecute terrorists it cannot or does not want to extradite. In order to facilitate the extradition of a person to Australia, the Attorney-General is now authorised to give a legally enforceable undertaking to a country as to the maximum sentence that could be imposed on a person.

In matters of AML/CTF, the authorisation process for the "proceeds of crime" investigative tools is simplified. The *Mutual Assistance in Criminal Matters Act* now allows the registration and enforcement of foreign non-conviction based proceeds of crime orders from any country. It also facilitates the granting of non-conviction based proceeds of crime orders, which are used for restraining and forfeiting the proceeds of serious crimes. In addition, it permits assistance in relation to serious corporate offences that may only carry monetary fines as penalties (rather than only those offences that carry an imprisonment exceeding 12 months).

These improvements come at a cost, in particular at the expense of privacy rights. To facilitate international cooperation and make the transfer and sharing of information more expeditious, the requirements of the *Privacy Act* 1988 are waived if the collection, use or disclosure of personal information about an individual is "reasonably necessary" for the purposes of the mutual assistance or extradition processes, even if no request has yet been formulated.[35]

34 *Extradition (Commonwealth Countries) Act 1966*, *Extradition (Foreign Countries) Act* 1966; *Extradition Act* 1988.

35 S 54A, *Extradition Act* 1988; s 43D *Mutual Assistance in Criminal Matters Act*.

1.5 Conclusion

Considering that money laundering legislation does not appear to have hampered the activities of organised crime significantly and its implementation is costly, it is surprising that it should have been chosen as a blueprint for countering the financing of terrorism. Reasons for the failure of the CTF measures are presented in Chapter 6 and suggestions are offered on making the prevention and detection of terrorism more cost-effective. The poor results of AML/CTF laws against organised crime and terrorism have not impeded their further extension against any type of financial crimes. Not only should AML/CTF legislation be reassessed but also its arguably detrimental impact on our democracy needs to be discussed.

At first sight, the implementation of AML/CTF laws may appear to enlarge democratic participation with the inclusion of the private sector in the fight against organised crime and terrorism. This is misleading. Financial institutions are legally compelled to cooperate (through heavy penalties) while private companies engineer the surveillance technologies that financial institutions and law enforcement agencies will be using. Instead of strengthening democracy, the involvement of the private sector in law enforcement task is actually the Achilles' heel of the AML/CTF apparatus. The relevance of the CTF provisions to fight terrorism and the justification of the limitation of criminal law principles they impose needs to be questioned given that the outcome of the new policies seems to have fallen short of the AML/CTF legislation's anticipated results. As evidenced by Australian court cases, CTF legislation has not been instrumental in preventing the commission of any terrorist act. AML/CTF provisions are used to track down previously identified terrorists or organisations. The "preventative justice" concept is challenged by the lack of efficacy of the "flagship" legislation designed to counter acts of terrorism.

Moreover, the emergence of non-elected bodies such as the UN Security Council, the G-7, the FATF and private organisations, in the legislative process and the reduction of the powers of parliament, the rising importance of law enforcement prerogatives and of the private sector conscripted as one of its arms, coupled with a reduction of the judicial review process destabilise the balance of powers and further amplify the weakening of the democratic systems which AML/CTF legislation claims to protect. This present study may not answer all the questions that AML/CTF legislation raises but it contributes significantly to exposing some of the problems and provides material for discussion and on-going debate on the changing paradigm of criminal law and the function of democracy.

CHAPTER 2

Australian AML/CTF Legislation in the International Context

> As devastating as terrorism can be, it is dwarfed by global organized crime and its implications. The world changes in even more dangerous ways. Counterfeit tender used to buy drugs can also be used to buy plutonium. Weapons of mass destruction abound – chemical, radiological, nuclear and biological. [...] As a result, the tiniest of unstable governments or parliamentary groups could extort the largest of countries.[1]
>
> KUPPERMAN

2.1 The Problem

The adoption of anti-money laundering (AML)[2] legislation is intrinsically linked to the rise of organised crime generally, and drug trafficking in particular. Portrayed as early as the 1920s, as a US phenomenon,[3] organised crime gained momentum with the rise of drug trafficking, prompting President Nixon to declare a "war on drugs" in 1969.[4] By the late 1980s, the American perception that the threat of organised crime was a worldwide menace more serious than terrorism was shared by the international community.[5]

At that time, the prevalent view of governments of industrial nations was that organised crime was a global threat not only to the development and stability of their own countries but to society as a whole,[6] because of the high risk

1 Kupperman (1994), p. 133.
2 AML stands for anti-money laundering and CTF for counter-terrorism financing.
3 Woodiwiss (2003), p. 7.
4 Martial metaphors have since been commonly used by American politicians (Sheptycki (2003), pp. 127, 128) to galvanise the public when seeking to implement new legislation and granting new powers to law enforcement agencies.
5 Kupperman (1994), p. 133.
6 See *Travaux préparatoires to the United Nations Convention against Illicit Traffic in Narcotic Drugs and Psychotropic Substances.*

 | DOI:10.1163/9789004359109_003

that corruption would spread, given the amount of illegally acquired wealth organised crime activities can generate. In contrast to common crime, the threat of organised crime lies in the particularly discrete and insidious ways it undermines institutions and society.[7] Hence, the effect of organised crime is described in terms of global harm, danger to democracy and national security rather than harm to the individual.

According to the UN Office on Drugs and Crime (UNODC),

> [o]rganized crime is being perceived as a threat to human security and the rule of law. In a growing number of cases, we can see a criminalization of the political process. The profits from organized crime are used to finance conflicts. This is not a new phenomenon, of course. But it is taking on worrying dimensions because of the large amounts of money available from crime.[8]

The European Union described organised crime as increasingly becoming a threat to society as we know it, and a danger to "democracy and the rule of law, for freedom, human rights and self-determination, values which are the *raison d'être* of any fight against organised crime".[9] This view was shared in Australia:

> With the accumulation of large sums of illegal profits comes power and institutional corruption. Such corruption is no longer a matter which this society can afford to take lightly, if ever it could. It calls for urgent action to be taken if it is not to destroy the capacity of our institutions to function in a proper and democratic manner.[10]

For the Australian government,

> [t]he security of Australia is the [...] highest priority, and maintaining that security and the safety and security of Australian citizens requires decisive action to target serious and organised crime.[11]

---

7 Volk (2002), p. 9.

8 Arlacchi (2001).

9 Recital, Council Resolution of 21 December 1998 on the prevention of organised crime with reference to the establishment of a comprehensive strategy for combating it, OJ C408, 29/12/1998.

10 Weinberg (1989).

11 Mcclelland (2009), p. 6964.

The increase in transnational crime was seen as a consequence of two factors: first, the introduction and spreading of new technologies; second, globalisation which abolishes internal borders and facilitates the free movement of goods, capital, services and persons.[12] This view was largely shared in Australia which saw the deregulation of the financial industry as providing new opportunities for money launderers.[13] This opinion is still held today.[14] However there is no suggestion to return to the *status quo ante*. The free movement of goods and services, including financial services, is considered part and parcel of the globalisation of the economy.

Some thought that the danger posed by organised crime had been largely exaggerated when it was first made, and that there was no evidence of an alleged "hegemony of global international crime",[15] given that, regardless of the veritable explosion in illicit trade, criminal organisations are more often than not competing with each other.[16] Unfortunately, the lack of reliable data on organised crime to determine the magnitude of the problem makes it amenable to various interpretations.[17] Hence, many commentators argue that most figures given in support of the claim of threat are detached from reality.[18] Accordingly, they suggest that the purpose of inflated figures is to capture the imagination of the audience and to legitimise policy decisions, rather than to assist in policy making.[19] Unfortunately, the absence of reliable data is hindering a global perspective on the reality of organised crime and precluding the development of an evidence-based policy.[20]

2.1.1 *What Is Organised Crime?*

Organised crime is hard to define. It is not a legal but a political, sociological and economic concept which draws from different perspectives.[21] Some prefer to speak of organised crimes,[22] hence "organised crime" can be considered as an umbrella concept. It is therefore difficult, if not impossible, to find a

12 1997 Action Plan on organised crime, point 1.
13 Costigan (1986), pp. 200–204.
Sherman (1991), p. 30.
14 Briggs (2010), p. 3.
15 Shelley (1995), p. 467.
16 Woodiwiss (2003), p. 29.
17 See Rec(2), 1997 Action Plan on organised crime, pp. 1–16. UNODC (2010), p. 2. Naylor (2003a), p. 36.
18 Reuter (1996), pp. 63–80. Clare (2013); Woodiwiss, Hobbs (2009), p. 111.
19 Pozo (1996), p. 2.
20 UNODC (2010), p. ii.
21 Manacorda (2002), p. 2. Schloenhardt (2009), p. 20.
22 Giudicelli-Delage (2002), p. 112.

definition that can be used in criminal law, so much that, though the 1988 *Convention against Illicit Traffic in Narcotic Drugs and Psychotropic Substances*[23] uses the expression "organised criminal group", it does not define it. Nevertheless, its main features can be described.

A criminal organisation is perceived to be different from previous criminal groups because of its structure and objective. Whereas the other groups would usually be formed for a limited amount of time to commit specific offences, a criminal organisation has a permanent structure. A criminal organisation is thought to organise itself towards a long-term objective of making substantial profits out of criminal activity. It is presumed that the organisation is run like a business.[24] It does not rely on particular members, whether foot soldiers or people at a senior level.[25] It may be compared to the Hydra; when one head is cut off, another one grows in its stead.

Because of its corrosive effect on society, the concept of organised crime requires that measures be taken before it is too late to reverse the trend.[26] Hence, effective legislation against organised crime must allow law enforcement to tackle the problem further upstream than ordinary criminal law permits. On this premise, legal provisions on controlled delivery, assumed identities, extended communication interception and entrapment have been adopted. However, they were considered insufficient and other measures were eventually needed.

2.2 The Strategies

Rather than emphasising prevention and strengthening political institutions to fight organised crime, criminal law has been made the weapon of choice.[27] While an international consensus on a legal definition of organised crime was slow to come about, the international community agreed on two strategies to tackle criminal organisations. The first one aimed to deprive them from the profits of their activities. The second was to strike at the organisation's structure.

---

23 1582 UNTS 95.

24 Morris (2008), p. 32. McClelland (2009).

25 Meagher (1983), p. 59.

26 According to the 2007 Confesercenti's annual report (Confesercenti is an association of 270 000 Italian retailers and small businesses), the mafia organisations' turnover amounts to EUR 90 billions – not counting drug trafficking (Le Monde.fr (2007)).

27 Mitsilegas (2003), p. 9.

2.2.1 *Depriving Criminal Organisations of the Profit of Their Crimes*

In 2009, transnational organised crime was estimated to generate USD 870 billion – an amount equal to 1.5 per cent of global GDP. According to the UNODC, drug trafficking is the most lucrative form of business for criminals, with an estimated annual value of USD 320 billion. Human trafficking is estimated to make annual profits of appreciatively USD 32 billion at least. Illicit trading in firearms brings in around USD 170 million to USD 320 million annually and identity theft generates around USD 1 billion each year.[28]

The greater the profits of criminal activities, the higher the risk of organised crime expanding its legal and illegal activities, thus controlling large sectors of the economy and corrupting officials. Consequently, confiscation has been made the main strategy against criminal organisations.[29]

> It is generally believed that confiscating the proceeds of crime is both an appropriate punishment and an effective prevention tool. Confiscation is a deterrent for criminals who try to maximize their profits, and it also prevents illicitly acquired assets from being reinvested into the legitimate economy. Confiscation can also serve as a mechanism to disrupt criminal activities, help create an image that crime does not pay and increase public confidence in the criminal justice system. In addition, confiscated assets can be used to compensate the damage suffered by trafficking victims.[30]

For centuries, criminal law has provided for the seizure and confiscation of the proceeds of crime. Nevertheless, law enforcement officers felt that the systems put in place by criminal organisations were preventing the identification of the criminal origin of their assets and that new legislation was needed to ensure that the proceeds of these organisations' activities could be seized.

The term money laundering first appeared in the 1920s in the vocabulary of United States law enforcement agents who were investigating mafia groups. The Mafiosi were giving the profits of drug trafficking a legitimate appearance by pretending it was the produce of their laundrette companies.[31]

---

28 UNODC (2016).

29 Adams (1986), p. 251.

30 UNODC (2014), p. 47.

31 Stessens (2000), pp. 82–83.

2.2.1.1 How Money Is Laundered

Money laundering is today understood as being the process by which funds of criminal origin are given the appearance of legitimate assets. Following the experts' classification, it can be broken down into three stages:

(1) The initial stage is the entry point of the illegitimate assets into the financial system. In case of drug trafficking, for instance, the notes in cash would be deposited in bank accounts. This is called the *placement stage*.

(2) In the second stage, the money launderer seeks to divert attention from the origin of the funds by transferring them to different accounts, companies, including front companies, within a country or more often internationally. The objective is to make it difficult to trace the assets back to an illicit origin, thus giving them a legitimate appearance. This is the *layering stage*.

(3) Once the assets are given a legitimate appearance, they are ready to be invested in legitimate business, for instance in shares, property, companies or luxury items. The *integration stage* is complete when the owner pays tax on his assets.

In the process of laundering, some of the assets may be lost or given away (as a payment or to corrupt an official), but on the whole the control over the proceeds by the owner remains intact. Consequently, it is estimated that the mafia derives more income from its legal ventures than it does from its illegal investments.[32]

Drug trafficking and human trafficking, like many organised crime activities, generates a lot of cash, often in small notes. Money laundering can therefore be considered as the "Achilles' heel" of organised crime,[33] as it compels criminal organisations to enter into contact with the financial institutions of the legal economy (called "the *gatekeepers*") to launder the profits of their crimes. Hence, AML legislation exploits this weakness of the criminal scheme in two ways. First, given that the criminal origin of the assets is hidden by the number of transfers and transactions, the offence of money laundering criminalises the process that enables the origin of the funds to be hidden. Secondly, AML law sets up a mechanism by which law enforcement agencies are enabled to follow the whereabouts of the assets by compelling financial instructions to make available to them various internal documents regarding the movements of the funds. This documentation is called the *paper trail.*

---

32 Sherman (1993), p. 13.

33 Bernasconi (1985).

Making business documents available to law enforcement officers may infringe on privacy. Therefore money laundering legislation includes provisions regarding the waiver of penalties attached to violations of the bank secrecy and commercial confidentiality.

Having found that the removal of bank secrecy was not leading to more convictions for money laundering and, thus, suspicious assets could not be confiscated, provisions regarding the easing or the reversal of the burden of proof, have also been introduced in AML related legislation.

2.2.2 *Making It an Offence to Participate in a Criminal Organisation*

After undermining the financial aspects of organised crime through the offence of money laundering, the attention focused on the structure of the criminal organisations. Given that in a criminal organisation, a foot soldier can easily be replaced without its operations being affected, the objective was to tackle its structures in the hope it would bring down the organisation, or at least curb its activities. To achieve this aim, a paradigm shift in the prosecution was created. Rather than relying on proving the involvement of an individual in the commission of a specific offence, which may be a difficult task, the emphasis was put on the relationship with the organisation.

The first steps can be traced back to the 1988 *Convention against Illicit Traffic in Narcotic Drugs and Psychotropic Substances* (thereafter 1988 Vienna Convention),[34] which required considering the commission of an offence on behalf of an organised group as an aggravating circumstance. Initially, common law States kept relying on their existing provisions on conspiracy. The European Union, whose members were mainly of civil law tradition, made a decisive impact by introducing in its legislation, in 1998, the offence of participation in a criminal organisation. The UN followed suit in 2000 with the adoption of the *Convention against Transnational Organised Crime* (UNTOC). When common law countries came to the conclusion that their conspiracy provisions were insufficient to address the problem,[35] they enacted provisions akin to the participation offence. In 2009, following Canada's example, Australia introduced Division 390 (Criminal associations and organisations) into the Criminal Code.

2.2.2.1 In Australia

Criminal organisations had certainly been active in Australia for many years.[36] From the 1970s, several Commissions of Inquiry and Royal Commissions

34 1582 UNTS 95.

35 Quaedvlieg (2009), p. 7.

36 Meagher (1983), pp. 18,19. Schloenhardt (2009), p. 92.

revealed the organised crime activities in Australia, particularly on the east coast.[37] They exposed a high level of corruption among public officials and the integrity of those that exposed it was attacked, most likely in an attempt to have their findings dismissed.[38] Most of the recommendations for tackling the problem were not implemented.[39] A major exception was Costigan's call for a money laundering offence.

Years later, it was the violence between motorcycle gangs that prompted a legislative reaction specifically designed to address criminal groups, firstly at the state level,[40] then at the Commonwealth level. Between 2003 and 2012, Australian states have adopted various statutes to curb the illicit activities of outlawed motorcycle gangs (OMGs).[41]

In what is considered a response to the introduction in South Australia of a controversial *Serious and Organised Crime (Control) Bill 2007*,[42] the Commonwealth initiated, 10 years after the EU, an *Inquiry into the future impact of serious and organised crime on Australian society*,[43] which was followed in 2008 by the launch of an *Inquiry into the legislative arrangements to outlaw serious and organised crime groups* to "examine the effectiveness of legislative efforts to disrupt and dismantle serious and organised crime groups and associations with these groups".[44] The fear that the absence of harmonised legislation would undermine the efficiency of law enforcement and possibly cause organised crime activities to be moved to less severe jurisdictions[45] echoes similar European concerns.

---

37 The Moffit Inquiry (1973–1974) which revealed the infiltration into NSW of overseas criminal organisations. Williams Inquiry (1977–1979), Woodward (1977–1979), The Steward Inqury (Nugan Hand) (1981–1983), Costigan Inquiry (1980–1984).

38 Moffitt (1985), p. 4.

39 Moffit (1985), pp. 22–24.

40 Schloenhardt (2009), p. 94. It must be noted however that in 2001 Queensland had enacted the *Crime and Misconduct Act 2001* (Qld). See Christensen (2004), p. 50. On 22 March 2009, a member of the Hells Angels Motorcycle Club was attacked and killed by a member of another rival gang, the Comancheros, at Sydney airport. A few days later, the New South Wales Government introduced the *Crimes (Criminal Organisations Control) Bill 2009* which was promptly passed into law by both Houses of Parliament.

41 *Statutes Amendment (Anti-Fortification) Act 2003* (SA), *Crimes Legislation Amendment (Gangs) Act* 2006 (NSW), *Legislation (Group Criminal Activities) Act 2006* (NT), *Serious and Organised Crime (Control) Act 2008* (SA), *Crimes (Criminal Organisations Control) Act 2009* (NSW), *Serious Crime Control Act 2009* (NT), *Criminal Organisation Act* 2009 (QLD), *Criminal Organisations Control Act 2012* (WA). See also Bartels (2010).

42 PJC-ACC (2009), p. 3. Schloenhardt (2009), p. 126. The *Serious and Organised Crime (Control) Act 2008* (SA) was adopted a year later.

43 PJC-ACC (2007).

44 PJC-ACC (2009), pp. 1, 2.

45 PJC-ACC (2009), pp. 134, 135.

In 2009, the Commonwealth developed its first *Organised Crime Strategic Framework*,[46] while the Standing Committee of Attorneys General (SCAG) issued a set of resolutions for a comprehensive national response to tackle organised crime.[47] It included recommendations regarding confiscation, intelligence, controlled operation, communication interception and legislative measures.

These recommendations were implemented in two stages, in June and September 2009. The two bills (*Crimes Legislation Amendment* (*Serious and Organised Crime*) *Bill 2009* and *Crimes Legislation Amendment* (*Serious and Organised Crime*) *Bill* (*N°2*) *2009*) were adopted speedily.[48] Given the importance of the proposed amendments, the rush was found unjustifiable.[49]

Inter alia, the first Bill broadens the scope of the Code's inchoate offences by adding joint commission and the second Bill facilitates the implementation of the previous Bill. It also introduced new offences in Division 390 of the Code (organised crime offences). The bills indicate a turn in criminal policy whereby the provisions on conspiracy are deemed insufficient to tackle organised crime. The introduced offences seek to extend the traditional boundaries of criminal liability to capture conduct that is not necessarily linked to the commission or planned commission of a specific offence but which is alleged to facilitate the criminal activity of an organisation.

In parallel with the adoption of specific anti-organised crime legislation, in which the mental element is often couched in broad terms and include wide use of strict liability, new provisions regarding evidentiary rules, such as the standard and the burden of proof, have also been introduced. Hence AML legislation is often applied in conjunction with anti-organised crime provisions to assist the prosecution to achieve conviction.

2.3 The Response: Towards Comprehensive AML Legislation

This section focuses, in chronological order, on the main factors which contributed to the growing awareness and development of international legislation against money laundering and terrorism financing.

---

46 Commonwealth Organised Crime Strategic Framework, Overview, 2009.

47 Crimes Legislation Amendment (Serious and Organised Crime) Bill 2009, Explanatory Memorandum, p. 1.

48 SLC-ALC (2009), p. 72.

49 The rush was justified by a minor amendment to the *Crimes Act 1914*. See Biddington, Spooner, Scully (2009), pp. 38 and 45.

2.3.1 *The 1970s*

2.3.1.1 The United States

Until the 1960s, the United States had used the conspiracy provisions on defrauding the Internal Revenue Services to sanction money laundering indirectly. However, the *Bank Secrecy Act* 1970 (BSA)[50] introduced a major innovation, the *cash transaction report*. Financial institutions were compelled to report every transaction above USD 10,000 to a central federal body, and to keep records of the transactions. These regulations were not properly enforced and the financial institutions ignored them until the 1980s, when the BSA was amended.[51] In 1986, laundering money derived from drug trafficking was eventually made an offence in the US legislation.

2.3.1.2 The Swiss Bankers Association (SBA)

The mere amount of funds being transferred every day through a busy financial centre makes it less conspicuous for criminals to transfer large amounts of money. Therefore, the more developed a financial system is, the more it is likely to be used by money launderers. In addition, sophisticated financial systems offer more opportunities for the layering stage. Though all the major international financial centres are concerned with money laundering, it is the Swiss Bankers Association (SBA) which first took the initiative of introducing measures to prevent the misuse of the Swiss banks by criminal organisations. Following the revelation that criminals had invested their assets in Swiss banks, giving the impression that, at best, the banks were taking advantage of ill-gotten gains and, at worst, were associated with criminal organisations, the SBA sought to protect their industry, restore its reputation of probity and regain the confidence of clients or potential clients. In 1977, the SBA issued an *Agreement on the Swiss banks' code of conduct with regard to the exercise of due diligence*.

One of the most important recommendations of the *Agreement on the Swiss banks' code of conduct* was the introduction of the *know your customer* standard (KYC) which requires the bankers to identify their customers as well as the beneficial owners of the funds. In addition, the banks committed themselves not to provide any active assistance to capital flight or to tax fraud. However, concerned about possible breach of client confidentiality laws, the *Agreement* stopped short of suggesting that its members inform the law enforcement authorities of possible cases of money laundering. Nevertheless,

50 It is now part of the *US PATRIOT Act*, Part III, International Money Laundering Control and Abatement Act, 2001.

51 Stessens (2000), p. 98.

given that no one can invoke bank secrecy in Switzerland when a criminal offence is being investigated, the adoption of the *Agreement* enabled the prosecuting authorities to collect important information (the paper trail) when a warrant was produced. Infringements of the *Agreement* were sanctioned by the SBA, which imposed fines. The industry supervisory body of the Swiss banks, the Swiss Federal Banking Commission, endorsed these recommendations, which were upheld by the Swiss Federal court.[52] Nevertheless, this private initiative was not sufficient to prevent money laundering and in 1990 the offence of money laundering was introduced into the Swiss Criminal Code.

2.3.2 *The 1980s*

2.3.2.1 The Council of Europe

The rise of acts of criminal violence, such as armed robberies and kidnappings, and terrorist attacks that took place in Europe in the 1970s and 1980s, prompted the Committee of Ministers of the Member States of the Council of Europe to recommend its first AML and counter-terrorism financing measures.[53] The objective was to prevent the "perpetration of further criminal acts and the spreading of the phenomenon". Terrorism financing was treated as an organised crime issue, not only because these terrorist organisations relied primarily on violent crimes to fund their operations,[54] but also because terrorism itself was dealt with within that context.

In June 1980, the Committee of Ministers issued a *Recommendation on measures against the transfer and safekeeping of funds of criminal origin*.[55] The Ministers recommended that the governments made it compulsory for the banking institutions to identify their customers when opening bank accounts, renting of safe-deposit and accepting cash transaction of a certain magnitude or transferring sums of a certain magnitude, keeping in mind the possibility of that transactions could take place in several parts. In 1986, the Ministers of Justice initiated the work leading to the adoption of the first AML convention, which was adopted in 1990. Australia took part in the *travaux préparatoires* and since 1997 is a party to the *Convention on Laundering, Search, Seizure and Confiscation of the Proceeds from Crime*.

52 ATF 109 Ib 146 ss.
53 CM/Rec(80)10E.
54 Pieth (2002), p. 365. Vlcek (2007), p. 100. Freeman (2011). Smith, Mccusker, Walters (2010), pp. 2–4.
55 CM/Rec(80)10E.

2.3.2.2 The United Nations

Though not directly requiring the criminalisation of money laundering, the 1988 *Convention against Illicit Traffic in Narcotic Drugs and Psychotropic Substances* (Vienna Convention) is nevertheless considered as a stepping-stone towards the development of AML mechanism. Its provisions on confiscation stipulate that the proceeds of drug trafficking should be traced and identified. Hence, the Convention indirectly advocates the adoption of the offence of money laundering. Further, bank secrecy should not preclude criminal investigations and mutual assistance, a core requirement in AML machinery.

2.3.2.3 Australia

Australia did not wait for the international community to act to introduce its first legislative package against money laundering. The *Proceeds of Crime Act 1987* (Cth) (POCA), which was promulgated following the adoption in the UK of the *Drug Trafficking Offences Act 1986*,[56] criminalised money laundering and provided for the confiscation of illegitimate assets. The *Cash Transaction Reports Act 1988* (Cth), which complemented it, sought to prevent the use of the financial system by money launderers. The provisions related to money laundering are now part of Division 400 of the *Criminal Code Act 1995* (Cth) (the Code). The declared objective of the 1987 Act was

> to strike at the heart of major organised crime by depriving persons involved of the profits and instruments of their crimes. By so doing, it [would] suppress criminal activity by attacking the primary motive – profit – and prevent the re-investment of that profit in further criminal activity.[57]

2.3.2.4 Basel Committee on Banking Regulations and Supervisory Practices (BCBS)

Another major step taken by financial institutions was the issuing in December 1988 of the *Basel statement of principles* by the Basel Committee on Banking Regulations and Supervisory Practices now called the Basel Committee on Banking Supervision (BCBS). The Basel Committee is part of the Bank for International Settlements. It is composed of representatives of the central banks and authorities responsible for the industry banking supervision from

56 This legislation was later replaced by the *Drug Trafficking Act 1994* (DTA).

57 Bowen (1987a), p. 2314.

twelve highly developed countries.[58] The *Statement of principles* was issued out of concerns that organised crime could infiltrate the legitimate sector of business, and possibly influence or control it. Along with most experts at the time, the Basel Committee was of the opinion that the corrupt power of criminal organisations constituted a major risk for democracies and therefore should not be minimised. Like the Swiss Banking Association, their main concern was to regain and maintain public confidence in banks and to avoid "direct losses from fraud either through negligence in screening undesirable customers or [...] association with criminals". The Basel Committee shared the view of the Council of Europe Committee of Ministers that "the banking system can play a highly effective preventive role while the cooperation of the banks also assists in the repression of such criminal acts by the judicial authorities and the police". The *Statement of principles* encouraged the banks' management to ensure that all clients are properly identified, that transactions which do not appear legitimate are discouraged, and that cooperation with law enforcement agencies is achieved. Over the years, the Basel Committee has kept formulating standards and best practice. One of its main contribution was to develop the concept of *customer due diligence* (CDD) for suspicious transactions.

2.3.2.5 The G-7

At the Paris Summit in 1989, the G-7 Heads of State or Government, and President of the European Commission set a Financial Action Task Force on money laundering (FATF) to determine which measures should be taken to combat money laundering.

2.3.3 *The 1990s*

2.3.3.1 Switzerland

In 1990, money laundering was introduced in the Swiss criminal code.[59] In contrast with the other States which had already criminalised money laundering and had limited it to specific offences (mostly drug trafficking,[60] sometimes also terrorism,[61]), Switzerland widened the scope of its legislation to any crime. This was also the approached taken by the 1990 Council of Europe Convention.

58 Belgium, Canada, France, Germany, Italy Japan, Luxembourg, the Netherlands, Sweden, Switzerland, the United Kingdom and the USA.

59 The new bill entered into force 1st August 1990. It was followed in 1997 by the adoption of the *Swiss Money Laundering Act*.

60 Australia, Canada, France, Italy, Luxembourg, UK, USA (cf. FATF (1990), p. 12).

61 Italy (terrorism and hijacking), United Kingdom (terrorism).

2.3.3.2 The Council of Europe

The Council of Europe was the first international organisation to adopt a convention against money laundering. Its main objective is to facilitate international cooperation "to the widest extent possible" not only between judicial authorities – the other conventions of the Council of Europe are sufficient in this regard,[62] but also – and this a novelty in a convention dealing with mutual assistance in criminal matters – between police and customs organisations (administrative cooperation). On the whole, the 1990 *Convention on Laundering, Search, Seizure and Confiscation of the Proceeds from Crime* (CETS 141) provides a complete set of rules, covering all the stages of the procedure from the first investigations (such as seizure and other provisory measures) to the imposition and enforcement of confiscation sentences.

The main characteristic of the 1990 Convention is the widening of the definition of the predicate offence that is the offence generating illegal proceeds. It is not limited to drug trafficking, but applies to any serious crimes such as terrorism, human trafficking and other offences generating large amounts of money. The Convention entered into force on 1 September 1993 and on 1 November 1997 it entered into force for Australia. Since its conclusion, the Council of Europe convention has been considered a cornerstone in AML policy and has significantly contributed to the work of the Financial Action Task Force, which is discussed below.

2.3.3.3 The Europe Union

The *Council Directive 91/308/EEC 10 June 1991 on the prevention of the use of the financial system for the purpose of money laundering* made the reporting of financial transactions mandatory whereas the FATF had recommended in 1991 to either authorise the reporting or oblige financial institutions to inform the competent authorities. In 1996, the Recommendation was changed to make the reporting mandatory.

2.3.3.4 The FATF

In April 1990, the FATF launched its 40 Recommendations. They were followed by Explanatory notes which were integrated into the 1996 revised version of the Recommendations.

---

62 Particularly, the *European Convention on Mutual Assistance in Criminal Matters* of 20 April 1959. This treaty is opened to non-European members states. Australia is not a party.

2.3.4 *The 2000s*

2.3.4.1 The United Nations

The most comprehensive international convention against organised crime to date is the 2000 UN *Convention against Transnational Organised Crime* (UNTOC or Palermo Convention). The treaty devotes two articles on money laundering, one on its criminalisation and the other on measures of administrative character. It reiterates the requirements found in 1988 Vienna Convention that bank secrecy should not prevent financial or commercial records to be made available and seized, or impede international mutual legal assistance.

The 2003 UN *Convention against Corruption* (UNCAC or Merida Convention) complements the UNTOC by expanding the preventive measures against organised crime by involving the private sectors and civil society. Its main focus is on corruption and economic crime. The articles devoted to money laundering are in essence the FATF recommendations. The originality of the UNCAC is therefore to include them in the treaty as well as provisions regarding international cooperation which, beyond traditional provisions on seizure and confiscation, significantly promote the restitution of illegally acquired assets and their repatriation. It contains specific provisions on information exchanges (including spontaneous information) and administrative assistance requirements. Australia was among the first signatories to the UNCAC, which entered into force in 2005.

2.3.4.2 The United Nations Security Council (UN SC)

Following the 9/11 attacks, the UN SC, acting under Chapter 7 of the UN Charter (Action with respect to Threats to the Peace), demanded that Member States criminalise the financing of terrorism (UNSCR 1373 (2001)). It also established a Counter-Terrorism Committee (CTC) to monitor the implementation of UNSCR 1373. In September 2005, it established the Counter-Terrorism Committee Executive Directorate (CTED) to conduct visits to ensure that Member States are implementing its Resolutions.[63]

In December 2006, the UN SC decided to impose economic sanctions on Iran to prevent the development of any nuclear weapons. UNSCR 1737 (2006) requires Member States to freeze the assets of particular individuals and companies with ties to Iran's nuclear programs. In 2016, following yet another nuclear test by the North Korea (DPRK, Democratic People's Republic of Korea), the UN SC urged Member States to apply the FATF Recommendations to implement the targeted financial sanctions it had imposed on individuals and entities (government agencies and banks) (UNSCR 2270).

63 UNSCR 1624 (2005).

2.3.4.3 The FATF

Following UNSCR 1373, the G-8 extended the FATF mandate to the financing of terrorism, a move backed up by the G-20. In early 2002, the FATF issued 8 Special Recommendations (SR) against terrorism financing. A 9th was added on later. The FATF Recommendations were updated in 2003. In 2007, pursuant to UNSCR 1737, the FATF added the financing of weapons of mass destruction (WMD) to the AML/CTF regime and published its first Guidance on the implementation of UNSCR 1737.

2.3.4.4 The G-8

In 2003, the G-8 set up the Counter-Terrorism Action Group (CTAG) to assist the CTC in its mandate, primarily through the provision of training, funding, expertise, equipment, technical and legal assistance to other countries. The CTAG is exclusively made up of Foreign Ministry officials of the G-8 Members States but representatives of other States such as Australia, Switzerland, and Spain have attended sessions.

2.3.4.5 The Council of Europe

In 2005, the Council of Europe adopted the *Convention on Laundering, Search, Seizure and Confiscation of the Proceeds from Crime and on the Financing of Terrorism* (CETS 198). It is the first international treaty covering both the prevention and the control of money laundering and the financing of terrorism. It also includes a monitoring mechanism to ensure its proper implementation by Parties. Although opened to accession by non-member States, Australia is not a Party.

2.3.5 *The 2010s*

2.3.5.1 The Global Counter-Terrorism Forum (GCTF)

Established at the instigation of the US Department of State's Bureau of Counterterrorism, the GCTF was launched in 2011 by 30 founding Members, including Australia. Its goal is to include civilian expert practitioners in the support the UN Global Counter-Terrorism Strategy, a move welcomed by the UN SC.

2.3.5.2 The FATF

In 2012, the 9 Special Recommendations (SR) against terrorism financing were integrated in the revised version of the 40 Recommendations. A rewritten Rec.7 addresses targeted financial sanctions related to the financing of weapons of mass destruction (called "proliferation financing"). The FATF continues to provide guidelines and best-practice papers on topical issues, such as the implementation of a risk-based approach (RBA), virtual currencies (VC)

(2015), financial inclusion (2017), and proliferation financing (2018). The 2018 40 Recommendations update has been entitled *International Standards on Combating Money Laundering and the Financing of Terrorism & Proliferation*, taking into account that the Interpretative Notes form an integral part thereof.

2.3.5.3 The G-20

At the Brisbane Summit in November 2014, G-20 leaders adopted *High-Level Principles on Beneficial Ownership Transparency*, making financial transparency a "high priority" issue.

2.3.5.4 The United Nations Security Council (UN SC)

The UN SC full endorses the work of the FATF and its new risk-based implementation. It regularly urges all Member States to implement the revised 40 Recommendations, insisting particularly on those dealing with targeted financial sanctions related to terrorism and terrorist financing. The initial Member States reporting system has been replaced in 2013 by the Overall Implementation Assessment (OIA) which gives the Counter-terrorism Committee Executive Directorate (CTED) more power over the Member states. With UNSCR 2395 (2017), the UN SC further expanded the Counterterrorism Committee (CTC)'s terms of reference. The new system allows the CTED to initiate visits, to collect information and to rank Member States' compliance.[64] Recently, in order to identify, arrest and cripple financially terrorists, and in particular foreign terrorist fighters, the UN SC has called for better interconnectivity between agencies and INTERPOL, as well as closer cooperation with the private sector.[65]

2.3.5.5 The Europe Union

In its 2015 AML/CTF legislative update (known as 4AMLD),[66] the EU included tax crime in its definition of serious crime and therefore as a predicate offence to money laundering. This move is likely to have an impact on a future revision of the FATF Recommendation, which presently does not formally consider tax crime as a predicate offence. Tax crimes are mentioned in the FATF glossary among a list of offences which each country may decide to consider as serious crimes.

---

64 For a discussion on the CTC's role, see Roele (2013).

65 UNSCR 2396 (2017), point 16.

66 Fourth Directive of the European Parliament and of the Council amending Directive on the prevention of the use of the financial system for the purposes of money laundering or terrorist financing, 08.05.2015.

The 4AMLD had not even been implemented when the EU decided on revise it. The 5AMLD, adopted in 2018, constitutes a major step toward financial transparency. Among the major modifications of the 5AMLD is the establishment, in each EU country, of a central register for ownership of bank accounts, enabling Financial Intelligence Units (FIUs) to identify account holders. The information will have to be "adequate, accurate and current" and accessible in real time. The sharing of information between FIUs is broadened. In due course, all these registers will be interconnected through a Central Platform.[67] A national register on beneficial ownerships (corporate and legal entities including trusts/trustees) will be managed centrally by the European Commission while the public (media, civil society i.e. NGOs) will be able to access it, under certain conditions, a clear move to counter tax evasion and tax avoidance, following the publication of the Panama Papers in April 2016. Furthermore, tax advisors and accountants will be brought within the scope of the directive. In addition, following the revelation that prepaid cards had been used in the preparation of the 2015 Paris terrorist attacks, the 5AMLD forbids the use of anonymous prepaid cards above EUR150, and addresses the risks related to virtual currencies. Also, it puts in place enhanced checks on transactions involving high-risk third countries.

2.3.6 *Two Different Approaches*

In his dissertation, *Money laundering – a New International Law enforcement model*, Guy Stessens contrasts the US approach with the Swiss one.[68] The American approach, which has been largely adopted by Australia, illustrates mistrust towards financial institutions. By contrast, the Swiss approach is more consensual and is based on a close cooperation between financial institutions and law enforcement agencies. These two initial systems constitute the backbone of AML mechanism. They have eventually merged into a more comprehensive approach which can now be considered as the world standard.

2.3.6.1 The US Repressive Approach

At first, US legislation defines precisely the requirements laid on the financial sector and sets in place an extensive transmission procedure. Such scheme presents substantial advantages, both for the financial institution and the client. It is clear for the financial institution what it needs to do; for instance, the guidelines provide an exhaustive list of what constitutes a suspicious transaction. The client is also clear about what to expect: for instance, every

67 Presently the date is set at 2021.

68 Stessens (2000). See pp. 108–112.

transaction of USD 10,000 or more will be reported. This regime therefore offers legal certainty and a most satisfactory application of the legality principle.

Unfortunately, this system presents two main drawbacks. First, it is always behind the crime reality. Criminal organisations are very creative in finding ways to circumvent the law. For instance, to evade the reporting rule of the USD 10,000 threshold, criminals made several bank deposits of less than USD 10,000, thus defeating the system. Hence, a major flaw of this scheme is that the list of requirements must constantly be adapted to the new realities of money laundering; consequently, regulations are never up to date. Secondly, the mechanism is inefficient at worst, very costly at best. The US method generated daily a huge amount of reports – over 12 million in 1997[69] – and, following a new approach, over 14 million in 2011.[70] In contrast, for the period 2014/2015, the total of transactions reports in Australia exceeded 96 million.[71] To analyse every report requires sophisticated software and a large workforce. If there are not enough people to analyse the reports, the system fails.

2.3.6.2 The Swiss Preventive Approach

By contrast, Swiss legislation did not list precisely what the financial institutions must do to prevent being complicit of money laundering, but rather left it to the financier to decide what behaviour or transaction is indicative of money laundering.[72] The employee has therefore a margin of appreciation. The Swiss approach can therefore be considered cost effective. It is economical for the State given that the financial institutions bear the costs of developing internal guidelines in accordance to the law; they must train their staff and check that the guidelines are being observed. It is also very efficient as it acknowledges that the financier is in the best position to assess if a transaction is suspicious or can be part of a money laundering scheme. Further, the involvement of the private sector ensures that the regulations are made by experts in a non-confrontational manner and can be issued very quickly.

However, the approach has four major drawbacks. First, the initial way chosen by Switzerland relies heavily on the financial industry. It lacks transparency for the non-expert. Second, given the regulations are developed outside the traditional prerogative of parliament which discusses and then adopts legislation, these regulations lack legal legitimacy and therefore they should not be enforceable penally. Third, this regime works well if the financier is honest

69 Stessens (2000), p. 99.
70 FinCEN (2011), p. 8. It is the last report available to date.
71 AUSTRAC (2015), p. 65.
72 Art.305ter Swiss Criminal Code.

and well trained. Therefore great attention must be paid to the supervision of financial institutions. Last, the Swiss approach does not foster client confidence in financial institutions as their employees can be considered as law enforcement agents.

2.3.6.3 In Sum

The different interests pursued by the legislators may explain why "the American model can be seen as predominantly repressive while the Swiss one is predominately preventive.[73] In the US, where organised crime is rife and the illegal drug market large, the main concern was to track and confiscate the assets of drug cartels in order to prevent them from expanding their illegal activities. Conversely, for Switzerland, which offers a small market for criminal organisations, the main concern was to prevent its financial institutions from being misused by criminals whose main operations are located outside the country. It is therefore not surprising that Switzerland became the first State to subject assets originated from any crime, and not just drug trafficking, to its AML legislation, even when the crimes had been committed outside the Swiss territory.

The American repressive approach, notably its incrimination of money laundering, has been internationalised by the UN *Convention against Illicit Traffic in Narcotic Drugs and Psychotropic Substances* and the Council of Europe *Convention on Laundering, Search, Seizure and Confiscation of the Proceeds from Crime*. The Swiss preventative approach is manifest in banking law and regulations. As industry regulations were translated into criminal legislation or upheld by criminal courts, the initial "twin track policy" consisting of a preventive style founded in banking law and a repressive stance founded in criminal law eventually merged into a more comprehensive course.[74]

The FATF Recommendations, considered as the world standard for the prevention of money laundering, which shall now be briefly examined, draws heavily on the US and Swiss experience.

2.4 The International Players

2.4.1 *The G-7, the UNSC and the FATF*

In 1989, the G-7 Heads of State or Government and the President of the European Commission expressed their concern regarding the threat posed by money laundering to the world financial system and established the Financial

73 Stessens (2000), p. 109.
74 Stessens (2006); Stessens (2000), pp. 108–112.

Action Task Force on money laundering (FATF). Its mandate was to examine money laundering techniques and trends, to review the action which had already been taken both at national and international level, and to recommend preventive measures that were still needed to combat money laundering, including the adoption of statutory and regulatory regimes to enhance multilateral legal assistance.

The FATF was originally composed of 15 States – the G-7 summit participants and 8 interested States, among them Australia.[75] It now includes 35 Members States and the two international organisations, the European Commission and the Gulf Co-operation Council. Although its secretariat is located in the OECD building in Paris, the FATF is a free-standing organisation; it is not part of the OECD.

In April 1990, the FATF issued a report containing 40 Recommendations for the prevention of money laundering. They are considered the "crown jewel of soft law".[76] They integrate the Council of Europe *Recommendation R(80)10 on measures against the transfer and the safekeeping of funds of criminal origin*, the *Basel Statement of Principles*, the recommendations of the 1988 UN *Convention against Illicit Traffic in Narcotic Drugs and Psychotropic Substances* and the 1990 Council of Europe *Convention on Laundering, Search, Seizure and Confiscation of the Proceeds from Crime* (1990 Convention on money laundering). They are the result of the work of various ministries (mainly justice, finance and foreign affairs), law enforcement authorities, bank supervisors and regulatory agencies. Because of their universal remit and the great variety and differences in national laws, the Recommendations are meant to be flexible and to be used as guidelines.

The Task Force's original mandate was for one year. It was extended several times, lastly in 2012, when it was prolonged until 2020. Following the 2001 terrorist attacks, the FATF mandate was enlarged to include the prevention of terrorism financing. In 2002, it issued Special Recommendations against the financing of terrorism, which were integrated in 2012 into the 40 Recommendations, alongside measures against the financing of weapons of mass destruction (called proliferation financing) which had been introduced in 2007.

During its annual meetings, the various FATF experts discuss issues of mutual concern. For instance, the law enforcement officers' group on typologies discuss the new technics, trends and patterns in money laundering they have discovered. These discussions are confidential. Only "sanitised" versions of

75 Australia, Austria, Belgium, Luxembourg, the Netherlands, Spain, Sweden and Switzerland.

76 Stessens (2000), p. 17.

their findings are made available to the public.[77] The Recommendations were revised and updated in 1996, 2003, 2012 and 2018 to reflect new trends and changes that had taken place in money laundering and terrorism financing methods.

After the FATF issued its Recommendations, its focus moved first to monitor the implementation of its recommendations by its Member States. To assist them, the FATF issued *Interpretative Notes* which were later integrated into the Recommendations. In addition, the FATF provides regular guidance on the implementation of the Recommendations and publishes best-practice guides. Teams of members of national delegations are sent in turns to another Member State to assess the level of implementation. Their findings are found in the *Mutual Evaluation Reports* (MER). Australia's AML legislation has been examined four times: in 1992, 1996, 2005 and 2015. In the next stage, the FATF strove to establish of a worldwide AML network. It opened its membership to other States; non-Members were encouraged to adopt and implement the recommendations. It developed FATF-style regional bodies and close cooperation with relevant international organisations, such as the Global Forum on Transparency and Exchange of Information for Tax Purposes (Global Forum). Practically, all these institutions are reinforcing each other's work.

The work of the Task Force constitutes a basic framework for the financial aspects of the fight against money laundering and has greatly influenced the subsequent national and international legislation, including Australia's. The Australian Government considers it as world standard and has modified its legislation accordingly. Since the 9/11 attacks, the UN SC has spearheaded the fight against terrorism and terrorism financing in particular. Its direction has given the FATF a new impetus to the AML apparatus as well as a focus on specific aspects.[78] Following the UN SC directions, the FATF has expanded the original scope of the Recommendations in regards to the financing of terrorism and the financing of weapons of mass destruction. It has emphasised, for example, the use of non-governmental, non-profit and charitable organisations by and for terrorists; the issue of foreign fighters and their families' travel expenses; the use of information technologies and the Internet; the need to develop a more effective international cooperation and transmission of data between the various actors. The current attention given to more transparency on ownerships is part of the general campaign to prevent the use of legal persons and arrangements (multiple shell and front companies) in ML/TF. The

77 Sanitised cases are cases which have had all specific identifying features removed.

78 UNSCR 2253 (2015), points 16,17; UNSCR 2354 (2017)_24.05.2017, points 17,18; UNSCR 2395 (2017)_21.12.2017.

focus has nevertheless been stressed as essential in the fight against proliferation financing and tax evasion. The more the scope of the AML/CTF has been expanded, the more institutions/ businesses and various actors, including the private sector, have been called to play a part.

2.4.1.1 The 40 Recommendations

The FATF 40 Recommendations, or international standards as they are now called, hinge on three axis: Legislation, prevention and cooperation.

2.4.1.1.1 *Legislation*

Member States are required to

- criminalise money laundering: At first, Member States were urged to ratify and implement the 1988 Vienna Convention and the 1990 Council of Europe Money Laundering Convention and to make money laundering a criminal offence. In 2003, States were invited to ratify also the 2000 UNTOC or Palermo Convention and the 2005 Council of Europe Money Laundering and Terrorism Financing Convention. Initially, only the proceeds of drug trafficking were subject to the FATF Recommendations. Gradually, the list of offences generating the proceeds (called *predicate offences*) was extended to all serious crimes. In a further stage, less serious offences committed on a commercial basis were included in the predicate offences and since 2012, tax crimes, which had traditionally been excluded from mutual criminal assistance, are listed among the designated serious offences;
- criminalise the financing of terrorism, including forms of participation. Since 2002, States are called to ratify and implement the 1999 UN *Convention for the Suppression of the Financing of Terrorism*;
- allow for the confiscation of laundered assets or of property of corresponding value, including non-conviction based confiscation;
- introduce criminal liability for corporations, a concept often unknown in the tradition of civil law States;
- grant international mutual assistance requests, including the freezing and confiscation of assets, extradition requests and provide for mechanisms of the confiscated assets with foreign agencies.

The sanctions for breaching the offences must be *effective, proportionate and dissuasive*. This wording has been taken from the European Union AML/CTF legislation.

2.4.1.1.2 *Prevention*

Initially, the FATF was set up to prevent the threat posed by organised crime to the banking system and to financial institutions. In a subsequent stage, the concern was enlarged to any channels that can be used for money laundering. Hence, the purpose of the AML regime is to ensure that money laundering is prevented and assets can be easily traced. The Recommendations focus mainly on measures to enhance the role of financial and not-financial institutions, but also on individuals. To achieve this, four basic requirements are imposed on them.

- *Know-your-customer*: The customer, the beneficial owner of the transaction and the source of the funds should be identified before the establishment of a business relationship (called the *know-your-customer* standard/principle or KYC). The purpose and nature of the business relationship should be identified and monitored on an on-going basis to ensure that the transactions are consistent with the information available.
- *Due diligence:* The financial institutions must give special attention to
  (a)
    - transactions suspected of being connected to money laundering, terrorism or proliferation financing (for instance complex, unusual and important transactions that do not seem to have an economic or legal justification or which use new and developing technologies, cash transactions above a defined threshold and virtual currency payment products and services (VCPPSs);
    - transactions which come from institutions based in States that do not or insufficiently apply the Recommendations (third risk countries) or from services that do not conduct adequate due customer diligence.

  (b) individuals and legal entities
    - designated persons and entities by the UN CTC;
    - beneficial ownerships (trusts, companies and other legal entities);
    - *politically-exposed persons* (PEPs). The politically-exposed persons are individuals who are or have been entrusted with prominent public functions, their family members or close associates, as well as their business relationships;
    - life insurance beneficiaries.

Since 2012, a *risk assessment analysis* has been introduced in order to adapt the measures to the actual risk of money laundering and terrorist financing. The introduction of a risk assessment has two main consequences: it permits the simplification of the *customer due diligence* (CDD) when there is clearly a reduce risk of money laundering or terrorism financing. It also demands a higher level of vigilance or "enhanced customer due diligence" in situations when the money laundering/terrorism financing risk is clearly greater. This is particularly the case in three situations: when there is no face-to-face contact with the customer, in cross-frontier banking relationship, and in relations with *politically-exposed persons* (PEPs). Transactions involving PEPs require enhanced CDD because of potential misappropriation of public assets and other corrupt practices.

- Records must be kept for at least five years.
- Guidelines and feedback: Institutions and persons covered by the Recommendations must develop internal policies, procedures and controls as well as train their personnel in order to carry out the requirements. This requires a specific knowledge and substantial means. Therefore those subject to the Recommendations need to be given access to up-to-date information on the practices of money launderers and terrorist financers, as well as on elements leading to the recognition of suspicious transactions, businesses and individuals. The FATF regularly issues "Best Practice guidelines" on various aspects of the requirements. In addition, given that implementing AML requirements is very costly, the private sector should see that the incurred costs are generating worthwhile results, even though the costs are passed onto customers. To that end, the FATF recommends that they be provided with "timely" feed back on the effectiveness of and follow-up to their reports of suspected money laundering / terrorist financing transactions.

2.4.1.1.3 *Cooperation*

The FATF requires measures on both domestic and international levels.

- *Domestic cooperation*

The implementation of the Recommendations requires extended cooperation between the private sector and the law enforcement authorities, as well as between various law enforcement agencies. National authorities must set in place domestic agencies which will collect, process and analyse the reports made by the financial and non-financial institutions subjected to AML/CTF regulations. These agencies need to set up registries with relevant and accurate information that can be accessed "in a timely manner" by other authorised entities, including tax agencies and financial institutions.

To assist those reporting entities, the competent authorities must establish guidelines to help them prevent money laundering as well as provide them with instructions regarding the reporting requirements. In addition, there should be a close working relationship between the central agency and domestic law enforcement and other units. In Australia, the central agency is AUSTRAC (Australian Transaction Reports and Analysis Centre) which works closely with federal agencies, such as ATO (Australia Tax Office), customs and immigration authorities, as well as with corresponding state agencies.

- *International cooperation* should be reinforced in two main areas: judicial and administrative.

Between judicial authorities. International mutual assistance in criminal matters is codified into strict rules contained in treaties. Such cooperation takes place mainly between judicial authorities, whose decisions are subject to appeal and review by an independent court. Since the 1980s, with the development of the AML machinery, many have called for a move away from the traditional forms of mutual assistance which are seen as too rigid and too slow.

The FATF recommends the widest possible range of mutual legal assistance, including on procedural and evidentiary aspects. The exception to legal assistance should be reduced to a minimum. For instance, it should not be hindered by the absence of dual criminality or on the ground of bank secrecy or because the offence has a fiscal character. Extradition procedures should be simplified. Further, the grounds for appeal should be limited so that the process can be accelerated.

The 1990 Council of Europe money laundering convention restricts spontaneous information to instrumentalities and proceeds and specifies that the requirement of confidentiality is the norm in mutual assistance, except when contrary to basic principles of the national law of the requested party. This exception has become the rule and a gateway to possible abuse. The general simplification of procedure which was advocated paved the way for an extensive form of administrative assistance. Procedural simplifications aim at facilitating the exchange of information, and therefore speed up criminal investigations.

In the area of administrative assistance, exchange of information is encouraged, provided it does not impede fair competition or discriminate between categories of financial institutions which would go against its Members' economic interests.

From the onset, in order to win the confidence of the financial sector, the suspicious transaction reports (STRs) made by financial institutions were treated confidentially and could not be transmitted spontaneously. Later, this was seen an impediment to an effective AML/CTF policy. Prevention depends on the quick accessibility of correct and pertinent information. Hence, in 2000s, the EU developed *the principle of availability*, which is included in the 2012 FATF recommendations. According to this principle, relevant information that may be pertinent to an investigation or analysis must be accessible to another equivalent authority in another Member State. In Australia, *Proceeds of Crime Act 1987* (Cth) (POCA) gives a clear mandate for the dissemination of information to other agencies.

The development of AML/CTF machinery has triggered a surge in administrative assistance (assistance on request) and automatic information transfer (spontaneous assistance) between law enforcement agencies which is a breakaway from the previously strict principles set forth in mutual assistance in criminal matters. New technologies have also made cooperation more broad and effective, allowing data to be collected on a wide-ranging scale, then processed and sent further to partner agencies. However, this type of information sharing erodes the safeguards put in place to protect human rights and fair trials. The main concerns stem from the fact that financial data are transmitted on individuals and companies that may have no connections with any crime. The transfer of information is not protected by the possibility of appeals not only because there are few appeal procedures in place in administrative assistance but also because most of the time the person concerned is simply not aware that data concerning him or her is being transferred; there is no obligation to inform that person. To avoid jeopardising a possible investigation, the transfer of data must remain confidential.

If the simplification of procedures can take place within a jurisdiction or between States of similar legal tradition upholding human rights, the risk of infringements on individual rights may be seen as minimal. However, the removal of procedural guarantees provided by the international treaties pose a serious risk of violation of the right of fair trial when dealing with States that do not uphold human rights. This is particularly the case when the accuracy of the information transmitted is not or cannot be verified beforehand or has been obtained illegally. Australia does not share this concern. For instance, in *Denlay v Commissioner of Taxation*, the court upheld the practice of using information that had been obtained illegally. In this case, the information had been stolen. Whether the information has been derived by legal or illegal means is no relevant criteria. According to the Federal Court of Australia, Logan J, the Commission of Taxation may authorise any agent "to have at *all* times *full and free* access to *all* buildings, places, books, documents and other papers for any of the purposes of the [ITAA]".[79] Even if an agent of ASIS were to commit all sorts of violations of a foreign banking secrecy law to obtain relevant documents, that would not rend that conduct unlawful under Australian law. Similarly, US legislation permits the Internal Revenue Service (IRS) to use information obtained from a third party in circumstances where that third party has illegally obtained that information.[80] The use of such information appears to be restricted to tax matters. Nevertheless, the rules regarding exchange of information have been further extended in terrorism financing matters.

By setting the conditions in which information and data could be transmitted, the international treaties' provisions protected not only the right of

---

79 *Denlay v Commissioner of Taxation*, [2010] FCA 1434 [91].

80 *Denlay v Commissioner of Taxation*, [2010] FCA 1434 [100] [103].

individuals against the overwhelming power of the State, they also ensure that it is appropriate to use the documents in judicial proceedings. Doing away with these rules opens the door to miscarriages of justice. Some of them are discussed in Chapter 5 in relation to terrorism financing. The Council of Europe, like the FATF, have partly acknowledged this problem and have accompanied their recommendations regarding administrative assistance with safeguarding provisions. The FATF stipulates that strict safeguards should be established to ensure that the exchange of information is consistent with national and international provisions on privacy and data protection, a lip service requirement given that some governments seem undisturbed when national legislation encroaches on human rights.

2.4.1.2 The Development of the Recommendations

2.4.1.2.1 *From Bank Secrecy to Mandatory Reporting and Risk-Based Approach* (*RBA*)

In the early days of the fight against money laundering, once a requested transaction had been deemed suspicious, it was understood that the banks should decline conducting it. Though this measure would keep intact the probity of the institution, it was not helping the law enforcement authorities to track the criminals, as the client would simply go elsewhere to perform the transaction; the paper trail would then be lost. Consequently, the FATF recommended that the technique of "controlled delivery" used in international drug trafficking should be applied in those involving suspected money laundering.[81] Hence, the financial institution was allowed to report the suspicious transaction to a competent authority, without informing the client and without risk of a sanction for breaching the privacy laws. The transaction would then be executed and all the documentation forwarded to the law enforcement agencies. In 1996, following the adoption of the EU first AML directive in 1991 which made it mandatory for financial institutions to report suspicious transactions, the FATF made the reporting to competent authorities mandatory, waiving the domestic confidentiality laws. Nearly a decade after the launch of the 40 Recommendations, the surge of the costs of the AML apparatus prompted the FATF to recommend a risk-based approach to reporting rather than "mechanistic and legalistic solutions".[82] This new approach relies on the financial institution's expertise in detecting suspicious transactions.

81 FATF (1993), p. 18.
82 Gilmore (2004), p. 41.

The RBA requires each country, firstly, to identify and assess the risk of money laundering, terrorism and proliferation financing per sector (institutions, activities, businesses or professions), then within each sector. Next, the financial and non-financial institution/business has to identify and assess the risk per client (for instance PEPs or not) and per transactions (the type of currencies involved). Secondly, they are required to tailor the implementation of the AML/CTF requirements proportionally to the risk thus identified. States with weak AML/CTF legislation also need to be identified so that appropriate RBA measures can be applied when dealing with financial transactions and institutions which come from these States. For instance, States with deficient AML/CTF legislation may be considered high-risk countries. However, if one of them is underdeveloped economically, it may not be considered attractive to money launderers and therefore not present a substantial risk for money laundering.

2.4.1.2.2 *New Payment Technologies and Virtual Currencies*

Over the years, there have been increased concerns regarding new payment technologies such as prepaid cards, mobile payments, internet casinos, internet banking and other electronic fund transfers which can be used to dissimulate the identity of the original ordering customer and/or the beneficiary. In Internet transactions, there is typically no face-to-face customer contact and thus no means to identify those involved. Prepaid cards can easily be passed on to third parties that are unknown to the issuer and allow third party remittances. However, the level of risk posed by anonymity is relative to the functionality of the card. One way to mitigate the risk is to fix funding or purchasing limits, reload limits, cash access, and to limit it to a given geographical area.

New forms of virtual currency (VC) such as bitcoins, zerocoins and darkcoins are considered as exhibiting a potential high risk of money laundering and terrorism financing, though the use of crypto-currencies have not been established.[83] Technically the use of bitcoins is transparent – their movements are traceable. However, they have been used for money-laundering purposes.[84] Hence, because convertible decentralised VC payment products and services (VCPPSs) pose difficulties to identify the persons involved, they are often regarded as presenting a higher risk of ML/FT. Consequently they should be subjected to enhanced due diligence measures.

---

83 Irwin, Milad (2016).

84 Theguardian.com (2016).

2.4.1.2.3 *From Banks to Non-financial Institutions, Charities and Independent Professionals*

Though the original preoccupation was to restore and preserve the integrity of the banking system, "experience showed that money launderers will utilise almost any form of corporate and trust activity to launder their profits", especially those which handle significant amounts of cash.[85] Ultimately any non-financial business can be used. Progressively, more institutions and businesses have been subjected to the AML/CTF regime. The increasing use of legitimate non-financial businesses (such as retail shops, import-export companies) and investments in gold and expensive goods led to an extension of the AML apparatus to non-financial institutions such as bureaux de change, currency exchange houses, casinos and betting agencies, auction houses, life insurance companies, building societies. Fiduciary transactions and alternative remittances systems such as hawala and hundi parallel banking systems, the Black Market Peso Exchange and the Chinese/East Asian systems have also come under scrutiny.

With the extension of the FATF mandate to terrorism financing, non-profit organisations (NPO), such as charities and non-governmental organisations (NGOs), were deemed "particularly vulnerable" to TF, despite a dearth of evidence, and been submitted to the Recommendations. The strong language was subsequently tuned down in 2015.[86]

Individuals and independent legal professionals such as lawyers, attorneys, notaries, accountants and estate agents are required to report suspicious transactions of which they have gain knowledge in the conduct of their business. This requirement has been slowly implemented given the conflict between professional secrecy and the AML/CTF obligations, but it has in recent years been gaining momentum, particularly in the context of a crack down on tax evasion.

2.4.1.2.4 *From Financial Activities to Trade*

The establishment of the Islamic State across Syria and Iraq in 2014 and its use of natural resources, such as oil and other commodities, and cultural goods to finance their activities, led to further attention given to international trade. Various international economic activities (such as the trade in oil and other natural resources), as well as assets which could be used to be exchanged against material necessary to develop WMD are increasingly scrutinised in order to prevent the financing of terrorism or of weapons of mass destruction.

---

85 Sherman (1993), p. 14; FATF (1991), p. 9.

86 See Romaniuk, Keatinge (2018).

2.4.1.2.5 *From Drug Offences to Tax Crimes*

The extension of the predicate offence (the offence which originates the proceeds) follows the development of the activities of criminal organisations. Starting with drug trafficking, it now includes all serious crimes, among which tax crimes, with definitions varying from State to State. There are similarities between money laundering and tax evasion in situations where criminal organisations do not fully launder their profits (manage to remove all connections between the assets and a predicate offence) but chose to keep the assets from the scrutiny of tax authorities. Evaded taxes must be disguised, and laundered money must be kept hidden from the tax authorities. In any case, the line between tax crime and legitimate tax planning may not be easily set and may vary according to jurisdictions.

The extension of the AML regime to tax offences may be considered a result of its failure to capture the great profits of the heads of criminal organisations, whereby corporate and individual tax evaders are sought for money laundering rather than only criminal organisations. It also prefigures a change of paradigm.

2.4.1.2.6 *From Criminal Proceeds to Criminal Funding*

Ten years after the 40 Recommendations were first issued, their paradigm has shifted. With the inclusions to the AML machinery of terrorism financing and the financing of weapons of mass destruction, the focus is no more on the predicate offence only, but also on the final destination of the assets. In this configuration, the origin of the funding may be legitimate, but it is the financed activities which constitute both the crime and a threat to security. However, so as to fit with the AML initial theoretical concept, the FATF has justified the inclusion of terrorism and proliferation financing into the AML/ATF apparatus by saying that they are both serious crimes. Consequently, they are constitutive of predicate offences to money laundering and subject to the AML/CTF arsenal.

2.4.1.3 The FATF Monitoring and Enforcement Mechanism

The question of the enforcement of the Recommendations has been in the centre of the discussions since the beginning of the FATF. It was thought that the credibility and reputation of the FATF would be at stake if it could not ensure the correct implementation of the Recommendations by its own members. Further, poor compliance would prevent the setting up of a worldwide network against money laundering, which has been the FATF goal since 1994. This section examines first how the FATF assesses the level of compliance of its own Members and the measures which have been taken to address their shortcomings; secondly, how the FATF reacted to the non-compliance of non-Member States as it sought to widen the fight against money laundering.

2.4.1.3.1 *FATF Member States*

Despite the marked development of international treaties in the field of criminal law after the WW2, there is still no proper mechanism to sanction their breaches. In this vacuum, there is room for creative alternatives. In order to monitor the correct implementation of the Recommendations, the FATF chose three methods. All stem from the observation that peer pressure can be an effective tool for enforcement. The findings are then discussed at FATF meetings.

Three methods

(a) The *self-assessment* procedure requires members to report annually to the FATF secretariat on their progress in implementing the Recommendations.

(b) The *cross-country evaluation* is conducted on the basis of questionnaires with the objective of finding out information on the nature and results of the measures taken so far regarding a specific Recommendation.

(c) Most importantly, the *mutual evaluation* process or a peer-to-peer assessment is the examination, by a team of experts from Member States, of one Member's complete set of AML/CTF measures (pertaining to legislation, industry, procedure, law enforcement, and cooperation). The first round of evaluation, which took 5 years,[87] was mainly concerned with the implementation of the Recommendations, while the second round (from 1996 to 1999) was concerned with the effectiveness of the measures adopted and the follow-up of the first report.[88] The third one, which started in 2004, focused on terrorism financing. The fourth round started in 2014: It is basically a follow-up of the previous one. As noted by Tom Sherman, then Chairman of the Task Force,

> this has proved to be a very effective mechanism as a large number of member countries are making significant efforts to introduce anti-money laundering measures in anticipation of a visit from a team of evaluators. This shows the value of external, pressure and peer scrutiny upon our membership.[89]

87 From 1991 to 1995.

88 The third round, a simplified form of the previous ones, was postponed till 2002 because in 2001 the FATF issued Special Recommendations pertaining to the financing of terrorism.

89 Sherman (1993), p. 19.

The monitoring regime put in place by the FATF has been widely followed in other arenas. For instance,

- in 1997 the Council of Europe set up the Committee of Experts on the Evaluation of Anti-Money Laundering Measures (PC-R-EV) later renamed MONEYVAL. It is composed of the Member States of the Council of Europe which are not members of the FATF i.e. former Eastern and Central European communist countries with limited experience in international financial exchanges.
- the Commonwealth Secretariat has also introduced self-evaluation of progress on the implementation of AML measures in the financial sector.
- in June 2000, the International Monetary Fund (IMF) launched an Assessment Program on Offshore Financial Centres. Contrary to the FATF practice, all assessments are voluntary, conducted by the IMF and not by the States.

The mutual evaluation process is also used in other fields than money laundering such as corruption[90] and human rights.[91]

Addressing non-compliance

From the onset, the issue of non-compliance has been debated in the FATF. Some Member States suggested that those members found not complying with the 40 Recommendations could be put onto a black list or be excluded from the international financial system (in accordance with then Recommendation 21, leaving it to each Member to decide if they would maintained financial relations with institutions from those non-compliant States and under what conditions. The FATF policy regarding non-compliant members was first applied, since 1995, to Turkey, Austria, Canada, Japan, and Singapore. The USA was treated differently, which might reveal a difference in treatment between FATF Members. Since then, non-compliance is addressed through the self-assessment and mutual evaluation exercises.

2.4.1.3.2 *Non-FATF Member States*

While still working on an effective implementation of the 40 Recommendations by its own members, the FATF launched a strategy towards a worldwide mobilisation against money laundering, which included persuading non-Member States to adopt its Recommendations.

The FATF feared that, once Member States started to enforce the AML regulations, criminal organisations would divert their capital towards non-compliant

90 See art.12, OECD *Convention on Combating Bribery of Foreign Public Officials in International Business Transactions*, 1997.

91 See the UN Human Rights Council (UNHRC) on the Members' compliance with the *International Covenant on Civil and Political Rights* (ICCPR).

or less compliant States such as countries in transition (for example the former Eastern European States) and emerging market economies. These economies were seen as particularly vulnerable to money laundering because they potentially offer opportunities for in-land investments, such as purchasing banks or other financial institutions for criminal organisations. In addition, the development of internet banking offered new opportunities for financial services to States whose financial sector was less regulated. Undoubtedly, these jurisdictions were also making unhealthy competition with States which had implemented the Recommendations.

Alleging that the lack of cooperation of certain States in abiding by the FATF rules, particularly a number of offshore jurisdictions,[92] could potentially jeopardise the whole AML system set up by the Task Force, the FATF considered implementing procedure akin to the one applicable to its own Member States. It was spurred into action by the enactment in 1995 of the Seychelles *Economic Development Act*, which provided immunity from prosecution for all criminal proceedings to investors bringing USD10 millions or more in approved investment schemes. Under the chairmanship of the USA, the FATF developed a formal policy regarding its relationship with non-members in order to assess their progress in combating money-laundering. In 1999, the FATF launched the *Non-Cooperative Countries and Territories* (NCCT) initiative. It consists of three steps. First, is the identification of the non-compliant jurisdictions (establishing the so-called "black list"). Secondly, there are the retaliatory measures to be applied to obtain a change (ranging from requiring FATF Members to provide closer scrutiny of transactions with NCCT to, *ultima ratio*, restricting or even imposing a financial embargo with those jurisdictions). Finally, there are the criteria for removing said jurisdictions from the list. In 2000 and 2001, the FATF identified 23 non-Member States whose money laundering provisions were said to be either non-existent, rudimentary or ineffective,[93] to which the FATF applied Recommendation 21. The States were each sent a report stating the reasons for their listing and indicating the steps that they should take to eliminate the negative aspects of their rules and practices. This procedure was widely criticised, namely by the IMF, specifically because the criteria for putting a jurisdiction on the black list were vague and inconsistent.[94] In response,

92 IMF (2000a), p. 2.

93 The Bahamas, the Cayman Islands, the Cook Islands, Dominica, Egypt, Granada, Guatemala, Hungary, Indonesia, Israel, Lebanon, Liechtenstein, the Marshall Islands, Myanmar, Nauru, Nigeria, Niue, Panama, the Philippines, Russia, St. Kitts and Nevis, Ukraine, and St. Vincent and the Grenadines.

94 IMF (2000a), pp. 5,6; IMF (2000b), pp. 2, 3.

the FATF abandoned this practice in 2006[95] and worked with the IMF to develop new criteria. Regularly, the FATF releases public statements identifying jurisdictions with strategic AML/CTF deficiencies. In 2015, only 3 States were on the NCCT list: The Democratic People's Republic of Korea (DPRK), Iran and Myanmar. In April 2018, two countries were on the high-risk list (DPRK and Iran) and nine others were still monitored.

Realising that the previous policy could foster the development of a parallel financial system, which would foreclose the traceability of all financial transactions, and therefore make the detection of terrorism and WMD financing more difficult, the FATF changed its policy from exclusion to inclusion.[96] Further, the FATF developed two less confrontational strategies based on

(1) the dissemination of the 40 Recommendations and cooperation with non-Member States which were offering financial havens and offshore centres. The FATF organises regional conferences in key regions like the Caribbean, East Europe and Asia-Pacific. These led to the setting up of FATF regional centres ("FATF-Style Regional Bodies"), composed of both Members and non-Member States.[97]
(2) the enlargement of its membership to strategically important States which are willing to implement the 40 Recommendations and can play a major role in their regions in the process of combating money laundering, irrespective of their level of economic development.

In order to ensure a worldwide AML/CTF network, the FATF maintains regular contacts with a number of governmental institutions.[98] Co-ordination meetings are also taking place in the margins of the FATF plenaries. In addition, the FATF has regular contacts with the private sector. Among the participants are national banking, financial and accounting associations, SWIFT, Western Union and the Offshore Group of Banking Supervisors.

---

95 Jakobi (2015), p. 400.

96 FATF (2017).

97 The regional FATF-style bodies are members of the FATF. They carry out mutual evaluations of their members and review regional money-laundering trends. Taking into consideration these jurisdictions, more than 130 States have adopted the FATF Standards. There are 9 FATF-Style Regional Bodies including the Asia/Pacific Group on Money Laundering (APG), created in 1997. Its secretariat is in Sydney.

98 UNODC (United Nations Office for Drug Control and Crime Program), the Council of Europe, the Commonwealth Secretariat, the International Monetary Fund (IMF), the International Organisation of Securities Commissions (IOSCO), the Offshore Group of Banking Supervisors, the World Bank, the World Customs Organisation, INTERPOL and the Inter-American Drug Abuse Control Commission (CICAD) and FOPAC (Fonds Provenant des Activités Criminelles, a division of INTERPOL which collects data about proceeds of criminal activities).

2.4.2 *The Financial Intelligence Units (FIU) and the Egmont Group*

2.4.2.1 The Financial Intelligence Units (FIU)

Traditionally, there is no obligation to report a crime – even a serious crime. Under AML/CTF legislation, reporting suspicion is mandatory. The reporting is not about a crime against life but a *suspicion* that assets *may* have a criminal origin. AML legislation initiated a trend that emphasises the importance of the financial aspects of a crime over the predicate offence or the crime itself. Under AML regulations, this trend has been further developed in such a manner that provisions pertaining to mutual cooperation, exchange of information, seizure and confiscation offer a wider scope of application than cooperation for other criminal offences.

One of the characteristics of money laundering is that it is a "crime without victim"[99] in the sense that there is no victim to report the offence to the police. It is therefore very difficult for law enforcement to find out that money laundering is taking place. Hence, the financial institutions' personnel is encouraged – rather compelled for fear of sanction – to cooperate with law enforcement agencies and even to be pro-active.

In order to facilitate the transmission of the requested information by financial institutions, a number of countries have set up "Financial Intelligence Units" (FIU). A FIU is a national agency responsible for receiving a variety of financial information received from the financial and non-financial institutions subject to AML/CTF regulations. It acts as an intermediary between the private financial sector and other authorities. The FIUs specialise in the analysis of financial transactions and offer advice. They transmit relevant information either to a law enforcement agency or to the prosecutorial authorities. The FIUs also communicate between each other and transmit information as suggested in the 1988 Vienna Convention and the 2000 UNTOC. The FATF regards the FIU as a "key body" in AML/CTF regime.[100]

The nature of the FIUs may vary according to each country's legal system. It can be a law enforcement agency, a judicial authority or an administrative agency, or an agency of an hybrid character.[101] Some common law States or in jurisdictions where the criminal justice system grants a greater role for the police, the FIU is a law enforcement agency. This is the case of the Australian Transaction Reports and Analysis Centre (AUSTRAC),[102] FinCEN (USA) and

99 STESSENS (2000), pp. 421,422.

100 FATF (2001a), para.64, p. 13.

101 Ecolef (2013), pp. 141–142.

102 AUSTRAC is Australia's anti-money laundering and counter-terrorism financing supervisory body which oversees the compliance of the "reporting entities" listed in the Act. It is also competent in areas of major crimes and tax evasion.

UKFIU (UK),[103] for instance. Some States have chosen a judicial authority to run the FIU since it fits well in their law enforcement tradition. Taking into account the reluctance of financial institutions or independent professionals to display a close collaboration with the police, some States, mainly European, have set up a body separated from the law enforcement authorities. They have opted for an administrative structure which is an "interface" between financial institutions and law enforcement authorities.

The FIU acts like a filter. It collects, processes and analyses data, retaining information which it considers pertinent, and transmits to law enforcement and judicial authorities that which, in its eyes, deserves police or judicial attention. Once this information is in hand of the FIU, it may be shared between other FIUs and partner agencies, domestically or abroad, according to a framework of a mutual administrative assistance agreement. Domestic legislation determines the level of cooperation the FIUs can provide.

2.4.2.2 The Egmont Group

The Egmont Group is an organisation which gathers FIUs.[104] Its objective is to develop among participants a more effective and practical co-operation. As from 1995, under the influence of FinCEN, the US Financial Intelligence Unit, several FIUs started to meet informally on regular basis to discuss matters of common interests, provide support and exchange expertise. The FATF recommends that national FIUs apply for membership in the Egmont Group. In 2008–2009, AUSTRAC CEO, Neil Jensen, was the Chair of the Egmont Committee.

2.4.3 *The Private Sector and the Wolfsberg Group*

Cooperation with the private sector is essential to ensure an effective AML/CTF implementation mechanism. Hence FIUs, and AUSTRAC in particular, have developed a close cooperation with the private sector non only to enforce the regulations, but also to discuss possible risks and ways to avert them. In Australia, the reporting entities are also consulted when new regulations are foreseen.

On the international scene, in the early stage of AML, the banking sector took some significant initiatives to fight money laundering in order to prevent the integrity of its industry. These measures were later translated into legislation. In 1999, assuming that the private sector was an essential stakeholder, some members of the civil society (NGOs representatives, an academic and a

103 UKFIU is attached to SOCA (Serious Organised Crime Agency).

104 Its name comes after their first place of meeting in a hotel in Brussels, the Egmont-Arenberg Palace.

former FinCEN director), gathered representatives from the banking sector to discuss ways of promoting better industry AML practices particularly in regard to corruption.[105] In 2000, the Wolfsberg Group, called after the name of their first meeting place, issued the *Wolfsberg Anti-Money Laundering Principles for Private Banking* (*Wolfsberg AML Principles*). It regularly issues Principles, Recommendations and Best Practice papers. It became the first industry body to issue recommendations to counter terrorism financing. Subsequently, the Wolfsberg Group invited FIUs' representatives to discuss their concerns regarding the increasing costs of AML/CTF machinery. It suggested allocating resources in accordance with the perceived risk. Eventually the Group was successful in winning the FATF over to follow a risk-based approach as opposed to a rule-based approach.[106]

The establishment of the Global Counter-Terrorism Forum (GCTF) in 2011 must also be read in the trend to associate more fully the civil society to the AML/CTF fight against money laundering and terrorism and proliferation financing. Though the Forum does not have the influence of Wolfsberg Group, its contribution in identifying emerging terrorism financing risks has been welcome by the FATF.

2.5 Confiscation and Assets Sharing

2.5.1 *Confiscation*

Considering that the international effort against organised crime is based on the assumption that the profits of criminal activities are immense, it was expected that the confiscated assets of criminal organisations following the implementation of AML system would be colossal. When that did not materialise, rather than question the figures of the profits of organised crime, it is legislation and criminal procedure as well as its implementation that became the focus of attention.[107] Calls were made to redraft the offence so as to allow a weaker mental element, to introduce strict or absolute liability and to redefine the evidentiary rules regarding the burden of proof.

The basis for these fundamental departures from the traditional criminal law principles was first laid in the 1988 Vienna convention. In regard to evidentiary issues, not only does the treaty recommend that the documentation regarding financial transactions (the paper trail) be made available to law

105 Aiolfi, Bauer (2012).

106 Pieth, Aiolfi (2003b), p. 362.

107 Freiberg, Fox (2000); Levi (1997), p. 228.

enforcement agencies, and advocate the abolition of bank secrecy and commercial confidentiality, it also suggests reversing the onus of proof regarding the lawful origin of the alleged criminal proceeds. In order to recoup the profits of criminal organisations, the Vienna Convention extends the traditional practice of seizing and confiscating assets of criminal origin by providing for the confiscation of property of a *corresponding value* and the confiscation of the *income derived* from these assets. Seizure and confiscation orders should also apply to property with which such proceeds of crime have been *intermingled*. Similar provisions have been inserted in the 2000 Palermo Convention (UNTOC). The 2001 terrorist attacks provided yet another opportunity to widen the scope of confiscation laws even more.[108]

Another significant change came with the adoption of the 2003 UN Convention against Corruption (UNCAC or Merida Convention) which promotes measures to allow confiscation of property without a criminal conviction in circumstances where the offender cannot be prosecuted due to death, flight, absence or *in other appropriate cases*. In addition, the UNCAC develops the concept of unexplained wealth laws. In sum, the onus is no more on the prosecution to prove that specific assets have a direct or even an indirect criminal origin, or to demonstrate, on the balance of probabilities, that the wealth has been obtained by criminal activity. Under unexplained wealth laws, it is the suspected offender or the defendant who must demonstrate the lawful origin of the contentious assets. These changes, also enshrined in the 2003 updated version of the 40 Recommendations, can be considered a response to the 1996–1997 FATF survey on confiscation. Members complained about legal and procedural difficulties to seize and confiscate and suggested explicitly the above ways to widen the scope of the seizure of suspected assets and facilitate their confiscation.

Undoubtedly, Australia is one of the front-runners in implementing the above changes. Following the UK example, the Australian government introduced the reversal burden of proof into the *Proceeds of Crime Act 1987* (Cth) (POCA 1987), which provides for conviction-based confiscation. The concept of civil forfeiture was first introduced in Commonwealth legislation in 1977 with a provision in the *Customs Act 1901*. However, it is the Australian States and Territories which took the lead in enacting civil forfeiture provisions. They were progressively adopted since 1989 to counter organised crime.[109] Civil forfeiture was introduced in the POCA in 2002 following the review of the *Act* by

108 Sherman (2006), pp. 10, par. 2.29.

109 Moffitt (1973–74), Williams (1977–79), Stewart (1981–83) and Costigan (1980–84); Lusty (2002).

the Australian Law Reform Commission to counter the failings of conviction-based provisions to capture the illegal gains from the heads of crime syndicates. For the Federal Government,

> [n]on-conviction based proceeds of crime orders are efficient and effective tools for restraining and forfeiting the proceeds of crime, especially where the identity of the person to whom the goods belong is unknown, the prosecution of the person is unsuccessful, the person has fled the jurisdiction, or where a prosecution is likely to be lengthy and that could prevent the timely forfeiture of criminal assets.[110]

Regarding the unexplained wealth laws, in his 2006 Review of the POCA, Tom Sherman, previous FATF chairman, questioned whether it was appropriate to adopt them given "the current tension between the rights of the individual and the interests of the community?"[111] On balance, he believed it would be inappropriate at this stage to recommend their introduction. Nevertheless, in 2010, despite the controversy regarding the effectiveness of unexplained wealth laws,[112] and with the Senate Standing Committee on Legal and Constitutional Affairs (SSC-LCA) endorsement, unexplained wealth provisions were enacted into the POCA 2002.[113] Upon the 2012 recommendations of the Parliamentary Joint Committee on Law Enforcement, the POCA 2002 was further amended by the *Crimes Legislation Amendment (Unexplained Wealth and Other Measures) Act 2015* in order to facilitate the implementation of the 2010 Act by removing judicial discretion and some procedural guarantees from the defendant. The Act may even apply retrospectively. The result is that the courts are required to order the confiscation of all assets which are disproportionate to the person's legitimate income.[114]

2.5.1.1 Discussion

The recent provisions regarding the reversal of the onus of proof, civil forfeiture and unexplained wealth laws are meant to circumvent the difficulty encountered, in organised crime cases, by the prosecution to prove that the assets are directly connected to a specific crime. The offences generating the proceeds are most often committed in another State which may not provide

110 Extradition and Mutual Assistance in Criminal Matters Legislation Amendment Bill 2011, Explanatory Memorandum, p. 132.

111 Sherman (2006), p. 37, par. 4.66.

112 Freiberg, Fox (2000).

113 *Crimes Legislation Amendment (Serious and Organised Crime) Act 2010* (Cth). Unexplained Wealth & other Measures) Bill 2014, Explanatory Memorandum.

114 ALRC (2015).

the level of mutual assistance required. The absence of a victim to report the offence and of witnesses to come to the bar compounds the difficulty in establishing the exact origin and amounts of the profits, making traditional evidentiary rules ineffective. However, these new provisions infringe on fundamental rights namely the presumption of innocence, the right of fair trial, the right to silence, property rights and the right to effective legal remedies for interested third parties, enshrined in international treaties that Australia has ratified. These infringements of fundamental crime law principles have raised the concerns of the Australian Law Reform Commission.[115] However by acknowledging that the minimum guarantees in criminal proceedings are not upheld by the legislation,[116] the Federal authorities concede that they pursue some different interests.

In 2000, FATF members reported "significant problems with the *mental element of the offence being set at too high a standard*".[117] In other words, the traditional judicial decision process is perceived as cumbersome at best, ineffective at worst while law enforcement agents' assessment of the criminal origin of the impugned assets is viewed as accurate. Their suspicions are deemed sufficient to warrant a seizure or confiscation order. In this configuration, criminal law guarantees are perceived as an obstacle to fighting crime. This thinking is based on the unverifiable allegations of the colossal profits of criminal organisations, and supported by political authorities keen to be seen actively engaged against organised crime. The prospect of more monies coming into the State's coffers during the economic downturn is another compelling argument. Eventually, the FATF succeeded in bringing the lawmakers to share their views. The underlying presumption of the veracity of the suspicions of law enforcement agents is the pivotal element in many of the provisions on organised crime of the last 20 years. It foreshadows the debate in the "war on terrorism" regarding the "balance" to be struck between human rights and security, in which these individual rights are often sacrificed in the name of the common good.

2.5.2 *Assets Sharing*

Confiscating the proceeds of international criminal organisations and money-laundered assets requires a high level of inter-agency and interstate cooperation. It is a complex, time-consuming and expensive operation. Moreover,

115 ALRC (2015), pp. 282; 495–519.
116 Crimes Legislation Amendment (Powers, Offences and Other Measures) Bill 2015 – EM p. 41.
117 FATF (2001a), para.60, p. 12.

when the seized assets are located in a different country, the State which has granted mutual assistance by providing evidence and information is often not in a position to issue a confiscation order and, thus unable to recoup its costs. Initially, given the frequency of mutual assistance cases, it was thought that over time, the States involved in money laundering cases would break even. However, some States are more often than others used in the layering stage rather than in the investment stage where the proceeds can be seized. To prevent a mutual assistance request from being declined or neglected on the grounds of lack of resources or disproportionate costs, the Vienna convention encourages the State in which the assets are confiscated to conclude agreements, either on a regular or case-by-case basis, to share the proceeds between those States involved in the investigation process. This mechanism is further underlined under the Palermo Convention (UNTOC). The US has actively pursued such a policy.[118] The FATF recommends such agreements.[119] Modern confiscation regimes provide for sharing or return of the proceeds and instrumentalities and compensation for victims.

In Australia, the POCA provides for the making of payments to States and Territories under the equitable sharing program. On the international level, Australia is a party to the UNCAC and in 2015, Australia had 29 bilateral mutual legal assistance treaties,[120] which generally include sharing provisions of confiscated assets. When no treaty is applicable, there is no formal mechanism in place. The requests are considered on a case-to-case basis by the Attorney-General.

2.6 Conclusion

The development of AML/CTF apparatus was built on the observation of the transnational expansion of organised crime. However, the magnitude of the problem has not been objectively quantified, and it is likely that it never will be given that criminal organisations operate secretively and their profits are concealed. The lack of quality data has been an internationally recognised problem, so much so that the FATF does not produce figures any more.[121] Thus, the

118 US Department of State (2015), pp. 20–21.

119 Rec. 38.

120 FATF (2015), p. 186. This figure was still current in March 2019.

121 In 1995, there was a general consensus that the total amount of money laundered worldwide ran each year into hundred of billions of US dollars (FATF VI, Annual Report 8 June 1995, p. 16) In 1997, the FATF decided to work out a reliable methodology to estimate the volume of laundered money and set up an ad hoc committee, which worked until 2000.

figures put forward by law enforcement agencies are an educated guess at best, and completely fabricated at worst. In 1998, the IMF stated:

> While we cannot guarantee the accuracy of our figures – and you have certainly a better evaluation than us – the estimates of the present scale of money laundering transactions are almost beyond imagination – 2 to 5 percent of global GDP would probably be a consensus range.[122]

Concerned for the integrity of their economies and democracies, the governments of some of the richest nations set in place a control of their financial systems, before extending it worldwide. The declared objective was to counter the rise of organised crime whose menace is described in terms proportional to its estimated profits. The FATF has thus emerged as an indispensable player in shaping legislation with its influence being felt widely beyond its Member States. Though AML legislation was founded on the provisions of predominantly the 1988 Vienna Convention, and the 1990 Strasbourg Convention, it developed significantly thanks to the work of the FATF and progressed further with the adoption of international treaties such as the 2000 UNTOC (Palermo Convention) and the 2003 UNCAC (Merida Convention). Since the beginning of the century, the UN Security Council has taken the lead in prompting the extension of AML apparatus to the financing of terrorism and weapons of mass destruction.

The action of the FATF has undoubtedly contributed significantly to a better understanding of money laundering and the measures that need to be put in place to tackle it. It succeeded in rallying financial institutions, professional and other persons in the collection of data and information on behalf of law enforcement agencies and led the path towards proactive investigation techniques, which have been extended later to different fields of operations of criminal organisations. Its creative way of ensuring the implementation of international agreements may even become a model for a new form of international governance.

For analytical reasons, the committee decided to limit its work to the proceeds of drug trafficking, but eventually had to renounce, as needed data were not available. Other organisations are still engaged in the same efforts: Europol, the European Monitoring Centre for Drugs and Drug Addiction, the IMF, and the UNODCCP, but so far no satisfactory and reliable methods have been found to provide an accurate estimate of the amounts of money laundered. See also Levi, Reuter, Halliday (2018).

122 FATF (1998a), Annex A (IMF).

Its major achievement is to have rallied governments, sometimes for fear of potential economic sanctions, to adopt the Recommendations it established. Nevertheless, on the premise of an imminent threat, and with the aim to have "effective legislation", the FATF has indirectly encouraged some already repressive governments to introduce new rules likely to restrict the political space in which NGOs and civil society actors operate"[123] and caused some national parliaments to pass laws weakening long held criminal law standards. The path to legislation standardisation is long and treacherous. Careful considerations should be given when downgrading internationally recognised principles. There is a risk, for instance when a lower standard of proof or a broad mental element is adopted for a particular offence, that the elements of the new definition will be introduced into other criminal offences.[124] This risk has been substantiated with the enactment of some anti-terrorism and anti-organised crime provisions. This has resulted in the present disquietude with domestic parliaments passing legislation encroaching on fundamental individual rights – which have been the privilege of free societies – and has the potential of eventually superseding the initial fear that the rise of organised crime poses to our democracies and our way of life.

123 Hayes (2012), p. 10.

124 Ashworth, Zedner (2008).

CHAPTER 3

A New Crime Type: Defining Money Laundering

> Money laundering is not *per se* a threat to the global economic and financial markets. Rather it is what the money laundering can do through the re-investing of the criminally gotten proceeds and the capacity to corrupt and negatively influence legitimate sectors of society. More particularly this threat can jeopardise the legitimacy of political and social systems.[1]
>
> BASSIOUNI M. CHERIF and VETERE EDUARDO

∵

3.1 Introduction

Criminal organisations have been active in Australia for many years.[2] Australia's awareness of organised crime activities grew progressively as Royal Commissions of Inquiry uncovered practices which were unknown to the general public. In the 1970s, there was a perception that criminal organisations were behind the rise of drug abuse but their scale and influence remained on the whole underestimated. The first inquiries, launched in Victoria and New South Wales reported organised criminal activities in fringe areas: The Moffitt Inquiry (1973–1974) brought to light the infiltration into NSW of overseas criminal organisations in the gambling and entertainment industry. It expressed alarm that the law enforcement agencies were ill-equipped to fight criminal organisations. In 1977, the assassination of Donald Mackay, a businessman who had been leading a campaign against drug trafficking in New South Wales, prompted the Woodward inquiry (1977–1979). The report alluded to a collusion between police officers, politicians and members of the 'Ndrangheta, the Calabrian "mafia". The Williams Inquiry (1977–1979) exposed the international ramifications of Australian drug trafficking organisations. It pointed also to the corruption of officials among police and other areas.[3] The report tries to assess the volume of drug trafficking but does not provide any substantiated figures.

1 Bassiouni, Vetere (1998), p. xxxiv.

2 Meagher (1983), pp. 18, 19. Schloenhardt (2009), p. 92.

3 Moffit (1985), p. 4.

 | DOI:10.1163/9789004359109_004

It relies on the estimation of a law enforcement officer that only 5% of all illicit drugs are confiscated, a figure which has been used commonly throughout the 1980s and 1990s.

The perception of organised crime changed significantly in the 1980s with the McCabe/Lafranchi inquiry (1978–1981), the Stewart Royal Commission (1981–1983), and the Costigan Royal Commission (1980–1984). They exposed the widespread use by criminal organisations of the Australian financial system to launder their profits as well as major tax frauds. Australia is a market for illegal drugs, and thus an entrance points for the proceeds of drug trafficking into the financial system. However its financial system is somewhat small compared to that of those located in Europe or the US. Its limited size may therefore explain why not many overseas criminal organisations use Australia to launder money. Hence, money laundering in Australia is mainly a domestic issue. The revelation of the scale of the tax avoidance schemes set in place by Australian companies – then being 6,688[4] – sparked radical social, judicial and legal changes. The public complacency regarding tax avoidance ended. It also prompted a departure from previous caselaw in the Federal and High Courts (The High Court's leniency on the matter was illustrated by the decisions of Sir Garfield Barwick).[5] Arguably, since then, the fiscal component of money laundered assets has been a major concern in Australia, playing down other considerations and introducing major reforms in legislation and in the way law enforcement agencies work.

The first warning shot came from Victoria where the McCabe/Lafranchi Inquiry investigated tax evasion schemes. Not only did the scale of the fraud surprise (over 3000 companies were involved, and a fiscal loss estimated at AUD 200 million) but it revealed that respectable lawyers were associated with the fraud. Moreover, that the Taxation Office had failed to take action shocked many. Soon after, the Stewart Inquiry reported the use of a NSW front company (Nugan Hand Ltd), directed by Frank Nugan, which offered a wide range of financial services without having money or skills.[6] It was estimated that the various breaches committed led to more than AUD 16 million being laundered. Allegedly, the primary goal of most clients was to evade tax laws.

The final wake-up call was the Costigan Inquiry, which uncovered Australia's largest corporate tax avoidance scheme. Initially, his mandate was to investigate the activities of the Federated Ship Painters' and Dockers' Union following a series of murders. It led him first to an associated company which

4 Freiberg (1988), p. 137.

5 Freiberg (1988), p. 139.

6 The Canberra Times (1985).

had a bank account in another state and then to a dozens of accounts throughout Australia.[7] The *bottom of the harbour* scandal, as it became to be known, involved the stripping of assets and accumulated profits from a company prior to the time its tax obligations were due leaving only an empty shell – dropping it figuratively to the bottom of the (Sydney) harbour. The stripped company was then transferred to another company or a person with limited means and who were insolvent when the tax was due.[8] It was estimated that the scheme defrauded the taxpayers of some AUD 1 billion, tens of billions in today's dollars.[9]

The authorities' failure to deal with this massive fraud i.e. to detect the problem and to prosecute with what legislation was available, coupled with the close relationship that some of the fraudsters had with the party in power eventually led in 1983 to a change of government. The systematic involvement of legal, accounting and bank professionals in these tax avoidance schemes shed a poor light on their ethics. This prompted the adoption of the *Crimes (Taxation Offences) Act 1980* which makes it a criminal offence to aid, abet or encourage the setting up of an arrangement leading to tax avoidance.[10]

Following the Costigan Inquiry and his recommendations, radical changes were implemented in law enforcement, in the judicial process and in substantive legislation. First was the creation of the Office of the Special Prosecutor with the introduction of the combination of investigation and ultimate prosecution function.[11] This led to the installation, in 1984, of the Director of Public Prosecutions (DPP) to coordinate investigations and prosecutions across Australia. Then, the same year, the National Crime Authority (NCA) was established. In addition, the culture of the Australian Taxation Office (ATO) changed from fostering compliance to deterrence with the opening of prosecutions. Furthermore, the secrecy provisions of the I*ncome Tax Assessment Act* were amended. They were viewed as another factor which had hindered the efficiency of the ATO. Originally, these provisions had been incorporated in the Act in the belief that the confidentiality of taxpayer information would enhance compliance with the law.[12] Full access to taxation records was progressively introduced so that relevant information could be shared between governmental agencies. Significantly, the Director of Public Prosecutions was granted authority to issue civil remedies in the form of seizure order even prior to the institution of a prosecution.

7 Costigan (1982), pp. 4–5.
8 Grabosky (1989).
9 West (2015).
10 S 6, *Crimes (Taxation Offences) Act* 1980.
11 Freiberg (1988), p. 149.
12 Grabosky (1989).

Secondly, in order to avoid delaying tactics, judicial review was restricted. The *Administrative Decisions (Judicial Review) Act 1977* was amended in 1987 so that pre-trial administrative procedures, like committal proceedings, would not generally be subject to review by superior courts. This change was a departure from the course of more than a century of settled law.[13]

Thirdly, sweeping legislation was introduced. In 1980, tax fraud was made a criminal offence. The governmental view at the time was that the *bottom of the harbour* tax avoidance scheme may not have been illegal. To prevent it reoccurring, the Government enacted, the *Crimes (Taxation Offences) Act 1980*, which made it a criminal offence for any person to set up a company or trust unable to pay tax debts. In 1984, penalties were increased. Under the Income *Tax Assessment Act 1936* (Cth) the sanction went from fines to an imprisonment period of up to 2 years whereas under the *Statute Law (Miscellaneous Provisions) Act* the penalty of the offence to defraud the Commonwealth increased to 10 years and the conspiracy to defraud to 20 years. In 1987, to ensure that the money and property involved in in tax evasion schemes could be seized and confiscated, the *Proceeds of Crime Act 1987* (Cth), was adopted. It was seen as a major tool against organised crime. Its declared objective was

> to strike at the heart of major organised crime by depriving persons involved of the profits and instruments of their crimes. By so doing, it [would] suppress criminal activity by attacking the primary motive – profit – and prevent the re-investment of that profit in further criminal activity.[14]

The provisions related to money laundering are now part of Division 400 of the *Criminal Code Act 1995* (Cth) (thereafter the Code). In 1988, to ensure that law enforcement would have access to all relevant documents in their investigations, the *Cash Transaction Reports Act 1988* (Cth) was adopted. It sets up reporting requirements such as the mandatory reporting of transactions of AUD 10,000 or more. It followed Costigan view that

> the most successful method of identifying and ultimately convicting major organized criminals is to follow the money trail. (…) Once you have identified and convicted them you take away their money, that is, the money which is the product of their criminal activities.[15]

13 Redlich (1984), p. 161.

14 Bowen (1987a), p. 2314.

15 Costigan (1984), p. 12.

In the 1980s and early 90s, Australia was at the forefront of the AML movement. By the time it took part in the *travaux préparatoires* to the 1990 Strasbourg Convention on Money Laundering, and the FATF, Australia had already enacted its first legislative AML package: The *Proceeds of Crime Act 1987* (Cth) and the *Cash Transaction Reports Act 1988* (Cth). Australia's AML/CTF legislation has been updated numerous times, mainly to implement the standards set by the FATF. In 1992, the *Cash Transaction Reports Act 1988* (Cth) was renamed *Financial Transaction Reports Act 1988* (FTR Act). The *Money Laundering and Counter-Terrorism Financing Act 2006* (AML/CTF Act) was passed shortly after the FATF's third evaluation of Australia's compliance with the Recommendations. The AML/CTF Act was implemented in stages with all provisions fully operational at the end 2008. The AML/CTF Act is complemented by the *Anti-Money Laundering and Counter-Terrorism Financing Rules Instrument 2007 (No.1)* (AML/CTF Rules) which are issued by the AUSTRAC CEO. They provide the detail for the broader obligations set out in the AML/CTF Act. To give effect to countermeasures regarding Iran and the DPRK, the Governor-General has issued *Regulations*. The Act and Rules' subsequent updates have led to an increase of the number of regulated (reporting) entities and designated services, an extension of their obligations, as well as an increase of AUSTRAC's enforcement powers, in line with the development of FATF recommendations. The 2015 FATF report on Australia and the 2016 statutory review of Australia's AML/CTF regime has led to the adoption to further amendments.

3.1.1 *Competence to Legislate*

Given the Australian Parliament's limited competence in criminal law under the heads of legislative power in the Australian constitution, the federal government had, and still has, no direct or sole competence to legislate on organised crime. It has therefore relied on its legislative powers conferred by sections 51(ii) (taxation) and 51(xii) (currency, coinage, and legal tender) to legislate on money laundering. Though this construction might seem weak in its attempt to combat an international scourge, it fits the domestic character of Australian AML scheme well. Upon examination of the constitutionality of the provisions of the *Financial Transaction Reports Act 1988*, the High Court of Australia noted that "the Act is not overly forthcoming in express provisions identifying its connection with taxation laws" but concluded nevertheless that "it is certainly with the matters reasonably incidental to the reach of that power".[16] Over the years, the convictions for violation of the AML legislation demonstrate that the provisions have indeed been used predominantly for financial purposes.

16 *Leask v Commonwealth* [1996] 187 CLR 579, 611 (Toohey J) and Kirby J [629] [637].

3.2 Defining Money Laundering

Money laundering (ML) is generally understood to be the process by which funds of criminal origin are given the appearance of legitimate assets. The AML provisions of the major international treaties – the 1988 Vienna convention, 1990 Strasbourg Convention, UNTOC[17] and UNCAC[18] – make the intention to *conceal* the illegal origin of the assets the core of the offence, as Table 1 shows,[19] but Australian legislation does not consider it a necessary element.[20]

TABLE 1 Defining money laundering (ML)

AUS – Code S 400.2	Definition of *deals with money or other property* A person deals with money or other property if the person does any of the following: (a) receives, possesses, conceals or disposes of money or other property; (b) imports money or other property into Australia; (c) exports money or other property from Australia; (d) engages in a banking transaction relating to money or other property.
AUS – POCA (1987) S 81(3):	A person shall be taken to engage in money laundering if, and only if: a. the person engages, directly or indirectly, in a transaction that involves money, or other property, that is proceeds of crime; or b. the person receives, possesses, conceals, disposes of or brings into Australia any money or other property that is the proceeds of crime and the person knows, or ought reasonably to know that the money or other property is derived or realised, directly or indirectly from some form of unlawful activity.
UN 1988 drug convention Art. 3	(b) (i) The conversion or transfer of property, knowing that such property is derived from any offence or offences established in accordance with subparagraph *a*) of this paragraph, or from an act of participation in such offence

17 UN Convention against Transnational Organised Crime (UNTOC) (Palermo Convention), 225 UNTS 20.

18 UN Convention against Corruption (UNCAC) (Merida Convention), 2349 UNTS 41.

19 See also Art.9, 2005 CoE *Convention on Laundering, Search, Seizure and Confiscation of the Proceeds from Crime and on the Financing of Terrorism*, CETS 198.

20 Sherman (1991), p. 10.

TABLE 1 Defining money laundering (*cont.*)

	or offences, for the purpose of concealing or disguising the illicit origin of the property or of assisting any person who is involved in the commission of such an offence or offences to evade the legal consequences of his actions; (ii) The concealment or disguise of the true nature, source, location, disposition, movement, rights with respect to, or ownership of property, knowing that such property is derived from an offence or offences established in accordance with subparagraph *a*) of this paragraph or from an act of participation in such an offence or offences; (c) Subject to its constitutional principles and the basic concepts of its legal system: (i) The acquisition, possession or use of property, knowing, at the time of receipt, that such property was derived from an offence or offences established in accordance with subparagraph a) of this paragraph or from an act of participation in such offence or offences;
UNTOC Art. 6.	(a) (i) The conversion or transfer of property, knowing that such property is the proceeds of crime, for the purpose of concealing or disguising the illicit origin of the property or of helping any person who is involved in the commission of the predicate offence to evade the legal consequences of his or her action;
UNCAC Art. 23.1 *Laundering of proceeds of crime*	(ii) The concealment or disguise of the true nature, source, location, disposition, movement or ownership of or rights with respect to property, knowing that such property is the proceeds of crime; (b) Subject to the basic concepts of its legal system: (i) The acquisition, possession or use of property, knowing, at the time of receipt, that such property is the proceeds of crime; (ii) Participation in, association with or conspiracy to commit, attempts to commit and aiding, abetting, facilitating and counselling the commission of any of the offences established in accordance with this article.

1990 CoE Convention on Money Laundering Art. 6	a.	the conversion or transfer of property, knowing that such property is proceeds, for the purpose of concealing or disguising the illicit origin of the property or of assisting any person who is involved in the commission of the predicate offence to evade the legal consequences of his actions;
	b.	the concealment or disguise of the true nature, source, location, disposition, movement, rights with respect to, or ownership of, property, knowing that such property is proceeds; and, subject to its constitutional principles and the basic concepts of its legal system;
	c.	the acquisition, possession or use of property, knowing, at the time of receipt, that such property was proceeds;
	d.	participation in, association or conspiracy to commit, attempts to commit and aiding, abetting, facilitating and counselling the commission of any of the offences established in accordance with this article.

The Strasbourg Convention, the UNTOC and the UNCAC mention four different types of conduct under money laundering, all requiring knowledge of the illegal origin of the assets. In the two first types of conduct, the intent to disguise the illicit origin of the assets or to assist the perpetrator of the predicate offence (that is the original offence that generated the proceeds) constitutes the core of the offence of money laundering. These types of conduct are, from a criminological perspective, the most typical form of money laundering.[21]

The third type of money laundering which is the *acquisition, possession or use of property*, while knowing at the time of receipt that such property was derived from a particular criminal activity has been described by Stessens as

> the most passive form of co-operation with the perpetrator of the predicate offence as it requires proof not of any kind of active engagement in illegal constructions of whatever kind, but merely the acquisition, possession or use of proceeds, and the knowledge, at the time of their receipt, that those proceeds were criminally derived.[22]

21 Vogel (1997), p. 340.

22 Stessens (2000), p. 115.

Initially introduced under section 81, POCA, it is, however, the main form retained by Australian law, a choice which has been criticised by academics.[23]

> Plainly s.81 should not have been drafted in a manner which permits the primary offender to be dealt with separately for the offence of money laundering when he [sic] alone has dealt with the proceeds of his crime. The section should have been drafted to make it clear that what is being attacked is the class of person who provides money laundering services for primary offenders by assisting them to conceal the fact of their criminality – by "washing" their money for them.[24]

In subsequent amendments, the Australian legislature has more or less retained the core ideas of the original version and has not embraced the typical form of money laundering found in the international definitions. Hence, under the Code, it is relevant that the person has no intention of concealing the criminal origin of the assets, or that he or she does not intend to assist a predicate offender in the evasion of legal consequences of his crime. One is therefore led to conclude that Australia does not criminalise money laundering proper, but rather different conduct which, as explained below, takes place *before* the laundering of funds *per se*.

Division 400 of the Code is more detailed, more comprehensive and more precise than the original version found in the *Proceeds of Crime Act 1987* (Cth). It presents three distinct scenarios depending on the money and property being proceeds of crime or not, or if it is reasonable to suspect that the money or property is proceeds of crime. In every case, the penalty varies according to the value of the assets:

- Assuming that the money and property are proceeds of crime, sections 400.3 to 400.8 make a distinction between various forms of *dealing with money or other property* according to the knowledge that the person has of its illicitness: the offender either knows that he or she is dealing with proceeds of crime or intends it to become an instrument of crime, or is either reckless or negligent as to that fact.
- Assuming that the money and property are not proceeds of crime, sections 400.3 to 400.8 make a distinction between various forms of *dealing with money or other property* according to the knowledge that the person has of the risk of it becoming an instrument of crime, according to three different fault elements: intention, recklessness and negligence.

23 Fisse (1988), p. 7.

24 Weinberg (1989), p. 216.

- Independently from whether the money and property are proceeds of crime, section 400.9 provides for sanctions in case it is reasonable to suspect that the money or property is proceeds of crime.

Upon examination of Australia's legislation and the international treaties, two main differences stand out: first, the Code does not always require an intent to *conceal* the illicit origin of assets; secondly, and remarkably, it provides for sanctions where money or property is at *risk* of becoming an instrument of crime. This last element is the cornerstone of the Australian AML mechanism. Given AML legislation is constructed around provisions regarding property derived from "*a crime*", the following section examines what this term means in their respective legal contexts.

3.2.1 *The Predicate Offence*

The predicate offence is defined as "the original offence that generated the proceeds in the first place",[25] or the crime underlying money laundering. From the onset, the Australian definition of the predicate offence of "dealing with the proceeds of crime" was far wider than the 1988 Vienna Convention. Australia realised very early that in order for the law to be an effective tool against criminal organisations, the predicate offence of its AML legislation could not be limited to drug trafficking offences. Australia followed the recommendations of the Commonwealth Law Ministers in provisions of the 1986 Commonwealth Scheme on Mutual Assistance in Criminal Matters which extended the predicate offence to offences other than drug trafficking, mainly in order to be able to fight tax evasion.

In 1996, the FATF recommended the extension of the predicate offence from a drug related crime to a *serious crime*, with a view to including the widest range of predicate offences. However, the Strasbourg Convention, to which all EU Member States and Australia are parties, does not define the predicate offence in relation to a "serious crime", rather it defines it as any criminal offence as a result of which proceeds were generated. The 2000 UNTOC defines a serious crime as conduct constituting an offence punishable by a maximum deprivation of liberty of at least four years or a more serious penalty. The four-year threshold was found in EU initial legislation. The EU AML legislation has then lowered it. Since 2015, serious crimes are all offences, including tax crimes, which are punishable by deprivation of liberty or a detention order for a maximum of more than one year or all offences punishable by deprivation of liberty or a detention order for a minimum of more than six months.[26]

25 Art.1e, CETS 141.

26 Art 3(4), Directive 2015/849 of 20 May 2015 of the European Parliament and the Council on the prevention of the use of the financial system for the purposes of money laundering or terrorist financing. OJ L141, pp. 73–112, 06.06.2015.

Under Division 400, the predicate and the subsidiary offences are offences against a law of the Commonwealth, or a law of a Territory that may be dealt with as an indictable offence or offences against a law of a foreign country constituted by conduct that, if it had occurred in Australia, would have constituted an offence against a law of the Commonwealth or a law of a State or Territory connected with the offence that may be dealt with as an indictable offence. Federal indictable offences are determined before a judge and jury, and so are usually reserved for more serious offences.[27] However, in some cases, the Code stipulates that an indictable offence may, in some circumstances, be dealt with as a summary offence, thus blurring the distinction. In other words, indictable offences can be serious or ordinary, depending on the characterisation by the legislature. The understanding of what constitutes a "crime" or a "criminal offence" may vary however between States. According to section 4G, *Crimes Act 1914*, indictable offences are offences against a law of the Commonwealth punishable by imprisonment for a period exceeding 12 months, unless the contrary intention appears. However, given that section 400.11 of the Code makes it is unnecessary to prove the existence of any fault element in relation to the type of these offences, the scope of these provisions is considerably reduce.

To summarise, Australian federal legislation does not strictly limit the predicate offences to *serious crimes* given that the penalty threshold of one year is rather low. In practice, for mutual assistance in criminal matters, the underlying offence of *dealing with the proceeds of crime* is likely to be somewhat similar to what is understood in most European jurisdictions by *serious crimes* for the purpose of AML legislation. From a law enforcement point of view, the three main predicate offences are drugs, fraud and tax evasion.[28]

In the next section, the nature of the offence of money laundering is discussed and its implementation by the courts is examined.

3.2.2 *Money Laundering, an Offence sui generis*

Since its inception, money laundering was considered as a distinct crime from the predicate offence. Under section 82 *Proceeds of Crime Act 1987* (Cth)) (thereafter POCA), the legislature created a less serious offence of money laundering called "possession etc. of property suspected of being proceeds of crime".[29] It has been expanded in section 400.9 of the Code and renamed "dealing with property reasonably suspected of being proceeds of crime etc". Conceiving money laundering as a distinct offence has two advantages: First, it allows law enforcement agencies to prosecute a person not only for participation in the

27 Bronitt, McSherry (2010), p. 111.

28 FATF (2015), 3.34, p. 55.

29 Sherman (1991), 5.12, p. 86.

predicate offence but also for money laundering. Secondly, in cases where the predicate offence has been committed abroad, it creates the legal basis to prosecute money laundering in the country where the assets are being "washed", even in part, without having to wait to receive a request for mutual assistance from the country where the illicit funds originate. To simplify the work of the prosecution further, section 400.13 states that it is not necessary, in order to prove that money or property is proceeds of crime, to establish that a particular predicate offence has been committed or by whom the predicate offence was committed.[30] The new offence triggered much debate among scholars to determine its type, and how to differentiate it from other offences such as the offence of receiving stolen goods.[31]

3.2.2.1 Proximity with the Offence of Receiving Stolen Goods

Since money laundering is an offence *sui generis*, it is not to be confused with ancillary offences such as receiving or handling stolen goods. Hence, the similarity of the Australian offence of possession etc. of property suspected of being proceeds of crime with the offence of receiving stolen goods has rightly given rise to criticism.

TABLE 2 Section 400.9 (1) + (1A), the Code

S 400.9 Dealing with property reasonably suspected of being proceeds of crime etc.
(1) A person commits an offence if: (a) the person deals with money or other property; and (b) it is reasonable to suspect that the money or property is proceeds of crime; and (c) at the time of the dealing, the value of the money and other property is $100,000 or more. Penalty: Imprisonment for 3 years, or 180 penalty units, or both. (1A) A person commits an offence if: (a) the person deals with money or other property; and (b) it is reasonable to suspect that the money or property is proceeds of crime; and (c) at the time of the dealing, the value of the money and other property is less than $100,000. Penalty: Imprisonment for 2 years, or 120 penalty units, or both. (2) (4) Absolute liability applies to paragraphs (1)(b) and (c) and (1A)(b) and (c).

30 Proceeds of Crime (Consequential Amendments and Transitional Provisions) Bill 2002 (Cth), Revised Explanatory Memorandum, p. 17.

31 Stessens (2000) pp. 121, 122, 128; Fisse (1988), p. 14. See Vogel (1997), p. 351. For a discussion on its proximity with an offence of subverting the course of justice.

It was the intention of the Government to include, in its AML legislation, an offence similar to the possession of goods reasonably suspected of having been stolen, which the Government claimed was very effective against theft.[32] There are, however, three main elements of the offence of receiving property suspected of being proceeds of crime (s 132.1) which have not been retained in the AML legislation.

Firstly, if money laundering is considered a form of receiving stolen goods, the perpetrator of the predicate offence should not be prosecuted for possessing proceeds of crime, in the same way a thief is not charged for being in possession of the goods he or she has stolen.[33] Although not precluded by law, the practice is not to overcharge the thief for possessing what he or she has stolen. However, Australia's "money laundering" legislation sanctions the predicate offender for being in possession of the property originating from his or her crime.

Secondly, under section 132.1 of the Code, as under the previous POCA provision, there is no offence of receiving stolen goods by mere criminal negligence. Nonetheless the legislature has introduced *dealing in proceeds of crime* by negligence, creating a different fault element for the money laundering offence and the offence of receiving stolen goods. Fisse criticised this position noting that

> [t]he mental element required for receiving is knowledge, or at least belief, that the goods received are stolen. The courts have assiduously refused to equate negligence or even wilful blindness with knowledge.[34]

Thirdly, in the traditional offence of handling stolen goods, a person is not punished if he or she finds out later that the goods have been stolen. This principle does not apply in AML legislation.[35] The title of the offence under section 400.9 "dealing with property reasonably suspected of being proceeds of crime etc". is therefore misleading. Given that absolute liability applies, – i.e. no fault element for any of the physical elements of the offence is required[36] – the offence does not require proof that the offender had any knowledge or belief as to the money or other property being the proceeds of crime.[37] Further, the

32 Bowen (1987b), p. 5.

33 The offence of possession has been redrafted under S 132.1 *Criminal Code Act* 1995 and renamed "receiving".

34 Fisse (1988), p. 14. Fisse (1992), p. 24.

35 Stessens (2000), p. 128.

36 Odgers (2010), pp. 41 and 97.

37 *Shi v R* [2014] NSWCCA 276 [41, 42].

crown is not required to prove that the money or property is derived or realised from an indictable offence; it is sufficient for the prosecution to prove a dealing with money or property which it is reasonable to suspect that it is the proceeds of an indictable offence.[38]

In *R v Yi-Hua Jiao*,[39] the crown submitted that section 400.9 was a "very serious offence involving a departure from the common law concept of offending because there is no element of mens rea". Whether section 400.9 should be viewed as a very serious offence is debatable since that it does not require criminality. Were serious offences created without an element of mens rea, that would signal a radical shift from the modern conception of criminal law laid down by Beccaria over two centuries ago in which criminality is a core component.

Given that Division 400 of the Code triggers the application of harsh confiscation laws, the proximity and yet different fault elements of the offences of receiving and dealing with proceeds of crime illustrate the intention of the Australian Government to create laws that strongly sanction emerging forms of financial crime, even if it means departing from well-established legal principles.

3.3 The Fault Elements

The international treaties state that money laundering is an intentional offence and that knowledge of the illegal character of the assets is constitutive of the fault element. The Strasbourg Convention on money laundering suggests the criminalisation of negligent behaviour, an option chosen by most European legislators.[40]

In broad terms, it could be said that the international treaties look at the past, while the Code looks ahead. The treaties are mainly concerned with the criminal origin of the assets, while the Code emphasises the future use of the assets. This appears clearly in the fault elements of Division 400 of the Code, one of which is the intent that the money or property will become an instrument of crime, or the risk of becoming so. The Australian perspective can be seen as incongruous given the internationally accepted concept of money laundering. It is understood that the assets need to be laundered because they are "dirty" by reason of their criminal origin. Australia's laws see such assets as "dirty" because those who handle them have a criminal purpose or there is a risk that the

38 *Heng-Sheng Lin v R* [2015] NSWCCA 204 [23] (unreported).

39 *R v Yi-Hua Jiao* [2015] NSWCCA 95 (unreported).

40 Stessens (2000), p. 124.

assets could be used for such a purpose. This view clearly identifies Australia's dealing with assets legislation as preventative tools against organised crime.

In Australia, the level of intent varies from "plain" intent to recklessness and negligence. The Australian provision rests on the *belief* that the money or property is the proceeds of crime, while the treaties refers instead to *knowledge*.

3.3.1 *Knowledge vs Belief*

Initially, the scope of knowledge that "property is derived from criminal activity or from an act of participation in such activity" depended on whether a crime could constitute a predicate offence in the legislation of a specific Party State. Mistake of fact regarding the predicate offence was a common defence. Gradually, as the list of predicate offences was enlarged to all serious crimes, mistake of fact has been more difficult to plead. This has considerably simplified the work of law enforcement.[41]

Rather than establishing knowledge, intent and purpose based on facts as required elements of money laundering activities, the international treaties specify that prosecution can infer the fault elements from "objective factual circumstances.[42] This lower threshold of proof is a standard clause in provisions on money laundering in all recent international treaties.[43]

In Australia, the prosecution does not have to prove the offender's knowledge of the illegal character of the proceeds but rather belief, recklessness or negligence, nor does the prosecution need to prove the offender's knowledge of the risk that the money or property will become an instrument of crime. In order to simplify the task of the prosecution even further, it is not necessary to prove the existence of any fault element in relation to whether an offence is an indictable offence or that a particular offence was committed or an intention or risk that a particular offence will be committed.

The Code provides definitions for knowledge, intent, recklessness, and negligence but offers no guidance on the meaning of belief. Commentators have consequently suggested definitions referring to the everyday meaning of the term.[44] According to Leader-Elliott,

> [w]hen existing or projected states of fact are concerned, the difference between knowledge and belief appears to reflect differences in the

41 Stessens (2000) p. 123, p. 14.

42 Art.3.3, 1988 *Convention against Illicit Traffic in Narcotic Drugs and Psychotropic Substances*, 1582 UNTS 95; Art.6.2.c, CETS 141; Art.6.2(f), UNTOC.

43 Art.9.2.c, CETS 198.

44 Odgers (2010), p. 4; Gillies (1997), p. 72.

> adequacy of grounds for being sure or certain about the facts. One believes rather than knows that something is so when the evidence is less than conclusive.[45]

It follows that a lesser degree of actual knowledge would be needed for belief, which in turn would be even less in order to establish mere suspicion. Since one may not be consciously aware of one's own beliefs, the prosecution does not need to prove that the defendant was consciously aware of the fact that the money or property are proceeds of crime or will become an instrument of crime.[46] The decision to refer to belief rather than knowledge in the fault element has rightly been seen as a tool to assist the prosecution, and a means "to qualify or dilute the uncompromising requirement of knowledge in some other way".[47]

3.3.2 *Value of the Assets*

In the Code, the penalties vary according to the significance of the assets and the fault elements. The prosecution must hence establish the value of the assets. In order to bypass the Code's requirements in relation to proof of fault, a subsection was introduced in sections 400.3 to 400.7 of the Code so that the prosecution does not have to prove that the defendant knew, or was aware of, the value of the dealing for him or her to be convicted of these offences. *Singh v R* establishes that the Code does not require the prosecution to prove that the suspicion that the money is proceeds of crime was contemporaneous with the accused's dealing with the money.[48] It follows that the defence for mistake of fact is restricted to cases where the person was under *a mistaken but reasonable belief about the value* of the property and if the value is AUD 1000 or more (s 400.10). Strangely this defence is absent for crimes of lesser value. Hence, *absolute liability* applies to the value of the money and other property at the time of the dealing. An offence of "absolute liability" does not require any fault element for any of the physical elements of the offence.[49]

In Australian AML legislation, the monetary element of the offence is paramount. It even overshadows the mental element. This is underlined in section 400.9. The difference of penalties under sections 400.9(1) and 400.9(2)

---

45 Leader-Elliott (2002), p. 69.
46 Odgers (2010), p. 43. Gillies (1997), p. 73.
47 Gillies (1997), p. 73; Leader-Elliott (2002), p. 69.
48 *Harmeet Singh v R* [2016] VSCA 163 [42–55].
49 Odgers (2010), pp. 41 and 97.

does not vary depending on the mental element – since absolute liability applies – but the according to the value of the assets involved.[50]

3.3.3 *Knowledge vs Recklessness and Negligence*

Under the Code, recklessness is defined as "awareness of a substantial risk that a specific circumstance exists, or will exist, while it is unjustifiable to take the risk". Recklessness is seen traditionally as more culpable than negligence.

The Model Criminal Code Officers' Committee (MCCOC) has chosen to define recklessness "in terms of a "substantial" risk rather than in terms of probability, or possibility, because they invite speculation about mathematical chances and ignore the link between the degree of risk and the unjustifiability of running that risk in any given situation".[51] The term "*unjustifiable*" was chosen rather than "*unreasonable*" in order *to avoid confusion between recklessness and criminal negligence.*[52] The definition of recklessness in the Code requires proof of conscious awareness of risk of a particular result or circumstance.[53] It is not enough to establish that the risk was obvious to others or to a reasonable person. In the absence of consciousness of risk, it is negligence at the most.[54]

Some civil law (European) jurisdictions have introduced in their legislation money laundering by wilful blindness or *dolus eventualis*, a fault element where the defendant harboured the suspicion that the funds might have a criminal origin but decided not to check further or ask any questions to clarify the matter, and hence consciously took the risk of dealing with possible criminal proceeds.[55] Wilful blindness goes beyond mere negligence in that it requires that the defendant has at least acknowledged the possibility that the proceeds could have a criminal origin.[56] By contrast, the MCCOC expressly rejected any formulation of a fault element in terms of "wilful blindness". According to Odgers,[57] "such a state of mind is likely to fall within the scope of recklessness" rather than knowledge or belief, if it falls anywhere.

50 See *R v Yi-Hua Jiao* [2015] NSWCCA 95 (unreported) and *Harmeet Singh v R* [2016] VSCA 163 [31–40].

51 MCCOC (1992), 203.3, p. 27.

52 Odgers (2010), p. 61.

53 This issue is discussed further in Webster (2007), pp. 272–286.

54 *Hann v DPP* (Cth) [2004] SASC 86 16 [26]; Leader-Elliott (2002), pp. 75, 77.

55 Money laundering by wilful blindness has bee adopted in Belgium, the Netherlands, the UK (s50 DTA 199 and s 93A CJA 1988) Switzerland and the USA (Stessens (2000), pp. 124, 125).

56 For a discussion on wilful blindness, see Bronitt, McSherry (2010), pp. 204–205.

57 Odgers (2010), p. 58.

3.3.4 *Negligence*

When civil law States legislation sanctions money laundering committed by negligence, the prosecution does not need to prove, for instance, that the defendant knew of the criminal origin of the funds. Rather, it suffices if, given the circumstances, the offender ought to have assumed that the property was proceeds derived from criminal conduct.[58] His/her behaviour will be compared to that of a diligent and prudent person in the same situation, or a "reasonable person" under common law.

In Australia, the initial version of the "money laundering provisions", section 81 POCA, included the fault element of "*ought to have known*" which is very similar to the European understanding of negligence. Following heavy criticisms,[59] this wording was removed and Division 400 of the Code uses the terms *negligent* and *reckless*. Even though, under the Code, money laundering by negligence attracts less severe penalties than under the POCA, the penalties are still high.[60] This indicates that money laundering is considered by the legislature as one of the most serious crimes.

In Australia, criminal negligence is defined as "a great falling short of the standard of care that a reasonable person would exercise in the circumstances" while such a high risk exists or will exist.[61] According to Leader-Elliott, "in general, Commonwealth criminal law tends to avoid prohibitions requiring proof of negligence. In more serious offences, the tendency has been to prefer prohibitions that are more specific in their requirements than a blanket prohibition of negligence".[62] Among the exceptions to the rule are the offences under Division 400 of the Code.[63]

Reflecting on the introduction of negligence in the *mens rea* of money laundering, Stessens rightly commented that "such a drastic move away from the requirement of intent seems more inspired by the desire to make convictions for money laundering easier than by motives regarding the blameworthiness of this type of negligent conduct".[64]

---

58 Stessens (2000), p. 123.

59 Proceeds of Crime (Consequential Amendments and Transitional Provisions) Bill 2002, Explanatory Memorandum, p. 3, Sherman (1991), 5.29; Weinberg (1989), p. 216.

60 The maximum penalty was 12 years' imprisonment. See *R v Chen* [2009] NSWCCA 66.

61 Odgers (2010), 5.5.100, p. 65.

62 Leader-Elliott (2002), p. 83.

63 Other exceptions are for instance manslaughter by negligence and negligent disease transmission.

64 Stessens (2000), p. 123.

3.4 The Physical Elements

The Australian legislation under Division 400 of the Code is complex. It has introduced a two-step mechanism which broadly consists firstly in establishing the possession of funds,[65] and secondly in the commission of a subsequent offence.

3.4.1 *Possession vs Intent to Launder Money*

The Code does not define the offence in terms of "money laundering". Rather, the offence is appropriately labelled "dealing with the proceeds of crime" though "*Money laundering*", nevertheless, appears in the Division heading. This difference reveals the fundamental concept of Australia's approach to the problem and the ideology underlying Australia's AML legislation. In Australia, the majority of prosecutions for money laundering are directed against the perpetrators of predicate offences.[66] This could be because both the predicate offence and the money laundering offence are judged concurrently. It may also be caused by money laundering legislation's ostensible preventive function.

By acting so early in the money laundering process, Division 400 produces the peculiar effect of penalising the predicate offender for being in possession of the proceeds of his or her crime, even when he or she has no intention of laundering them. Under the terms of the offence, keeping the cash from drug sales at home for daily usage, for instance, a drug dealer would also be liable for the most stringent form of "dealing in proceeds of crime" which carries a penalty of at least 12 months imprisonment if the value is less than AUD 1000 (s 400.8). In interpreting the above offence, Australian courts have taken the view that a literal interpretation would be contrary to the legislator's intention.[67] On several occasions, the court held that in order to charge an offender under Division 400, the prosecutor had to bring evidence that there was an additional criminality to the predicate offence. In *Thorn v R* (2009),[68] where the applicant accessed through an ATM the proceeds of frauds he had himself committed so he could gamble, the court noted that the applicant

65 "*Possession*" has been redefined several times to gain in precision and to include new forms of money laundering. These definitions shall not be discussed here.

66 FATF (2005b), 83, p. 28.

67 In *Nahlous v R* [2010] NSWCCA 58 [18].

68 *Thorn v R* (2009) 198 A Crim R 135.

> (…) was doing nothing to hide the source or to change the nature of the funds. He was simply gaining access to them. The activity came within the scope of the offence under s 400.4, because the offence is so widely drawn. But it was a highly technical version of the offence.
>
> This was an unusual use of a money laundering offence. To the extent that there was an overlap with the fraud offences the charge represented the use of the funds that had been dishonestly obtained under those offences. The criminality was very much in the obtaining of the funds not in their use. It is somewhat analogous to a robber being sentenced for both the robbery and being in possession of the stolen goods. (…).[69]

The New South Wales Court of Criminal Appeal held that dealing with money that was the result of some other person's criminal activity so as to hide its source was "money laundering in the true sense of that term and clearly the type of activity that the legislature had in mind in creating the offence".[70]

Nahlous v R,[71] where the defendant was charged with the sale of unauthorised decoders and possession of money received from that sale, underlines that offences of "dealing with the proceeds of crime" under Division 400 should be considered as offences distinct from the predicate offence. In *Schembri*, the Court of Criminal Appeal stated that it opposed charging the predicate offender with a money laundering offence when there was no separate act of criminality that warranted a separate charge.[72] They should not be prosecuted concurrently with the predicate offence if the offender has not taken any step towards disguising their illegitimate origin. To prosecute a person for a principal offence and also for dealing in the proceeds of crime from that offence is an abuse of process.[73]

The breadth of Australian legislation is, however, softened by the judiciary which rarely sentences the predicate offender for a money laundering offence.[74] Most convictions for "dealing with the proceeds of crime" fall on the predicate offender, whose sentence is not usually increased because the "dealing" does not reflect a different criminality from the predicate offence. Nevertheless, in order to avoid the risk of double punishment because a person in possession of the proceeds of his/her offence can also be found guilty of

69 *Thorn v R* (2009), [31] and [27].
70 *Thorn v R* [2009], [30].
71 *Nahlous*[2010] NSWCCA 58.
72 *Schembri v R* [2010] NSWCCA 149 [16].
73 *Schembri v R* [2010] NSWCCA 149) [17].
74 Sherman (1991), p. 97 (5.64); FATF (2005b), 83, p. 28.

money laundering, Tom Sherman suggested modifying the qualification of the act of possession by limiting it to third parties alone.[75] However, the Attorney-General's Department decided that it was preferable to do just the opposite and proposed, in 2008, an amendment to clarify that the definitions of "receives", "possesses", "conceals" and "disposes" include the right to access money or property, whether it is in his/her possession or not. In 2010, the New South Wales Court of Criminal Appeal underlined the judicial practice:

> The decisions of the Court of Criminal Appeal in *Thorn v R; Nahlous v R; R v Jones; R v Hili and Schembri v R* constitute strong reminders by the Court of Criminal Appeal to prosecutors that the money laundering offences in s 400 are to be used in a measured way. An assessment is required, in the circumstances of each particular case, as to whether a money laundering charge ought be brought, or a combination of charges including a money laundering offence and other offences.[76]

Eventually, in 2014, the Federal Prosecution Office gave instructions to avoid charging both the predicate offence and a money laundering offence, unless it reflected the whole criminality of the accused.[77] To improve clarity, it would be preferable for the Australian federal AML provisions to be aligned to the core international definition and to make the concealment of the criminal origin of the proceeds of crime the characteristic element of any type of money laundering offences. This would mean a complete revamp of the legislation, since the Australian approach is conceptually different from the main types of money laundering as it considers the risk that the proceeds could become an instrument of crime.

3.4.2 *The Risk Factor as a Physical Element of the Offence*

Consistent with its very strong preventive approach, Australian legislation adopts penal sanctions where money or property is at *risk of becoming an instrument of crime*.[78] This offence applies independently of the legitimate or criminal origin of the assets. There is no corresponding provision in the main international conventions dealing with AML. This preventative approach was introduced into the Code by the *Proceeds of Crime (Consequential Amendments and Transitional Provisions) Act 2002* (Cth) upon the recommendations of the

---

75 Sherman (1991), p. 87.

76 *R (Cth) v Milne* (No 1) [2010] NSWCCA; 259 FLR 42, [165].

77 CDPP (2014), CDPP (2017), para 7–16.

78 *Ansari v R, Ansari v R* [2007] NSWCCA 204 [24].

Australian Law Reform Commission,[79] in response to the "considerable frustration" of law enforcement agencies. In cases of on-going criminality, such as drug trafficking, assets in the hands of a suspected money-launderer may not be proved beyond reasonable doubt to be the proceeds of a specific offence and therefore could not be seized. Yet, the likelihood that those assets will be further invested into the organisation's illegal activities is high. If the assets are in the hands of a suspected member of a criminal organisation, the risk of the funds being used to finance further crime may be easily established; the same cannot be said of a financial institution.

Division 400 of the Code obliges the person or institution that deals with money to examine not only the possible criminal origin of the assets, which is already a challenging task, but also its likely use, making it even harder for the person or institution dealing with money or property since the final destination of the goods is even more problematic to ascertain. The purpose of such provision is preventive. It seeks to alert anyone dealing with money or property, even of legitimate origin, to be vigilant for a possible involvement with an illegal activity. This provision is, however, more than a wake up call since heavy penalties are attached to its violation. In the case where a professional money-launderer working for a drug trafficking organisation who intends that the money or property will become an instrument of crime is convicted, the penalty can be up to 25 years. In a case of negligence and recklessness, an employee of a financial institution may face up to 12 years imprisonment. Hence, the provision raises two questions in particular. The first pertains to the level and type of vigilance required when dealing with assets. This issue is closely linked to the determination of the risk and the scope of negligence and recklessness. The second question relates to the nature of the subsidiary offence.

3.4.2.1 Assessing the Risk

The Code uses the term "physical element" to describe the various aspects of the *actus reus*. They are the *conduct, a result of conduct or a circumstance in which conduct, or a result of conduct, occurs*. In Division 400, the risk that money or property will become an instrument of crime is a physical element. It is not a result of the person's conduct but a circumstance in which that conduct occurs. The existence of this risk is thus a matter of fact. That a person was reckless with respect to a risk is, however, a fault element (*mens rea*). Thus, depending on the case and the offence, a risk can be a physical element (when

79 ALRC (1999), p. 128.

the situation is *in fact* risky) or be paired with a fault element as in recklessness (when the person is aware of the risk).[80]

The idea of risk is a likelihood of something existing between the spectrum of highly probable to mere possible or remote.[81] In the case of recklessness, the risk must be substantial, unjustifiable, and not unreasonable.[82] The question whether taking a risk is unjustifiable is one of fact. However, the Code does not define what is to be understood by "substantial" for the purpose of determining the fault element requiring substantial risk. Based on the onlooker principle, Leader-Elliott states that

> [t]he risk is substantial if a reasonable observer would have taken it to be substantial at the time when risk was taken i.e. before it materialised. [...] The standard is obviously vague. It also involves significant conceptual problems. [...] The Code requirement of "substantial risk" appears to have been chosen for its irreducible indeterminacy of meaning.[83]

When discussing "substantial risk" for the purpose of the section 5.4 recklessness fault elements tests, Odgers remarked that

> [i]t is not possible to provide greater precision regarding the concept of "substantial risk". As MCCOC[[84]] stated, this is partly because the lower the justifiability of taking a risk in any given situation, the lower the level of risk that will be regarded as "substantial". For example, if there is no justifiability in taking any risk in a particular situation, the tribunal of fact is likely to regard a relatively small risk as a substantial one. (...) Conversely, if there are reasonable justifications for taking some risk, the tribunal of fact is likely to require a relatively high risk in order to classify it as a substantial one.[85]

Hence, in a context where money laundering is considered as one of the most serious crimes – as demonstrated by the penalties it carries – there is the

80 For further discussion on this issue, see Bronitt, McSherry (2010), pp. 203–206, Odgers (2010), pp. 59–63.

81 Bronitt, McSherry (2010), p. 205.

82 Odgers (2010), p. 41.

83 Leader-Elliott (2002), p. 73. A definition of "*substantial risk*" can be found in Carswell's Words and Prases, an American legal dictionary, Odgers (2010) n°5.4.140.

84 MCCOC (1992).

85 Odgers (2010), p. 60.

possibility that the risk may too easily be deemed "substantial" and "unjustifiable". The application of the dealing with assets offences therefore requires a particular vigilance to ascertain that the transaction will not constitute a crime.

3.4.3 *The Subsidiary Offence*

A subsidiary offence is a crime that the offender envisages committing after a predicate offence. The Australian Federal Police (AFP) and the National Crime Authority (NCA) justified the need for a "pro-active" definition of money laundering so that the financing of the activities of a criminal organisation could be prosecuted in cases where the criminal origin of the funds could not be undoubtedly ascertained.[86] Hence, the amended definition of money laundering is wide and captures a large range of conduct, not only the offence that conspirers intend committing, but even the laundering of money.[87] The broad definition of the "crime" under section 400.1 – which notably is not restricted to an offence under the Code, or federal law more generally – is an essential aspect of the Australian legislation as underlined in section 400.13. It provides that there is no requirement (1) to prove that a particular predicate offence has been committed and (2) that there is an intent or a risk to commit a particular offence with the money or property. Under the Code and the *Proceeds of Crime Act 2002* (Cth), money or property can hold, at the same time, both the character of an instrument of crime and of proceeds of crime. J Greg held that

> [t]hat money might have originally been derived from another crime is essential for it to be the subject of a money laundering offence but that does not mean it is not derived also from a money laundering offence involving a dealing with the money, that is, the instrument of a money laundering offence nor does that mean, in the common use of language, nor the terms used and defined by application in the Act and Code that it is not also properly described as the proceeds of the offence.[88]

In Australia, the subsidiary offence would more often be an offence against the *Financial Transaction Reports Act 1988* (FTRA), a tax offence or a conspiracy offence. Hence, the FTRA is an intrinsic tool in the Australian AML legislation.

---

86 ALRC (1999), pp. 124–131.

87 *Ansari v R* [2007] NSWCCA 204 [23]. See also Chapter 5.

88 *DPP v In the matter of S19 of the Proceeds of Crime Act 2002 Re Sunshine Worldwide Holdings Ltd*). [2005] NSWSC 117, 400, [59].

3.4.3.1. Example 1: Structured Transactions (s 31, FTRA 1988)

The offence of structuring transactions so as to avoid reporting requirements ("*smurfing*",[89]) was introduced in section 31 of the *Cash Transaction Reports Act* (*Cth*), now section 31 of the *Financial Transaction Reports Act 1988* (FTRA). It attracts a maximum imprisonment period of 5 years.

TABLE 3 Section 31, FTRA 1988

S 31 FTRA – Offence to conduct transactions so as to avoid reporting requirements

(1) A person commits an offence against this section if:
(a) the person is a party to 2 or more non-reportable cash transactions; and
(b) having regard to:
(i) the manner and form in which the transactions were conducted, including, without limiting the generality of this, all or any of the following:
(A) the value of the currency involved in each transaction;
(B) the aggregated value of the transactions;
(C) the period of time over which the transactions took place;
(D) the interval of time between any of the transactions;
(E) the locations at which the transactions took place; and
(ii) any explanation made by the person as to the manner or form in which the transactions were conducted;
it would be reasonable to conclude that the person conducted the transactions in that manner or form for the sole or dominant purpose of ensuring, or attempting to ensure,
that the currency involved in the transactions was transferred in a manner and form that:
(iii) would not give rise to a significant cash transaction; or
(iv) would give rise to exempt cash transactions.
(2) (...)
that no report in relation to the currency involved in the transfers would be made under section 15.
(3) A person who commits an offence against this section is punishable, upon conviction, by imprisonment for not more than 5 years.

89 In *Leask v Commonwealth* [1996] 187 CLR 579, 592, 593, Kirby J refers to an American definition: "[T]o break up a single transaction above the reporting threshold into two or more separate transactions – for the purpose of evading a financial institution's reporting requirement". Fisse, Fraser (1992), p. 173.

Fisse and others vehemently criticised the initial provisions and called for a thorough revision.[90] The Senate Standing Committee on Legal and Constitutional Affairs endorsed these criticisms and made recommendations,[91] which were not followed. Despite the many subsequent amendments of the Act and its replacement by the FTRA, given that the wording of the provision has not changed, most of these criticisms remain valid. Two criticisms are worth mentioning here, both pertaining to the fault element.

3.4.3.1.1 *A Strict Liability Offence*

The main criticism is that the formulation creates a strict liability offence i.e. the proof of the fault element is not expressly required, which represents a departure from currently accepted criminal law principles, despite section 6A FTRA stating that Chapter 2 of the Codw (except Part 2.5) applies to all offences against the Act.[92] According to Fisse and Fraser,[93]

> the wording of the section sets out an objective test, namely that it is reasonable to conclude from the matters stipulated in s 31(1)(b)(i) and (ii), or 31(2)(b)(i) and (ii) that the sole or dominant purpose of the person charged was to evade the reporting requirements. This is hardly the same as requiring that the accused acted with an intention to evade the requirement. [...] On a literal interpretation of the section, an accused is subject to liability whether or not he or she acted with an intention (sole, dominant, or incidental) to evade a reporting requirement.

In *Leask v Commonwealth,* Toohey J agreed that the way the offence under section 31(1) was drafted was unusual.

> It must be acknowledged that the manner in which s 31(I) goes about establishing criminal liability is unusual. It avoids the conventional means by which an offence is created, that is, simply by the proscription of identified conduct. The sub-section creates an offence, but not just by reference to conduct. Rather, if the manner and form in which the non-reportable cash transactions were conducted make it *reasonable to*

90 Fisse, Fraser, Coss (1992), p. 175. Fisse, Leonard (1997), pp. 22–25.

91 SSC-LCA (1988).

92 See SSC-LCA (1993), point 10.34.

93 Fisse, Fraser (1992), p. 175.

> *conclude* that they were conducted for the sole or dominant purpose of ensuring, or attempting to ensure, that the reporting requirements of the Act were inapplicable, then the person has committed an offence.[94]

Further, Brennan CJ commented that "section 31(1) is not a provision imposing strict liability but the fault element of the offence (mens rea) is extremely limited".[95] He said that:

> The mens rea required for criminal responsibility for the commission of a statutory offence has to be ascertained by reference to the text which creates the offence. The mens rea required by section 31(1) is confined, in my opinion, to the elements of the offence prescribed in par (a) [the person is a party to 2 or more non-reportable cash transactions].[96] A person who engages in the conduct mentioned in s 31(1)(a) is liable to conviction only if he voluntarily conducted the two or more "non-reportable cash transactions" therein mentioned and knew the facts which gave the transactions the character of "non-reportable cash transactions". [...] It is immaterial whether the offender knew that his conduct was unlawful [...].[97]

Section 6A of the FTRA includes a reference to the general principles of criminal responsibility of the Code, which should imply that intent and recklessness should be applied by operation of the Code. Section 5.1(2) of the Code states that a law may specify a different fault element to those provided by the Code, which is the case in section 31 FTRA.[98] However, section 6A has not led to a different interpretation of section 31 since 1995 when the Code came into force.[99]

In *Lee v R*,[100] Spigelman CJ expressed the opinion that in section 31 "purpose" is not used as an equivalent to "intention"; "the actuating purpose is

94 *Leask v Commonwealth* [1996] 187 CLR 579, 610.

95 *Leask v Commonwealth* [1996] 187 CLR 579, 598.

96 S 31(1)(a) provided: "A person commits an offence against this section if: (a) the person is a party to 2 or more non-reportable cash transactions".

97 *Leask v Commonwealth* [1996] 187 CLR 579, 592, 593.

98 In *Lee v R* [2007] NSWCCA 71 [14], Sully J was of the opinion that *purpose* should be understood as "intention". Spigelman CJ disagreed: [15] "[...] the reference to "purpose" in s31(1)(b) of the FTRA, should be understood to be a reference to an actuating purpose, rather than to a result which the person "means to bring about".

99 See for instance Spigelman CJ in *Lee v R* [2007] NSWCCA 71 [19] and [26].

100 *Lee v R* [2007] NSWCCA 71.

itself a matter indicating fault".[101] It follows that the standard of proof for each element of the offence is proof beyond reasonable doubt, however the standard of proof for "reasonable to conclude" is not beyond reasonable doubt.[102] According to Sully J, [t]he words "reasonable to conclude" and the words following them in s 31(1)(b) do not describe a standard of proof but rather a test that has to be satisfied before a finding of guilty can be made.[103] As Dawson J noted, "[t]he only effect of the words it would be reasonable to conclude" is [...] to lower the standard of proof from that of beyond reasonable doubt to that of a reasonable conclusion.[104] Such practice illustrates, once again, the breadth of Australian money laundering legislation. The provision was criticised by the court for its unclear wording and its unusual approach to the standard of proof[105] but, as Brennan CJ concluded, "it does not follow from the limitation of the required mens rea that section 31(1) is not constitutional".[106]

Stessens correctly pointed out that negligence is more easily established when abstract rules of conduct, such as guidelines provided by the financial institutions or a supervisory body regarding the customer's identification or record keeping, have not been observed.[107] Hence, the definition of dealing with property reasonably suspected of being proceeds of crime was further extended with section 400.9(2) to include key requirements of the FTRA. However, in contrast with other sections of Division 400 in which negligence is a mental element, the extension of FTRA rules in the Code does not require any mental element.

A dealing with money or property which it is reasonable to suspect to be the proceeds of an indictable offence can be proved when any conduct listed under 400.9(2) has been established. This demonstrates, according to the Supreme Court of New South Wales "that the purpose of s 400.9(2) is to expand the operation of s 400.9(1)(b) in order to encompass conduct that does not fall within the definition of 'proceeds of crime'".[108]

101 *Lee v R* [2007] NSWCCA 71, [15], [16] and [84].

102 *Lee v R* [2007] NSWCCA 71 [67].

103 *Hannes v The Director of Public Prosecutions* (Cth) (No. 2) [2006] NSWCCA 373; quoted by Sully J in *Lee v R* [2007] NSWCCA 71 [79].

104 *Leask v Commonwealth* [1996] 187 CLR 579, 597. See also Toohey J's comments on the background of the Act, pp. 611, 612.

105 Toohey J in *Leask v Commonwealth* [1996] 187 CLR 579, 611.

106 *Leask v Commonwealth* [1996] 187 CLR 579, 593.

107 Stessens (2000) p. 124.

108 *Heng-Sheng Lin v R* [2015] NSWCCA 204 [23] and [26] (unreported).

TABLE 4 Section 400.9 (1) + (2), the Code

S 400.9 Dealing with property reasonably suspected of being proceeds of crime etc.
(1) A person commits an offence if: (a) the person deals with money or other property; and (b) it is reasonable to suspect that the money or property is proceeds of crime; and (c) at the time of the dealing, the value of the money and other property is $100,000 or more. Penalty: Imprisonment for 3 years, or 180 penalty units, or both. (…) (2) Without limiting paragraph (1)(b) or (1A)(b), that paragraph is taken to be satisfied if: (a) the conduct referred to in paragraph (1)(a) involves a number of transactions that are structured or arranged to avoid the reporting requirements of the *Financial Transaction Reports Act 1988* that would otherwise apply to the transactions; or (aa) the conduct involves a number of transactions that are structured or arranged to avoid the reporting requirements of the *Anti-Money Laundering and Counter-Terrorism Financing Act 2006* that would otherwise apply to the transactions; or (…) (ba) the conduct amounts to an offence against section 139, 140 or 141 of the *Anti-Money Laundering and Counter-Terrorism Financing Act 2006*; or (c) the value of the money and property involved in the conduct is, in the opinion of the trier of fact, grossly out of proportion to the defendant's income and expenditure over a reasonable period within which the conduct occurs; or (d) the conduct involves a significant cash transaction within the meaning of the *Financial Transaction Reports Act 1988*, and the defendant: (i) has contravened his or her obligations under that Act relating to reporting the transaction; or (ii) has given false or misleading information in purported compliance with those obligations; or (da) the conduct involves a threshold transaction (within the meaning of the *Anti-Money Laundering and Counter-Terrorism Financing Act 2006*) and the defendant: (i) has contravened the defendant's obligations under that Act relating to reporting the transaction; or (…) (4) Absolute liability applies to paragraphs (1)(b) and (c) and (1A)(b) and (c).

(5) This section does not apply if the defendant proves that he or she had no reasonable grounds for suspecting that the money or property was derived or realised, directly or indirectly, from some form of unlawful activity.
Note: A defendant bears a legal burden in relation to the matter in subsection (5) (see Section 13.4).

3.4.3.1.2 *An Offence for Which There Is No Defence of Reasonable Mistaken Belief*

Given that the proof of the fault element is not expressly required, the FTRA does not provide any defence of reasonable mistaken belief,[109] which contrasts with section 400.9 (5).

3.4.3.1.3 *Aggregation of Structured Dealings*

Section 400.12 is used to sanction multiple structured dealings. Its purpose is to allow the prosecution to take into account the total value of multiple structured dealings so as to prevent the offender from pleading separate counts with a view to manipulating the value based penalty scheme.[110]

TABLE 5 Section 400.12, the Code

400.12 Combining several contraventions in a single charge

---

(1) A single charge of an offence against a provision of this Division may be about 2 or more instances of the defendant engaging in conduct (at the same time or different times) that constitutes an offence against a provision of this Division.
(2) If:
(a) a single charge is about 2 or more such instances; and
(b) the value of the money and other property dealt with is an element of the offence in question;
that value is taken to be the sum of the values of the money and other property dealt with in respect of each of those instances.

---

109 Fisse, Fraser (1992), pp. 177, 178. The introduction of S 6A into the FTRA has not modified this.

110 Proceeds of Crime (Consequential Amendments and Transitional Provisions) Bill 2002 (Cth), Revised Explanatory Memorandum, p. 17.

Sections 400.3 to 400.7 provide that absolute liability applies to the value of the money and property, i.e. it is not necessary for the prosecution to prove that the defendant knew of the exact value of the assets with which s/he was dealing. In contrast, section 400.12 does not do that; it is not a special liability provision. Nonetheless, when combined with sections 400.3 to 400.7, section 400.12 has a transforming effect. In *Tan v R,* the Supreme Court of Victoria held that "s 400.12 is a substantive provision which 'transforms' an individual dealing with money under $1m in value into a contravention of s 400.3 if it is made in the context of a number of dealings, the sum of which is $1m or more".[111]

Hence, section 400.12 can be applied to dealing with money intending that it be an instrument of future crime (*Trandy*[112]), and to dealing in what the offender knew was proceeds of drug offending (*Tan*).

3.4.3.2 Example 2: A Tax Offence

In Australia, the money laundering offence is often used in conjunction with tax laws to sanction tax avoidance. In many cases, the origin of the money or property may be legitimate but the income is concealed. In this configuration, AML legislation does not sanction a predicate offence but the subsidiary offence.

Not all financial transactions which have been concealed from the tax authority or incorrectly reported may lead to a conviction for money laundering. In *Milne v R,*[113] the High Court of Australia impugned previous court rulings for having convicted Milne for money laundering. Milne had swapped shares and reported a smaller profit than he should have done in his income tax return. The prosecution alleged that Milne had dealt with money or other property which was used or intended to be used to become an instrument of crime, in this case a tax offence. Though acknowledging that the purpose of Division 400 was to create offences of broader application than existing money laundering offences, the Court found that the prosecution's understanding of the physical element was beyond the Code's definition. French CJ held that the Crown had given to the term "use" a meaning which the text of the Code will not bear and which its purpose does not require.[114] The HCA clarified the meaning of "instrument of crime".

111 *Tan v R* (2011) 35 VR 109; [2011] VSCA 427 [33].

112 *Trandy v R* [2009] VSCA 321.

113 *Milne v R* (2014) 305 ALR 477; [2014] HCA 4.

114 *Milne v R* (2014) 305 ALR 477; [2014] HCA 4 [2] [8].

> The definition of "instrument of crime" and the deployment of that term in s 400.3(1)(b)(ii) require a temporal separation between the requisite dealing and the intended use of the property. They also require an instrumental connection between the intended use of property and the commission or facilitation of the commission of an offence. Conduct involving property which is no more than a necessary condition of the commission of a subsequent offence does not on that account amount to the use of the property in or to facilitate the commission of that offence. Nor is the instrumental connection demonstrated merely by an intention to take advantage of circumstances arising after and as a result of the requisite dealing. A fortiori, that is the case where that property has been put beyond the reach of the accused by sale to a third party.

The disposal of the shares which held a higher value was the relevant dealing. However they could not possibly be considered an instrument of crime because they had transferred. They were not Milne's anymore when he filed his tax income. Hence, it is expected that the requirement for a temporal separation will reduce the scope of AML provisions offences for prosecuting tax offences.[115]

3.4.3.3 Example 3: Conspiracy

Prior to 2010, Australian federal legislation did not have a corresponding provision to *participation in a criminal organisation* found in UNTOC and hence relied on the concept of conspiracy. The use of conspiracy in the context of money laundering or *proceeds of crime* presents difficulties, particularly in matters of recklessness for recklessness does not constitute a sufficient fault element.[116]

The two-step construction of the Australian offence of "dealing with money" is made more complex in the case of a conspiracy because it is a composite construction, since it consists of an agreement, of which the fault element is the intention to commit an offence which must be of a non-trivial character. Conspiracy to commit an offence of "dealing with money" becomes thus a three-step offence.

The issue of recklessness in "dealing in proceeds of crime" has been discussed in two cases: *Ansari* and *R v LK and R v RK*.[117] The risk factor which is

115 Leighton-Daly (2015), p. 11.

116 *Giorgianni v R* [1985] CLR 473 [506] per Wilson, Deane and Dawson JJ.

117 *R v LK*; *R v RK* [2010] 241 CLR 177 and *Ansari v R* [2010] 241 CLR 299. See also *A Ansari v R, H Ansari v R* [2007] NSWCCA 204. Dobraszczyk (2010), pp. 64–66.

part of the circumstance contained in the definition of "dealing with money" is the key element which explains a different solution to two seemingly similar cases.[118] In both cases, the defendants were charged with conspiring to commit money laundering. The *Ansari* brothers had agreed to collect a large sum of money and to deposit it in several amounts of less than AUD 10,000, while *LK* and *RK* had agreed to transfer a large sum of money, reckless as to the fact that it was the proceeds of crime.

The differences between the two cases stem from the circumstance defined in Division 400 and to the structure of the offences. It is not possible to enter recklessly into an agreement to conspire since the Code specifies that the fault element must be intent; it is possible, however, to conspire to commit an offence for which the mental element is recklessness.

In *Ansari v R* [2010], the defendants were found reckless, not so much as to the fact that there was a risk that the money might become an instrument of crime, but by creating such risk by their conduct ("structuring" / "smurfing").[119] To understand the risk, it is necessary to keep in mind that the FTRA makes it compulsory for financial institutions to report to designated authorities any significant cash transaction i.e. AUD 10,000 and above.[120] Making several transactions of less than AUD 10,000 is considered to be "smurfing" or "structuring cash transactions".[121] By agreeing to deposit a large number of non-reportable amounts, the prosecution established the defendants' intention to elude the requirements of the FTRA, thus committing a money laundering offence.[122]

The appellants held the view that the offence of conspiracy, defined under section 11.5, does not carry the fault element of recklessness, but a fault element of intention. Consequently, in their view, "the charges set out in the indictment disclosed an offence [not] known to the law". They thought that there was "a logical incoherence in applying the intention that an offence be committed, which is necessary to make out a conspiracy, to an offence of which recklessness is an element – in this case, an offence against s 400.3(2) of the Code".[123] Their appeal was dismissed.

Simpson JA observed at [34] that:

---

118 LK and RK were acquitted while the Ansari brothers were found guilty.

119 *Ansari v R* [2010] 241 CLR 299 [14] [18].

120 Art.15, FTRA.

121 Fisse, Leonard (1997), p. 22.

122 Art 31 FTRA; *Ansari v R* [2010] 241 CLR 299 [14].

123 *Ansari v R; Ansari v R* [2010] 241 CLR 299 [23] [24].

> The flaw in the appellants' argument is in failing to identify who the Crown alleged was (or would have been) "reckless" and to what aspect of the facts alleged the recklessness attaches. The appellants' argument attributes recklessness to themselves, in the formation of, or entry into, the criminal agreement. I accept that recklessness is insufficient for that. But that is not the correct analysis. It is not recklessness as to the agreement that is in question; it is agreement (intentionally entered into) that an offence will be committed that might, inter alia, be done with a reckless state of mind. The recklessness attaches, not to the formation of, or the entry into, the agreement, but to the offence that is to be committed pursuant to the agreement.[124]

French CJ stated that

> [t]he requisite intention on the part of the conspirators that the offence against s 400.3(2) be committed extends to an intention that the person committing it will be reckless as to the fact that there is a risk that the money dealt with will become an instrument of crime. Such an intention may exist where the contemplated repository of the reckless state of mind is a third party. But if it be the alleged conspirator who is said to intend to carry out the offence, that person may intend to deal with the money with knowledge of the risk that it will become an instrument of crime. Alternatively, such a person may intend to deal with the money intending that there will be a risk that it will become an instrument of crime. These states of mind are logically consistent and reflect the application of the extended meaning of recklessness under s 5.4(4) of the Code. Once that is accepted, no incoherence is introduced by reason of the particular offences of structured transactions and tax evasion relied upon to support the characterisation of the possible use of the money as an instrument of crime.[125]

In *R v LK; R v RK*, the defendants were accused of conspiring to commit the offence of dealing with money while being reckless as to the fact that the money was proceeds of crime. Both the trial judge and the Chief Justice were of the opinion that *Ansari* cannot support a charge of conspiracy where, in order to satisfy the test of intention with respect to the entry into an agreement to

124 *Ansari v R, Ansari v R* [2007] NSWCCA 204 [23].

125 *R v LK; R v RK* [2010] 241 CLR 177, [26].

commit an offence, the accused must *know* the facts that constitute the offence (emphasis in original).[126]

The plurality judgement upheld the previous decisions, taking the view that

> [t]here cannot be a conspiracy in which the parties to the agreement are reckless as to the existence of a circumstance which is a necessary element of the offence said to be the subject of the conspiracy. Such recklessness would be inconsistent with the very intention that is necessary at common law and under the Code to form the agreement alleged. In this case that intention is an intention to deal with money which is proceeds of crime. Recklessness as to whether the money is proceeds of crime is recklessness about a term of the agreement constituting the conspiracy.[127]

"In *R v LK and R v RK*, at the time the agreement was made, the money may, or may not, have been (or have become) proceeds of crime. The agreement, if carried out in accordance with LK's and RK's intention, may not have involved dealing with money that is proceeds of crime".[128] In the eyes of the trial judge, *Ansari* is to be understood as accepting

> that the Crown can charge a person with conspiring to commit an offence the mental element of which is recklessness where it relies on intention or knowledge to prove the element of recklessness or where a third party is to commit the relevant offence. Neither of these circumstances was alleged in the present case.[129]

In *R v LK and R v RK* the defendants were reckless as to the fact that the money *was* proceeds of crime which was a necessary element of the conspiracy; in *Ansari* the defendants were reckless as to the *risk* that the money would be used in the commission of an offence, namely smurfing. The evidence was in "[t]heir receipt and their contemplated receipt of the money, intending to 'launder' it by deposits of less than $10,000, [since it] was said to have created the relevant risk".[130]

126 *R v LK; R v RK* [2010] 241 CLR 177, [7].

127 *R v LK; the Queen v RK* [2010] 241 CLR 177, [77].

128 *R v LK; the Queen v RK* [2010] 241 CLR 177, [122].

129 *R v LK; the Queen v RK* [2010] 241 CLR 177 [69].

130 *Ansari Ansari v R; Ansari v R* [2010] 241 CLR 299 [14].

Ansari was confirmed in *Tan v R* where a plurality of offenders was found guilty of laundering proceeds of drug trafficking by structuring transactions. The question was whether section 400.12 applies to a conspiracy, so that the individual dealings of the conspirators may be aggregated to determine the precise extent of the substantive offence for which they are to be punished. The Supreme Court of Victoria held that the offence that the offenders conspired to commit was a single offence of section 400.3.

> The consequence of s 400.12 is that the substantive offence may be committed where there are multiple dealings each of which involves an amount less than $1m but which in aggregate equal or exceed that amount. As the acts which constitute the offence include dealings in amounts of money less than $1m, an agreement to deal in such amounts can constitute a conspiracy to commit the substantive offence. That is to say the conspiracy will encompass those acts which are in law capable of establishing that offence. Accordingly, the prosecution must establish the conspirators' agreed intention was to deal in such amounts as in law would constitute the commission of the substantive offence.[131]

The conspiracy provisions have often been used in money laundering cases. *Ansari* ensures that it will remain so. It also opens the door for a wider application as *Ansari* provides the prosecution with a clear basis to charge defendants for conspiring to commit offences which the mental element is recklessness. The prosecution would find this extension of the legislation's scope particularly useful in organised crime offences which provide recklessness as a fault element. *Ansari* may also be applied in conjunction with terrorism offences, and the new joint commission provision. In sum, the Code's emphasis on the fault element of recklessness and negligence reinforces the preventative character of Australia's dealing with assets provisions.

3.5 Corporate Liability

By virtue of Part 5.2 of the Code, Division 400 applies to bodies corporate in the same way as it applies to individuals. Hence, a body corporate may be found guilty of a money laundering offence, including one punishable by imprisonment. The physical element of an offence committed by an employee, agent or

131 *Tan v R* (2011) 35 VR 109; [2011] VSCA 427 [37].

officer acting within the actual or apparent scope of his/her employment, or within his/her actual or apparent authority is then attributed to the body corporate. However, there is a major difference regarding the fault element in that a corporation cannot be guilty of negligence unless the body corporate is held negligent when viewed as a whole, for instance when there is inadequate corporate management control or supervision of the employee, or the employee was not properly informed.

TABLE 6 Section 51, AML/CTF Act 2006

S 51 Division 400 and Chapter 5 of the Criminal Code
If a person, or an officer, employee or agent of a person, communicates or gives information under section 41, 43, 45 or 49, the person, officer, employee or agent is taken, for the purposes of Division 400 and Chapter 5 of the *Criminal Code*, not to have been in possession of that information at any time.

The *Anti-Money Laundering and Counter-Terrorism Financing Act 2006* also provides for the criminal liability of corporations.

If an entity subject to AML/CTF requirements complies with its reporting obligations (suspicious transactions (s 41), threshold transactions (s 43), international funds transfers (s 45) or as instructed by AUSTRAC (s 49), it cannot be held criminally liable, even if it carries out the transaction. It is therefore difficult to prosecute a financial institution. So far, corporations have not been successfully prosecuted for money laundering.

3.6 Penalties

AML legislation is essentially composed of two parts: substantive provisions criminalising money laundering which are found in Division 400 of the Code, and provisions implementing AML measures: the *Financial Transaction Reports Act 1988* and the *Anti-Money Laundering and Counter-Terrorism Financing Act 2006*. Both contain penal sanctions.

Violations of the *Anti-Money Laundering and Counter-Terrorism Financing Act 2006* can incur up to 10 years imprisonment or 10,000 penalty units, or both, and violations of the *Financial Transaction Reports Act* can go up to an imprisonment period of 5 years or a fine. Under the Code, penalties for money laundering offences vary according to the value of the assets and the fault elements of intention, knowledge, recklessness and negligence. The most serious penalties are reserved for those offenders who deal with very large sums of money, an evidence of a link with organised crime.[132] Hence, with the mental element being constant, the penalty is increased with the value of the dealt property. For instance, if at the time of the dealing the value is less than AUD 1,000, the penalty can go up to imprisonment for 12 months, or 60 penalty units, or both (s 440.8). By contrast, if the money or property is worth more than AUD 1 million, the penalty can reach imprisonment for 25 years, or 1500 penalty units, or both (s 400.3). It is noteworthy that, since the Code does not provide for an increased penalty in case of offences committed in company or as a member of a criminal organisation, the court appears to use the wide imprisonment period found in Division 400 to sanction an offender acting in association with someone else.[133]

TABLE 7 Penalties for money laundering offences[a]

Australia	A fine and/or 6 months to 25 yrs
Belgium	15 days to 5 yrs
Denmark	18 months to 6 yrs
Finland	A fine or max of 2 yrs / 6 yrs for "serious" ML
France	Up to 5 yrs and a fine, raised in case of aggravated ML
Germany	3 months to 5 yrs max rises to 10 yrs in very serious cases[b]
Luxembourg	A fine or up to 1 to 5 years or both/Double if re-offending and up to 20 yrs in organised crime cases[c]
Spain	6 months to 6 yrs and a fine proportional to value of proceeds
Sweden	Max 2 yrs / 6 yrs for "serious" ML
The Netherlands	A fine or alternatively a max of 4 yrs
UK	A fine or up to 14 yrs or both
Ireland	A fine or up to 14 yrs or both

a Deloitte (2011), pp. 127–134, European Commission (2012).
b i.e. when the perpetrator acts professionally or as a member of an organisation formed for the continued commission of money laundering.
c The maximum is raised to 20 years if the conduct implies participating in a criminal organisation.

132 *R v Van Loi Nguyen* [2010] NSWCCA 226 [59].
133 *Nahlous v R* [2010] NSWCCA 58 [15].

At international comparison, provisions for money laundering offences vary considerably according to whether they are issued in a civil law or common law State. In continental Europe, the imprisonment period is usually notably shorter than in the common law States. In comparison to these States, Australian maximum penalties for the same offence are twice as severe.

3.6.1 *Legal Exemptions*

In Australian substantive money laundering legislation, there is no provision regarding the case of dealing with money or property while being mistaken as to its criminal origin. Although the general provisions of the Code apply, Division 400, which sanctions recklessness and negligence, leaves very little scope for the application of circumstances involving mistake or ignorance, as the defendant can easily be found to have been reckless or negligent even if he or she was unaware of the risk. Stessens rightly pointed out that

> [t]his can obviously lead to grave injustices and it may indeed be one circumstance where the application of anti-money laundering law may violate the legality principle, precisely because the incrimination will not provide "effective safeguards against arbitrary prosecution, conviction and punishment". [...] [d]omestic legislation [...] should provide the person who becomes aware of the criminal origin of the proceeds only after he has taken them into possession with a legal "escape route".[134]

Under the POCA (1988), the only "escape route" granted was to financial institutions or one of their officers, employees or agents provided they informed law enforcement agencies *as soon as practicable*. This follows FATF recommendation that financial institutions, their directors, officers and employees be protected by legal provisions from criminal and civil liability for breach of any restriction on disclosure of information imposed by contract or by any legislative, regulatory or administrative provision. Nowadays, the protection is still only available to financial institutions and their agents.

3.7 Conclusion

The construction of the Australian AML regime sits at odds with the rhetoric used to initiate AML legislation as a means to prosecute organised crime.

134 Stessens (2000), pp. 128, 129.

However this can easily been explained by the circumstances which prevailed in the years leading to its adoption. From a constitutional perspective, Australian legislation is not directed against the most serious forms of organised crime. Its principal object is to facilitate the administration and enforcement of taxation laws. The contribution of the AML legislation against organised crime is thus indirect. Hence, the comment by the FATF team that "money laundering is perhaps excessively seen in Australia as a revenue issue",[135] could not be more justified.

Australia's offence against money laundering is correctly called "dealing with assets" rather than "anti-money laundering". It differentiates itself in three respects from the major international conventions on the topic. First, it does not make the concealment of the criminal origin of the assets the core element of the offence. Secondly, Division 400 of the Code emphasises the risk that the assets, even legitimately acquired, could be used as an instrument of crime. Thirdly, Division 400 includes the fault element of recklessness and negligence, broadening considerably the already wide scope of the provisions.

The emphasis on the risk, which is further stressed by offences that include recklessness and negligence as a fault element, gives to Australia's dealing with assets legislation a very strong preventative character. This feature is in stark contrast with the civil law's traditional understanding of the function of criminal law which is seen as a purely punitive tool, not a preventative one.[136] According to this tradition, the intention is only punishable if it has led to the attempt to commit a crime. Under the Code, it is not only the (commission of a) crime that is sanctioned but (taking) the risk that one could be committed. Furthermore, the Australian offences are liable to very high penalties, which may appear disproportionate given that they do not sanction crimes against life, limb or personal freedom.

Although it is understandable to draw attention to the risk of being part of a crime, the severity of the penalties may have the unforeseen consequence of dissuading all risk-taking, even in circumstances when the funds are not going towards a criminal activity, just to avoid being told by a court that there was a substantial risk and that therefore the conduct was reckless.[137] It cannot be excluded that the provisions on the risk that the assets could become an instrument of crime paired with the breadth of the fault element would work as a deterrent for cautious and honest businesspersons to deal financially with

135 FATF (1996b), point 84.

136 According to the principle *nullum crimen sine actu* (there is no crime without an action, a conduct).

137 Leighton-Daly (2015), p. 15.

Australia. It may be one of the many elements that need to be factored in when striking a deal with an Australian partner. If it were the case, the provisions would be disproportionate to the legitimacy of the aim pursued.

Upon the adoption of the *Proceeds of Crime Act 1987* (Cth), Fisse had already expressed his concern regarding the legislation:

> [...] recent Commonwealth prohibitions on money-laundering are unparalleled in their departure from basic principles of criminal liability. The so-called war against organised crime has generated a new despotism in criminal legislation, a new despotism wherein serious offences are defined in such scattershot terms that the scope of liability depends very little on law and very much on administrative discretion. This despotism is not only ethically indefensible, but has gone to the extent of exposing lawyers, accountants, stockbrokers and financial institutions to an unwarranted risk of prosecution in their everyday professional or business lives.[138]

In addition, by criminalising the risk that the assets could be used in a crime as part of its AML provisions, the Australian legislature makes dealing with assets a "dirty" operation. It introduces thereby a moral element. Australia's money laundering legislation may illustrate a very particular understanding of criminal law as a tool for social control. Given the extensive breath of AML legislation and the widespread use of strict liability provisions, a particular vigilance is required by the judiciary.[139]

The Code's view not only puts Australia's dealing with assets legislation squarely in the preventative apparatus, it also prefigures the breadth of the Code's organised crime and terrorism offences and foreshadows the pro-active law enforcement measures that will be taken against terrorism.

---

138 Fisse (1987), p. 60.

139 See *R (Cth) v Milne* (No 1) [2010] NSWSC 932 [165] and [166].

CHAPTER 4

Money Laundering Post-9/11: Defining Terrorism Financing

> We have entered into the "risk society", marked more and more by the fear of dangers, or disasters, being natural or man-made (inter-human violence or ultra-power of technologies).[1]
>
> MIREILLE DELMAS-MARTY

4.1 Introduction

Despite having been one of the first States to introduce comprehensive legislation against money laundering, Australia did not update the FTRA 1988 (Cth) or the topical provisions of the Code. As a result, in 2005, Australia was found in the main to not comply with the international benchmark.[2] Bringing Australian legislation back in line with international standards was a considerable task which was undertaken in stages in conjunction with the adoption of counter-terrorism financing legislation. Starting with an overview of Australia's terrorism legislation in the international context, this chapter sets its development and stresses, *inter alia,* the similarities of the CTF provisions with AML legislation, particularly with regard to its preventative character, and its aversion of risk.

Terrorism has existed since antiquity.[3] Contrary to the later attacks in the second part of the 20th century, the former acts of aggression were carried out by nationalists or anarchists who had local support. In the 1960s, different forms of terrorist acts such as plane hijacking, hostage taking, prompted an international reaction. These acts were mainly conducted by movements seeking independence from colonial powers. The political context made it

1 *Nous sommes entrés dans la "société du risque", de plus en plus marquée par la peur de dangers, voire de catastrophes, d'origine naturelle ou humaine (violence interhumaine ou surpuissance des technologies*). Delmas-Marty (2010), pp. 223, 224.

2 FATF (2005b).

3 Chaliand, Blin (2004); Laurens, Delmas-Marty (2010), p. 12.

 | DOI:10.1163/9789004359109_005

difficult for the international community to agree on a concerted action. Within the Security Council, the permanent members were conducting a cold war through independent or nationalist movements. Unable to agree to a common and comprehensive definition of terrorist acts, the international community resorted to adopting several multilateral treaties in reaction to certain forms of terrorism. Still today, there is no international comprehensive convention on terrorism. There are fifteen international treaties which are considered to form the nucleus of the international legislation against terrorism. They can be grouped according to their scope.

TABLE 8 15 international treaties on terrorism

Scope	Year	Title
Air travel	1963	*Convention on Offences and Certain Other Acts Committed on Board Aircraft*
	1970	*Convention for the suppression of Unlawful Seizure of Aircraft* *Convention for the suppression of Unlawful Acts against the Safety of Civil Aviation*
	1971	*Protocol for the Suppression of Unlawful Acts of Violence at Airports Serving International Civil Aviation Supplementary to the Convention for the Suppression of Unlawful Acts against the Safety of Civil Aviation*
	2010	*Protocol Supplementary to the Convention for the Suppression of Unlawful Seizure of Aircraft*
	2010	*Convention on the Suppression of Unlawful Acts relating to International Civil Aviation against civil aviation*
Maritime navigation, vessels and fixed platforms	1988	*Convention for the Suppression of Unlawful Acts against the Safety of Maritime Navigation.*
	1988	*Protocol for the Suppression of Unlawful Acts against the Safety of Fixed Platforms Located on the Continental Shelf*
Persons, based on their status	1973	*Convention on the prevention and punishment of crimes against internationally protected persons, including diplomatic Agents*
	1979	*Convention against the taking of hostages*
Dangerous materials	1980	*Convention on the physical protection of nuclear material*
	2005	Amendment to the convention replaces the 1980 convention which is provided with a new title: *Convention on the physical protection of nuclear material and nuclear facilities*
	1991	*Convention on the marking of plastic explosives for the purpose of identification* is related to the aircraft conventions
	1997	*Convention for the suppression of terrorist bombing*
Financing	1999	*Convention for the Suppression of the Financing of Terrorism*

In the 1970s and 1980s, some European States saw the rise and fall of anarchist and right wing terrorist groups: *Die Rote Armee Faktion* (Red Army Faction – RAF), in Germany, and a neo-fascist group and the *Brigate Rosso* (BR, Red Brigade), in Italy. France was the scene of several attacks by various terrorist groups (such as *Action directe*) and Middle-Eastern organisations. These events prompted the Council of Europe in 1977 to adopt the *Convention on the Suppression of Terrorism* and in 1980 to recommend AML measures to tackle terrorist activities.[4]

Outside Europe, the increase of terrorist aggression after WW II did not elevate the issue of terrorism financing to the forefront of the international agenda until 1998 which was the year the US embassies in Kenya and Tanzania were attacked. As a result, a draft *International Convention for the Suppression of the Financing of Terrorism* (thereafter UN Convention on terrorism financing) was initiated. Its objective was to cover all means of financing and to focus on the financing of the most serious terrorist acts. Despite a prompt adoption, in 1999, the ratifications were slow to come: By the end of August 2001, only four states had ratified it (Botswana, Sri Lanka, UK and Uzbekistan).

A decisive turn took place with the strikes of 11 September 2001. Within two weeks, the UN Security Council passed Resolution 1373 (UNSCR 1373) calling for a number of specific measures to be taken against the financing of terrorism, terrorists and in favour of inter-State cooperation. These measures were deemed necessary for two reasons. First, the UN *Convention for the Suppression of the Financing of Terrorism* and the UNTOC had not come into force. Secondly, these conventions would only be binding on the State Parties, whereas the Security Council Resolutions passed under Chapter 7 of the UN Charter are binding on every UN Member State.

In Australia, at the end of the 20th century, there have been several acts of political violence committed by ethno-nationalists (mainly connected with Yugoslavia), including three deadly "terrorist incidents". The first was in 1978; an explosive device in a bin outside the Hilton Hotel in Sydney where Commonwealth Heads of Government were meeting was detonated, killing three people. The offender has officially never been identified.[5] The second was the assassination of a Turkish diplomat and his body guard by an Armenian group in Sydney in 1980. The third was the explosion of a car bomb in the Turkish consulate killing the offender in 1986.[6] Australia has also been used as a base

4 CoE, Committee of Ministers, Recommendation R(80)10 on measures against the transfer and the safekeeping of funds of criminal origin, 27.06.1980.

5 *Alister Alister v R* [1983] HCA 45, (1984) 154 CLR 404; *R v Anderson* (1991) 53 A Crim R 421; *R v Evan Dunstan Pederick* [1996] NSWSC 623.

6 *R v Demirian* [1989] VR 97.

TABLE 9 UNSCR 1373

UNSCR 1373 – point 1
(a) Prevent and suppress the financing of terrorist acts; (b) Criminalize the wilful provision or collection, by any means, directly or indirectly, of funds by their nationals or in their territories with the intention that the funds should be used, or in the knowledge that they are to be used, in order to carry out terrorist acts; (c) Freeze without delay funds and other financial assets or economic resources of persons who commit, or attempt to commit, terrorist acts or participate in or facilitate the commission of terrorist acts; of entities owned or controlled directly or indirectly by such persons; and of persons and entities acting on behalf of, or at the direction of such persons and entities, including funds derived or generated from property owned or controlled directly or indirectly by such persons and associated persons and entities; (d) Prohibit their nationals or any persons and entities within their territories from making any funds, financial assets or economic resources or financial or other related services available, directly or indirectly, for the benefit of persons who commit or attempt to commit or facilitate or participate in the commission of terrorist acts, of entities owned or controlled, directly or indirectly, by such persons and of persons and entities acting on behalf of or at the direction of such persons.

to prepare for attacks outside the country (Yugoslavia, Japan).[7] In 1990, ASIO noted that the only discernible domestic threat of politically motivated violence in Australia came from the racist right.[8] At that time, terrorism financing seemed more a domestic issue and only a matter of concern for the States affected by terrorist attacks.

At the eve of the 21st century, with the exception of the Northern Territory, there was no specific anti-terrorism legislation in Australia. However every state and territory had enacted legislation that could be used to prosecute acts of terrorism. At the federal level, there was a mosaic of legal provisions in various acts that could be applicable; most of them implemented Australia's obligations under the international terrorism conventions, arguably "in the anticipation of and response to an act of international terrorism that directly or

7 Harris-Hogan (2017), pp. 2–3.

8 Human Rights and Equal Opportunity Commission (1991) p. 223.

indirectly affected Australia".[9] However, there were no adequate provisions to act preventatively against terrorism, particularly on the domestic scene. Some of the existing provisions were originally taken from English law and inserted in the *Crimes Act 1914* (Cth). Other provisions were expanded or introduced to cover domestic offences against the Commonwealth in a period where communism was seen as a major threat to democracy.[10] Following the 1978 Sydney Hilton Hotel bombing,[11] the Government ordered several legislation and policy reviews. The recommendations that were issued only concerned particular aspects of terrorism. None suggested the enactment of specific terrorism offences. On the contrary, Hope J was of the opinion that, on the whole, "domestic intelligence gathering and law enforcement bodies were given adequate powers under existing legislation".[12] The term "terrorism" appeared for the first time in Australia in law enforcement legislation, the *Australian Security Intelligence Organisation Act 1979*, but was replaced in 1986 by "politically motivated violence",[13] which is the basic concept which underlies Australia's current terrorism law. Although not all politically motivated violence is terrorism, it is the use of fear as a means that distinguishes acts of terrorism from other forms of politically motivated violence.[14] There were also some provisions under the *Crimes (Foreign Incursions and Recruitment) Act 1978*. However they were limited to foreign activities (financing of hostile acts against foreign States by Australians or persons using Australia as a base).

In September 2001, the Australian Government initiated a legislative process that spanned many years to ensure that the country had comprehensive legislation against terrorism. Having to write legislation from scratch, Australia took for a model for its legislation the *UK Terrorist Act*. It did not follow the *Model Legislative Provisions on Measures to Combat Terrorism* that the Commonwealth Secretariat was preparing at the time.[15] Within 5 years, thirty pieces of legislation were passed by the Commonwealth Parliament.[16] Since the constitutional

9 Hancock (2002), p. 1; Ricketts (2002), pp. 145–148; SLC-ALC (2002). In contrast, see Rose, Nestorovska (2007). Cornall AO (2007).

10 Barwick (1960).

11 The various subsequent convictions were overturned. Since no author has been identified and no motive uncovered, there are still speculations as to the reasons for the explosion.

12 Hope (1979), pp. 3 and 33–34.

13 See National Anti-terrorism Plan (NATP). Hancock (2002), p. 4.

14 Hansch (1996), p. 92.

15 This is even more surprising when Australia had a representative in the Director of the Legal and Constitutional Affairs Division of the Commonwealth Secretariat in the person of Dianne Stafford. Commonwealth Secretariat (2002).

16 Jull (2006), p. 52. For an overview, see Sheller (2006), pp. 33–35.

basis for legislating in domestic terrorism matters was questioned, the Federal government sought an Agreement with the states and territories to be granted the necessary legislative powers to legislate in domestic terrorism matters. It was signed on 5 April 2002. Although the need to adopt terrorism legislation was not really disputed by the opposition, the haste with which the legislation was prepared gave rise to many criticisms and subsequent modifications.[17] With the 2002 package of legislation, the foundation of anti-terrorism legislation was laid, creating terrorism offences (terrorist act and terrorist organisations) and introducing a system for listing organisations related to terrorist activities. The Commonwealth issued its first National Counter-Terrorism Plan in June 2003.[18] The procedure for proscribing terrorist organisation was developed in 2004. The 2005 amendments introduced control orders and preventative detention. On the law enforcement front, the Terrorist Financing Intelligence Unit (TFIU) was established within the AFP in 2010. Composed of representatives of several agencies, both at federal (AUSTRAC, AIC) and State levels, it focuses on terrorism financing investigations and intelligence, as well as education and liaison. The potential threat of Australian jihadists returning home (estimated at 150 in 2014)[19] to pursue their fight prompted the adoption of the *Counter-Terrorism Legislation Amendment (Foreign Fighters) Act 2014*.

Prompted by the Security Council stance, the FATF issued, on 31 October 2001, eight Special Recommendations (SR) on Terrorist Financing, and added a ninth in 2004. They are regarded as complementary to the 40 Recommendations. In order to determine the added value of counter-terrorism financing (CTF) legislation and whether it is intrinsically different from AML legislation, the following sections focus first on the examination of the FATF Special Recommendations.

4.2 The FATF Special Recommendations on Terrorism Financing

4.2.1 *Introduction*

Although the declared justification of the FATF Special Recommendations is to set out the basic framework to detect, prevent and suppress the financing of terrorism and terrorist acts, a close examination shows that, except for

17 Ricketts (2002); Williams (2003), p. 191; Williams (2002), p. 212. Sheller (2006); Jull (2006).

18 National Counter-Terrorism Committee (2003). The Government White paper on *Transnational Terrorism: the threat to Australia* was only released in 2004.

19 Grattan (2014).

aspects of SR VIII on non-profit organisations, the Special Recommendations pertain more to money-laundering than specific anti-terrorism measures. The latest 2012 revision of the FATF Recommendations has integrated the *Special Recommendations against Terrorism* and added measures against the financing of the proliferation of weapons of mass destruction into the *Forty Recommendations.*

TABLE 10 The special recommendations on the financing of terrorism

SR I:	Ratification and implementation of the 1999 UN International Convention on the Suppression of the Financing of Terrorism and UN resolutions relating to the prevention and suppression of the financing of terrorist acts, particularly UNSCR 1373
SR II:	Criminalising the financing of terrorism and associated money laundering
SR III:	Freezing and confiscating terrorist assets
SR IV:	Reporting suspicious transactions related to terrorism
SR V:	International cooperation
SR VI:	Alternative remittance
SR VII:	Wire transfers
SR VIII:	Non-profit organisations
SR IX:	Cash couriers

Since the FATF had already recommended extending the predicate offence of money laundering to serious offences, which include terrorism,[20] the addition of special recommendations against terrorism does not appear *prima facie* to be justified. Insofar as the Recommendations prescribe reporting obligations, seizure and confiscation measures as well as international cooperation, they are a mere extension of the AML regulations to the financing of terrorism. This is particularly the case as regards SR I to V.[21] The following sections examine briefly SR VI, VII, VIII and IX, and their contribution against terrorism financing and their impact.

20 FATF (1999); FATF (1996), para.18, p. 6: para.71, p. 47.

21 SR I has been integrated in former Rec 35 and renamed Rec 36, SR II is now Rec 5, SR III is Rec 6, SR IV has been integrated in former Rec 13 and renamed Rec 20, SR V has been integrated in former Rec 36 and renamed Rec 37.

4.2.2 *Difficulties in Implementing SR VI, VII, VIII and IX*

4.2.2.1 Alternative Remittance (SR VI)[22]

Alternative remittance systems have been an on-going concern for the FATF, at least since 1996. Although there is no broadly-agreed definition, they are known on several continents under different names (hawala, hundi, giro houses, black market peso exchange) and are sometimes referred to as "underground" or "parallel banking systems", though they are mostly legitimate. Generally they have developed according to specific ethnic, cultural or historical factors. In some cases, they are a traditional method for moving money that pre-dates the spread of Western banking systems in the 19th and 20th centuries.

Since the financial transactions which funded the attacks against the USA were not detected before 11 September 2001, it was (mistakenly[23]) thought that the terrorists had used a parallel banking system. Hence, the FATF issued a SR on Alternative Remittance Systems. Nevertheless, SR VI cannot be seen as specific against the financing of terrorism since the FATF has debated this issue for years.[24] Before the end of the 20th century, the development of money laundering techniques and the use of different forms of financial activities and businesses had called for new measures to restrict the flow of illegitimate assets. In addition, the FATF had extended legal obligations to other non-regulated finance sectors and non-financial sectors. With the FATF Special Recommendations on terrorism financing, the list of organisations subject to the new rules was extended even further. The implementation of the Special Recommendations is seen as adversely affecting the non-bank money remitters' business viability.[25]

4.2.2.2 SR VII – Wire Transfers

According to the FATF, wire and funds transfer refer to any transaction carried out on behalf of an originator person (both natural and legal) through a financial institution, by electronic means, with a view to making an amount of money available to a beneficiary person at another financial institution.[26] SR VII is not particular to terrorism financing. The use of wire transfers in money laundering schemes has been the concern of law enforcement agencies for many years as the use of internet banking and other "e-money transfers" increased. The measures required to counter the anonymity of the transactions were

---

22 SR VI is now Rec 14 (Money or value transfer services), 2012 version.

23 Warde (2007), p. 170.

24 FATF (1998b), points 22 and 67. Vlcek (2007) p. 109.

25 Neilsen (2006) p. 4.

26 SR VII is now Rec 16, still called wire transfers in the 2012 version.

considered for years to be an excessive burden for the financial sector.[27] The objective of this SR VII is to ensure that basic information on the payer of fund transfers is immediately available to appropriate law enforcement agencies to assist them in their work. Hence the 2003 FATF's initial minimum threshold went from "no higher than USD 3000" to EUR 1000/USD 1000 in 2005.[28]

Making the transfer of funds to poor countries cumbersome or restricting the flow of money could fuel anti-Western feelings and thus create a breeding ground for terrorism. Somalia typifies the negative impact of CTF legislation on poorer countries. Local Somalis are deprived of overseas finance since no international banks are operating in Somalia and they need to rely on alternative remittance services provided from outside the formal banking system. The main remittance service used by Somalis overseas (Al-Barakaat) was suspected – ultimately wrongly – of financing Al Qaida. Consequently, its directors were arrested, its assets frozen and its 700 employees laid off. This led to long-term consequences since "the company was the country's biggest employer and ran the biggest bank, the biggest phone system, and the only water-purification plant".[29] Many Somalis felt unfairly treated. A few years later, Somalia saw the rise of Al-shabab, an Islamic fundamentalist group linked to Al Qaida.[30] There has also been a resurgence of acts of piracy in the international waters near Somalia, as well as abductions for ransom. Whether there is a connection between these two situations remains to be established, but the possible link is troubling. Notwithstanding the above, the 2014 tightening of AML/CTF regulations has prompted Australian banks to close their services to remittance operators, and so affecting about 10,000 Somalis living in Australia.[31]

4.2.2.3 SR VIII – Non-profit Organisations[32]

Though the example of misuse of non-profit organisations (NPOs) for terrorism financing (TF) purposes are few and far between, great concerns have been voiced regarding the use that terrorists could make of them. They could be used in three different ways: as a front for fundraising, as a channel for financing terrorists or terrorist activities, and as a means to launder funds of criminal origin on behalf of a terrorist organisation. Charities are seen to be most at

27 Pieth, Aiolfi (2004), p. 4.

28 FATF (2005a), 15, p. 8.

29 See Warde (2007), pp. 93 and 102; Golden (2002); Michaelsen (2009).

30 They have claimed responsibility for several terrorist attacks in Somalia and in Kenya. Al-shabab is considered a terrorist organisation by the Australian Government.

31 Armitage (2014); Armitage (2015); Safi (2015); De Koker, Singh, Capal (2017).

32 SR VIII is now Rec 8, still called Non-profit organisations in the 2012 version.

risk of abuse for TF when they engage in programmes of providing housing, social services, education, or health care in areas of conflict where terrorist activities are rife, but also in countries where there is no conflict, when terrorist groups actively targeted a population for support and cover. Consequently, SR VIII urges States to ensure that NPOs cannot be misused for terrorism purposes.

SR VIII distinguishes itself from other Recommendations by addressing the way an organisation is working rather than by monitoring its financial transactions. Its objective is to ensure that non-profit organisations are run in a transparent manner so that they cannot be a conduit for terrorist financing or for the purpose of circumventing the law. One way to reach this objective is to set up national registration or licensing procedures and to identify precisely the persons who ultimately control the NPOs. Thus, the focus is not so much on the "cleanness" of the financial transaction as on the probity of the institution. Nevertheless, they are required to keep financial records five years to be able to demonstrate this. There is no requirement on NPOs to identify each donor, in the way the financial sector must know its clients. Best practice requests the identification of individuals in management positions, the proper monitoring of activities and having transactions processed by approved financial institutions. However, financial institutions dealing with NPOs as clients must apply the CDD (customer due diligence) requirements. Where the ML/TF risks cannot be mitigated, for instance because of lack of transparency, as a last resort, it is the responsibility of the financial institution, on a case-by-case basis, to refuse a customer relationship or to terminate it.

The FATF and Australia's definition of non-profit organisations are very similar.[33] NPOs primarily engage in raising or disbursing funds for charitable, religious, cultural, educational, social or fraternal purposes. Some designated services of some NPOs are subject to the *Anti-Money Laundering and Counter-Terrorism Financing Act 2006* (Cth) (Act).[34] Aware that terrorist organisations may seek to infiltrate the NPO sector and misuse funds and operations to provide cover for or support of terrorist activities, the *Australian Charities and Not-For-Profits Commission Act 2012* introduced a regulatory framework to "promote transparency and confidence across the sector and the general public that charitable funds and services are applied for legitimate purposes, and are not contributing to terrorist or other criminal activities (from an

33 See Australian Government (2009), p. 7, though the Australian *Charities and Not-for-profits Commission Act 2012* does not provide a definition.

34 Bricknell, McCusker, Chadwick, Rees (2012).

Australian perspective)".[35] Registration is voluntary. It offers tax incentives for those registered. The Act also establishes the Australian Charities and Not-For-Profits Commission (ACNC). However the Commissioner has no specific mandate regarding terrorism financing. In 2015, the FATF blamed Australia for not having conducting a risk assessment of the NPO sector. Subsequently, the Australian Transaction and Reports Analysis Centre (AUSTRAC) and the Australian Taxation Office (ATO) in consultation with the ACNC undertook a national risk assessment on NPOs and published a report in August 2017.[36] The extent to which NPOs are being used in Australia as a conduit for money laundering is unknown. Currently, it is unlikely that Australian NPOs are being used for terrorism financing. Nevertheless, vigilance is required.

It is alleged that the threat of terrorism demands a low threshold.[37] In the EU, data transmissions of NPO above EUR 150 are closely monitored. Determining the proper threshold for transactions to charitable organisations is particularly difficult given the tension between the need to exercise surveillance and control, and the necessity to allow the free flow of money to developing countries, even where terrorist organisations may have a base, in order to permit economical development. Australia, to date, has not implemented a similar threshold for NPOs.

The initial measures recommended by the FATF had non-intended negative consequences for the economically most vulnerable. The Task Force has since softened its stance against the NPOs sector and a dialogue has been institutionalised with NPO representatives.[38] However, the FATF has been accused for having "endorsed some of the most restrictive NPO regulatory regimes in the world, and strongly encouraged some already repressive governments to introduce new rules likely to restrict the political space in which NGOs and civil society actors operate".[39]

4.2.2.4 SR IX – Cash Couriers[40]

A large portion of organised crime proceeds is generated in cash form. Initially, the FATF recommended that Member States monitor the cross-border

35 Australian Charities and Not-For-Profits Commission Bill 2012 / Australian Charities and Not-For-Profits Commission (Consequential and Transitional) Bill 2012, Explanatory Memorandum. para 5.58 p. 64.

36 AUSTRAC – ACNC (2017), pp. 9–10.

37 FATF XVI (2005a), p. 8.

38 Romaniuk, Keatinge (2018).

39 Hayes (2012), p. 10.

40 SR IX is now Rec 32, still called Cash couriers in the 2012 version.

movements of cash while financial institutions exercised enhanced diligence when receiving large amounts in cash. The UNTOC contains similar recommendations on monitoring cross-border movements of cash.[41] The FATF requirement was softened in the 2003 revised version of the Recommendations and eventually deleted.

In October 2004, the FATF added a ninth SR on the financing of terrorism which made it mandatory to introduce the monitoring of cash movements. It may, therefore, seem surprising to have included a revised Recommendation on cash couriers among those regarding the prevention of terrorism financing. It would have been quite feasible to insert this modification in the body of the 40 Recommendations. It is argued that the adoption of the control of cross-border transportation of cash is not primarily a measure against terrorism financing but serves other purposes. It seems to have been inserted among the SR in order to circumvent controversy. The issue of controlling cash movements can conflict with a free trade which requires a free flow of capital while the prevention of money laundering and fiscal considerations plead in favour of a control over cash movements.

The FATF recommends threshold of USD/EUR 15,000 for customer due diligence (CDD) requirements and for occasional transactions. Australia had introduced a control of international cash movements for amounts of AUD 10,000 whether by travellers or through mail and cargo, as part of its AML scheme. For casinos, Australia has kept the AUD 10,000 threshold in breach of the FATF Recommendations which prescribe a threshold of USD/EUR 3,000. Despite its wording, SR IX does not specifically target terrorism financing. It does not make a distinction between cash that could be linked to serious criminal activities – either stemming from crime or aimed at financing it – and other illegal activities such as fiscal infringements – or legitimate income. SR IX rather leans towards the US/Australian threshold reporting systems by which assets above a given amount are deemed to be potentially suspicious and must therefore be reported.

4.2.3 *Conclusion*

Bringing Australian legislation in line with international standards was undertaken in stages. The first main step was taken in 2002 with the adoption of the *Suppression of the Financing of Terrorism Act 2002* (Cth) and the second in 2006 with the adoption of the *Anti-Money Laundering and Counter-Terrorism Financing Act 2006* (Cth) which specifically implemented SR VI (remittance services), SR VII (wire transfer funds services), and SR IX (cash couriers). SR VIII has not

41 Art.7.2, UNTOC.

been implemented as such though some services provided by non-profit organisations are covered by the *Anti-Money Laundering and Counter-Terrorism Financing Act 2006* (Cth).[42] In part to comply with the FATF's requirement, the Government enacted the *Australian Charities and Not-For-Profits Commission Act 2012* (Cth). Special Recommendations VI, VII and IX are the only SR specifically implemented in the *Anti-Money Laundering and Counter-Terrorism Financing Act 2006*.

The arguments for legislating against the financing of terrorism were marred by wrong data and preconceived ideas. As in the USA, the adoption of the legislation was characterised by a lack of proper analysis of terrorism funding.[43] The Australian Government believed that the attacks on the USA required "substantial resources" and that "confiscation of the instruments and proceeds of terrorism [...] [wa]s likely to produce a net gain to Commonwealth revenue"[44] when in fact studies of terrorist attacks reveal that their costs are very low compared to the damage caused.[45] Nevertheless, in the following years, the budget of agencies charged with investigating and prosecuting the new terrorism offences was regularly increased as the number of mandatory reports rose rapidly. For instance, AUSTRAC's budget for 2003–04 reached AUD 19.943 million. For 2016–2017, the estimated expenses were devised over AUD 68 million with the government/taxpayers contribution at nearly AUD 58 million. ASIO's budget exploded from AUD 62.7 million in 2001 to AUD 304 million in 2008 (a 485% increase). It has continued to grow, reaching AUD 477 million in the 2016–2017 budget.

The Australian Government, like those of the USA and the EU, created a momentum generated by the "moral panic" which allowed them to introduce controversial legislation without proper analysis of the new crimes.[46] For instance, the adoption in 2002 of the *Suppression of the Financing of Terrorism Act*, a revision of the 1987 *Proceeds of Crime Act*, as part of the legislation against the financing of terrorism, was the opportunity to introduce civil forfeiture of property, which had long been the wish of law enforcement.[47] The purpose of the *Suppression of the Financing of Terrorism Act* (2002) (Cth) was to enable Australia to meet its international requirements, but it goes far beyond them, particularly when it introduces recklessness as a fault element, by contrast to

42 Neilsen (2006), p. 3.

43 Warde (2007), p. 36.

44 Criminal Law Branch (2002), 8, p. 3.

45 Smith, McCusker, Walters (2010), p. 4. Freeman (2011), p. 462.

46 McSherry (2004), p. 356.

47 Criminal Law Branch (2002), p. 5; Australian Law Reform Commission (1999), pp. 54–56.

the international treaties which only require knowledge and intention. There are, therefore, strong parallels between the Code's AML and CTF provisions in their approach to criminality, which opens the door to the same criticisms.

Even though the FATF Special Recommendations have been issued to provide for a basic framework to detect, prevent and suppress the financing of terrorism and terrorist acts, they tackle money laundering rather than serve as specific CTF measures. Moreover, they had long been discussed before September 2001 and cannot be considered as targeting terrorism specifically. SR I to V merely extended the AML regime to CTF. SR VI to XI extended the machinery even further. The only Special Recommendation that does not appear to have a link with money laundering is SR VIII which requires a particular surveillance on non-profit organisations.

Some CTF measures such as SR VI (remittance services), SR VII (wire transfer funds services), SR VIII (Non-profit organisations) impact socially and economically on already disadvantaged sections of the global society by restricting funds transfers by migrants (remittances) and towards the work carried out by charities in developing countries. It is estimated that, worldwide, migrants transferred about USD 351 billion in 2011 to their families abroad.[48] Hence, Vlcek observed, "constraining the informal value transfer system has the potential of a far more detrimental impact upon developing states than it has for any likelihood to identify and isolate terrorists".[49] Although intended specifically to prevent acts of terrorism, the SR may be criticised for being both hasty and ill-conceived, producing serious and unintended consequences for the poorer members of the world community and only further antagonising them, ultimately making the measures counter-productive.

Subjecting sectors such as lawyers, accountants and notaries to these regulations have been disputed as the new rules infringe on lawyer-client confidentiality and legal professional privilege. This extension of the circle of entities subject to AML/CTF regulations was so controversial that the adoption of the new law has been delayed in Australia. Until today it has not taken place. The new legislation was, however, adopted elsewhere, for instance in the EU, because it was included in a package of measures against the financing of terrorism. Some suggest that had it not been the case, the law would not have been passed.[50]

---

48 RSR.ch (2011).

49 Vlcek (2007), p. 110. Jonsson, Cornell (2007), p. 75. McCulloch, Pickering, McQueen, Tham, Wright-Neville (2004), p. 71.

50 Vlcek (2007), pp. 106–107.

Analysis of the features of terrorism financing shows that the trend to assimilate the financing of terrorism within the framework of money laundering law is not supported by sound theoretical or practical grounds. The ability of FATF Special Recommendations to effectively address terrorism financing, which usually deals with small amounts of money, needs to be raised. This examination suggests that the Special Recommendations were mainly adopted for two reasons: first, symbolically, to demonstrate that the international community and national authorities were not powerless against terrorism and that they were taking action against it. Second, the Special Recommendations also provided authorities with the opportunity to adopt legislation that would not have been accepted had it not been presented as a means to combat terrorism.

The Special Recommendations also highlight the danger of hastily transplanting laws from one field to another due to political pressures. Before adopting any legislation, there is a need to assess the effectiveness of the proposed measures, undertake an evaluation of the possible risk that these measures could have negative and counterproductive side effects. It is also important to determine what would be the "mitigation strategies", their costs, and have a public debate. This process should not be rushed. Unfortunately, the Special Recommendations were not the only measures which were enacted swiftly in the wake of the September 2001 terrorist attacks, so were also Australia's CTF offences.

4.3 Defining a Terrorist Act

To understand what terrorism financing means, it is necessary to outline what is terrorism under the Code and to set it in the international context, namely the 1999 UN *Convention against the financing of terrorism* (UNCFT), to which both the UN Security Council resolutions and the FATF refer. In particular UNSCR 1373 requires Member States to take specific measures against the financing of terrorism.

In Australia, the substantive provisions on terrorism are found mainly in Part 5.3 of the Code and in the *Charter of the United Nations Act 1945* (Cth) (COTUNA). COTUNA gives effect to the UN Security Council Resolutions which impose sanctions on individuals and organisations suspected of involvement in terrorism. Broadly, in the Code, Division 100 defines "terrorist act", Division 101 "terrorism", Division 102 "terrorist organisations" and their respective related offences, Division 103 "financing terrorism", Divisions 104 and 105 pertain to control orders. A provision on "urging violence" has been introduced in Division 80. The *Counter-Terrorism Legislation Amendment (Foreign Fighters) Act 2014* created *inter alia* a new offence of "advocating terrorism" and makes it

TABLE 11 Defining a terrorist act

The Code – Section 100.1 (Definitions)	UNCFT – Article 2
terrorist act means an action or threat of action where: (a) the action falls within subsection (2) and does not fall within subsection (3); and (b) the action is done or the threat is made with the intention of advancing a political, religious or ideological cause; and (c) the action is done or the threat is made with the intention of: (i) coercing, or influencing by intimidation, the government of the Cth or a State, Territory or foreign country, or of part of a State, Territory or foreign country; or (ii) intimidating the public or a section of the public. (2) Action falls within this sub-section if it: (a) causes serious harm that is physical harm to a person; or (b) causes serious damage to property; or (c) causes a person's death; or (d) endangers a person's life other than the life of the person taking the action; or (e) creates a serious risk to the health or safety of the public or a section of the public; or	Article 2 1. Any person commits an offence within the meaning of this Convention if that person by any means, directly or indirectly, unlawfully and wilfully, provides or collects funds with the intention that they should be used or in the knowledge that they are to be used, in full or in part, in order to carry out: (a) An act which constitutes an offence within the scope of and as defined in one of the treaties listed in the annex; or (b) Any other act intended to cause death or serious bodily injury to a civilian, or to any other person not taking an active part in the hostilities in a situation of armed conflict, when the purpose of such act, by its nature or context, is to intimidate a population, or to compel a Government or an international organization to do or to abstain from doing any act. […] 3. For an act to constitute an offence set forth in para.1, it shall not be necessary that the funds were actually used to carry out an offence referred to in para.1, sub-para. (a) or (b). 4. Any person also commits an offence if that person attempts to commit an offence as set forth in para.1 of this article. […]

The Code – Section 100.1 (Definitions)	UNCFT – Article 2
(f) seriously interferes with, seriously disrupts, or destroys, an electronic system including, but not limited to: (i) an information system; or (ii) a telecommunications system; or (iii) a financial system; or (iv) a system used for the delivery of essential government services; or (v) a system used for, or by, an essential public utility; or (vi) a system used for, or by, a transport system. (3) Action falls within this subsection if it: (a) is advocacy, protest, dissent or industrial action; and (b) is not intended: (i) to cause serious harm that is physical harm to a person; or (i) to cause a person's death: or (iii) to endanger the life of a person, other than the person taking the action; or (iv) to create a serious risk to the health or safety of the public or a section of the public.	**Treaties listed in the annex:** 1. Convention for the Suppression of Unlawful Seizure of Aircraft, The Hague, 16.12.1970. 2. Convention for the Suppression of Unlawful Acts against the Safety of Civil Aviation, Montreal, 23.09.1971. 3. Convention on the Prevention and Punishment of Crimes against Internationally Protected Persons, including Diplomatic Agents, 14.12.1973. 4. Int'l Convention against the Taking of Hostages, 17.12.1979. 5. Convention on the Physical Protection of Nuclear Material, Vienna, 03.03.1980. 6. Protocol for the Suppression of Unlawful Acts of Violence at Airports Serving International Civil Aviation, supplementary to the Convention for the Suppression of Unlawful Acts against the Safety of Civil Aviation, Montreal, 24.02.1988. 7. Convention for the Suppression of Unlawful Acts against the Safety of Maritime Navigation, Rome, 10.03.1988. 8. Protocol for the Suppression of Unlawful Acts against the Safety of Fixed Platforms located on the Continental Shelf, Rome, 10.03.1988. 9. Convention for the Suppression of Terrorist Bombings, 15.12.1997.

an offence to join a listed terrorist organisation overseas. It also provides additional powers for security agencies.

The Code's definition of a terrorist act is that of an action (or a threat of an action) listed, coupled with a specific intent and purpose. Under the UNCFT, the terrorist act is defined in two ways: (a) in reference to nine international conventions on terrorism which were adopted prior 1999, and (b) by a number of different criteria. It covers a wide range of conduct from the act of a single person to the activities of a large organisation. Given that, at the end of last century, Australia was a party to all these treaties but one, the *Convention for the Suppression of Terrorist Bombings,* the offences under the conventions are not criminalised under Part 5.3, though the conduct overlaps. In both cases the fault element is intent. Under the UNCFT, the fault element pertains to the offences under (a) and (b). The next section outlines the conduct's physical elements.

4.3.1 *Under the Nine Terrorism Conventions*

The main characteristics of these terrorist conventions can be thus summarised:

- The listed Conventions require the contracting Parties to criminalise a number of specific acts, such as offences against life, freedom, property. The conventions always criminalise the attempt and complicity. The threat, to commit one of the offences listed, is criminalised in four conventions, but curiously not in the 1997 *Convention for the suppression of terrorist bombing.* Since 1997, all the conventions require the criminalisation of the participation in the commission of the offence, including its financing. The States are required to prohibit on their territories what may be called criminal or terrorist organisations ("illegal activities of persons, groups and organisations that encourage, instigate, organise, *knowingly finance* or engage in the perpetration" of the listed offences).
- All conventions but three criminalise the intent to compel a person, an international organisation or a State to do or to refrain from doing any act. Those conventions which do not are the early conventions on the safety of air travel.

4.3.2 *Under the UNCFT and the Code*

The list of actions that fall under the definition of terrorist act under the Code and the UNCFT intersect but do not coincide. The UNCFT is wider in some aspects and on the whole more precise than its Australian counterpart. Moreover, the UNCFT specifies that the terrorist act must be *unlawful* and *wilful.* This requirement may exclude the acts of violence perpetrated by security forces. Further, the Code defines the terrorist act as an *action* and a *threat of action* of the widest possible kind.[51] Defining a threat of action as a terrorist act considerably widens the scope of the offence. In contrast, the UNCFT does not include threat (outside some of the 9 conventions). In essence, under the Code, the focus is on the political, religious or ideological intention of the act rather than on the conduct. In contrast, under the UNCFT, the focus is mainly on the protection of human life.

4.3.2.1 The Terrorist Character

Both the UNCFT and Australian legislation require what can be called a "terrorist character" to distinguish terrorist offences from other criminal acts. Under the Code, given that the crimes listed are already sanctioned penally as criminal offences, it is the motive and intention of the perpetrator. The UNCFT couches the terrorist character in terms of *purpose* to intimidate a population, or to compel a Government or an international organisation to do or to abstain from doing any act, coupled with the *nature or context* of the attack.[52]

Under the Code, the motive (subjective element) is the intent of advancing a political, religious or ideological cause. The intention is to coerce, influence by intimidation a government or intimidate the public or a section of the public ("objective element"). It has been argued that the inclusion of motive in terrorism legislation is essential to distinguish acts that are penalised under criminal law from terrorist acts because terrorist acts are "crimes that are conceptually and morally different because they involve political or religious coercion of the public or government".[53] It is however not the view of the UNCFT. Albeit an ideological motive can clearly be inferred from the purposes of the conduct that is criminalised under the UNCFT, it is not an element of the offence. Hence the UNCFT allows for other motives, such as financial gain or greed. Therefore, on this point, the UNCFT has a far broader scope than the Code since it could include acts committed by a criminal organisation which are profit driven. Attacks against politicians by drug trafficking organisations could come under UNCFT as ways of compelling a Government to release their imprisoned leaders or prevent public authorities from prosecuting them, or intimidate a population to extortion.

---

51 *R v Lodhi* [2006] NSWSC 584 [75–76]. The breadth of the Commonwealth's definition has been criticised. See Law Council of Australia (2013), pp. 37–38.

52 There is a debate among scholars about whether motive is a sufficient element to distinguish a criminal group from a terrorist group since their methods and motives are often shared. See Shelley, Picarelli (2005).

53 Saul (2007), p. 34; Sheller (2006), p. 57.

The Code's intent of advancing a political, religious or ideological cause is not to be confused with the intention of the offender to commit the terrorist act (fault element) for it is a physical element, a "circumstance", of the offence.[54] Hence, under the Code, the intention of coercing, intimidating etc. is intrinsic to the act itself. There is no requirement that the intention of the perpetrator would be to terrorise the government or intimidate as long as he or she intended to do a terrorist act.[55] The intention to commit a terrorist act would encompass the intention to coerce or intimidate, hence removing some of the difficulties in proving an added *mens rea*.[56]

4.3.2.2 The Circle of Protection

Both section 100.1 and the UNCFT aim to protect persons, Government, and property. The UNCFT adds international organisations. However, only under 1(b) does the UNCFT protect property.

4.3.2.2.1 *Property and Infrastructure*

According to Whealy J, the range of public utilities and government services is not limited to those mentioned in section 100.1(2)(f).[57] The UNCFT defines *State or government facility* as "any permanent or temporary facility or conveyance that is used or occupied by representatives of a State, members of Government, the legislature or the judiciary or by officials or employees of a State or any other public authority or entity or by employees or officials of an intergovernmental organization in connection with their official duties". Compared to some of the 9 conventions which list property offences, it appears that a less severe level of damage satisfies the Australian definition, when the impact of the act is taken into account.

4.3.2.2.2 *Government*

Under the Code, "Government" is to be understood as "the established system of political rule".[58] The focus is on the running of state functions. It should be stressed that neither the UNCFT nor Australian legislation distinguishes whether the "government" is a democratic one or not. Australia specifically excludes political activities and industrial action from falling under terrorism

54 *R v Lodhi* [2005] NSWSC 1377 (23 December 2005) at [55]. *Lodhi v R* (2006) 199 FLR 303 at [90]. See also Gani, Mathew (2008), p. 276, 7.

55 Law Council of Australia (2002), pp. 6 and 34.

56 McSherry (2004), p. 361.

57 *R v Lodhi* [2006] NSWSC 584 [73].

58 See Dixon J in *Burns v Ransley* (1949) 79 CLR [101, 115].

legislation provided there is no intention to cause serious harm, endanger life or create a risk to health or safety to the public. Interestingly, the UNCFT limits the intention to compel a Government to perform or abstain from performing any act and does not include intimidation. Further, it would seem, only a population can be intimidated. By contrast, in the Code, a terrorist act may include the intention to "influence by intimidation" governmental authorities. Hence under the Code, the scope of a terrorist act is broader than its international counterpart when directed against a "government".

4.3.2.2.3 *Public v Population*

The terms "public" (Code) and "population" (UNCFT) are not defined but indicate that the legislation's focus is on "masses" rather than small groups. A population has reference to a geographic component (a place), which distinguishes a "population" from a scattered group of people. It could also mean "the number or body of inhabitants of a particular category" sharing common ethnicity, interests or beliefs or ethnicity in a place. On this point again, the Code is broader than the UNCFT. Under the Code's terrorism provisions, only "serious harm that is physical harm to a person" is taken into account. This means seriously bodily injury and not psychological harm. Taking into account that the Australian definition of a terrorist act includes "a serious risk to the health or safety", in contrast with the UNCFT, the Code's scope is broader than the UNCFT.

4.3.2.2.4 *International Organisations*

Contrary to the UNCFT, the Code does not protect "international organisations" under its terrorism provisions. However, the UNCFT does not define them. The term should be defined in domestic legislation and could include private international organisations, such as NGOs.

4.3.2.3 The Nature and Context Element

The nature and context element under the UNCFT is absent from the Code. Being undefined, this element opens the door wide to subjectivity. What act in itself is likely to intimidate a population or to compel a government?[59] One may think that an attack against a Parliament that would kill a large number of members or ministers would meet the requirement. However, which government would readily admit that it has lost its independence and is compelled? The attacks that the USA suffered in 2001 can hardly be seen as having compelled the US government. As regards the 2003 attacks against the UN headquarters

59 See Flore (2005), p. 213.

in Baghdad which killed UN High Commissioner for Human Rights Sergio Vieira de Mello, and 22 others, one can also wonder if it compelled the UN to do or abstain, though it undoubtedly had a substantial impact on its operation in Iraq. It would seem that the contextual element refers more to hostage taking, hijackings, extortion, which were some of the major terrorist acts that were prevalent during the second half of last century rather than to the terrorist attacks which have occurred these last 18 years. Arguably, these crimes apart, only major acts of war would compel a country, however the UNCFT does not apply in armed conflict. Strictly, unless the conduct cannot, *given its nature or context, compel a government or an international organisation* then it is not a terrorist offence under the UNCFT. Given that this circumstance does not exist under the Code,[60] the Australian definition is broader than its international counterpart.

4.3.2.4 Conclusion

The definition of the terrorist act under the Code is more restricted in its scope than under the UNCFT, for the Code makes it mandatory that the offender has an intention of advancing a political, religious or ideological cause. Furthermore, international organisations are not protected under section 100.1. In a diverse, politicised and religious international community, the requirement to advance a political religious or ideological cause is likely to restrict mutual legal assistance. Therefore, the absence of such an intention coupled with the focus on severe harm to civilians is a most conducive way to secure international cooperation.

4.4 Defining Financing

Australian legislation on terrorism financing is found in two major Acts: the Code, with Division 103 introduced in 2002, and the *Anti-Money Laundering and Counter-Terrorism Financing Act 2006* (Cth) (AML/CTF Act).[61]

4.4.1 *Financing Terrorism*

4.4.1.1 In the AML/CTF Act

The definition under the AML/CTF Act is not straightforward. It includes offences under the Code, COTUNA, under state or territory legislation, and under

60 Rose, Nestorovska (2007) (p. 25) speak of a "context of political conflict", this expression is misleading for there is no such requirement under the Code.

61 Australia's legislation is drawn from the UK *Proceeds of Crime Act* 2002, see Tyre (2010), pp. 77,78.

foreign legislation. For the purpose of this study, only the relevant provisions of the Code and COTUNA shall be examined.

TABLE 12 Financing terrorism under AML/CTF Act and UNCFT

Section 5, AML/CTF Act	Article 2, UNCFT
financing of terrorism means conduct that amounts to: (a) an offence against section 102.6 or Division 103 of the Criminal Code; or (b) an offence against section 20 or 21 of the Charter of the United Nations Act 1945; or (c) an offence against a law of a State or Territory that corresponds to an offence referred to in paragraph (a) or (b); or (d) an offence against a law of a foreign country or a part of a foreign country that corresponds to an offence referred to in paragraph (a) or (b).	1. Any person commits an offence within the meaning of this Convention if that person by any means, directly or indirectly, unlawfully and wilfully, provides or collects funds with the intention that they should be used or in the knowledge that they are to be used, in full or in part, in order to carry out: (a) An act which constitutes an offence within the scope of and as defined in one of the treaties listed in the annex; or (b) Any other act intended to cause death or serious bodily injury to a civilian, or to any other person not taking an active part in the hostilities in a situation of armed conflict, when the purpose of such act, by its nature or context, is to intimidate a population, or to compel a Government or an international organization to do or to abstain from doing any act.

4.4.1.2 In the Code

Australian legislation goes beyond the requirements of the UNCFT. Not only is the Australian definition of financing different, so also is its definition of "terrorism". The structure of the Commonwealth offence is partly similar to the offence of *dealing with proceeds of crime*. The major differences between Australia's legislation and the UNCFT pertain to the physical and fault elements of the offences and to the type of funding. The UNCFT limits the physical elements (*actus reus*) to *providing* and *collecting* funds to carry out a "terrorist act". By contrast, the Code adds *making funds available to another person* under "financing a terrorist" (s 103.2), and *receiving funds* under section 102.6 (Getting funds to, from or for a terrorist organisation). "Funds" are broadly defined and cover property and assets of every kind, including "equipment or weapons".[62] The definition under the UNCFT is also wide:

> "Funds" means assets of every kind, whether tangible or intangible, movable or immovable, however acquired, and legal documents or instruments in any form, including electronic or digital, evidencing title to, or interest in, such assets, including, but not limited to, bank credits, travellers cheques, bank cheques, money orders, shares, securities, bonds, drafts and letters of credit.

TABLE 13 Financing terrorism under the Code – Section 103.1.

(1) A person commits an offence if:
- (a) the person provides or collects funds; and
- (b) the person is reckless as to whether the funds will be used to facilitate or engage in a terrorist act.

Penalty: Imprisonment for life.
Note: Intention is the fault element for the conduct described in §(1)(a). See subs5.6(1).

(2) A person commits an offence under subsection (1) even if:
- (a) a terrorist act does not occur; or
- (b) the funds will not be used to facilitate or engage in a specific terrorist act; or
- (c) the funds will be used to facilitate or engage in more than one terrorist act.

Australia's fault element requirements are broader compared to the UNCFT requirements for section 103.1(1)(b) of the Code includes intention and recklessness as to whether the funds will be used to facilitate or engage in a terrorist act. This contrasts with the UNCFT which requires that the offender must act with *intention* that the funds should be used or in the *knowledge* that they are

62 Anti-Terrorism Bill (N°2) 2005, Explanatory Memorandum, p. 10.

to be used, in full or in part, to carry out a terrorist act.[63] The UNCFT looks at the purpose of the funding not the channel, whether it is an organisation, a person or even a terrorist. It follows that section 103.1(1)(b) is similar to the money laundering offences in subsections (2)(c) of sections 400.3 to 400.7. The following sections examine these three different offences under the Code and two offences under the *Charter of the United Nations Act* (s 20, dealing with freezable assets and s 21, giving an asset to a proscribed person or entity).

4.4.2 *Financing a Terrorist*

The offence of financing a terrorist under the Code (s 103.2) enacted in 2005 contains identical fault elements to the offence of financing a terrorist act (i.e. terrorism) found under section 103.1. Recklessness as to whether the other person will use the funds to facilitate or engage in a terrorist act is also criminalised.

TABLE 14 Financing a terrorist under the Code – Section 103.2.

(1) A person commits an offence if:
- (a) the person intentionally:
- (i) makes funds available to another person (whether directly or indirectly); or
- (ii) collects funds for, or on behalf of, another person (whether directly or indirectly); and
- (b) the first-mentioned person is reckless as to whether the other person will use the funds to facilitate or engage in a terrorist act.

Penalty: Imprisonment or life.

(2) A person commits an offence under subsection (1) even if:
- (a) a terrorist act does not occur; or
- (b) the funds will not be used to facilitate or engage in a specific terrorist act; or
- (c) the funds will be used to facilitate or engage in more than one terrorist act.

63 Initially the Security Legislation Amendment (Terrorism) Bill (n°2) 2002 (Cth) included absolute liability offences. Recklessness and knowledge were introduced as a response to the critics raised by the Senate Legal and Constitution Legislation Committee (SLCLC). See Sheller (2006).

Although section 103.2 criminalises the financing of a terrorist, the law does not provide any definition of what is a terrorist. The definition can of course be inferred (a terrorist is a person that commits a terrorist act) but it may be very difficult for another person to determine if someone is a terrorist or not, particularly when no terrorist act has yet been committed and the potential terrorist does not divulge his or her intention. In any case, it should include financing the overseas travel of terrorist fighters and their families. Assisting financially or providing support to those who are travelling unlawfully to a region where a listed terrorist organisation is engaging in a hostile activity (declared areas by the Minister of Foreign Affairs pursuant to Division 119 of the Code) could come under Division 103 or sections 102.6 and 102.7. However, to avoid a potential conflict with the requirement of a mental element to demonstrate criminality, the provision of funds or other assets to an individual terrorist "for any purpose" must not be criminalised. Hence, according to the FATF, the offence of "financing a terrorist" should not include financing a terrorist for purposes which does not contribute to terrorism in any way (e.g. basic sustenance).[64]

There are two substantive differences between sections 103.1 (Financing terrorism) and 103.2 (Financing a terrorist). First, the physical element of "providing funds" in section 103.1(1) is replaced by "making funds available" in section 103.2(1)(i). Both "providing" and "collecting", though not defined imply intent, while "making funds available" does not necessarily imply an intention. The Security Legislation Review Committee (SLRC) suggested that to bring the text into line with UN instruments, the fault element should be a specific intent.[65] Secondly, section 103.2 adds that the funding is done "to another person" whose usage of the funds is not clear, for it is not known "whether the other person will use the funds to facilitate or engage in a terrorist act". The provider must therefore make an assessment of the risk that the funds could be used towards a terrorist activity and if it is unjustifiable to take such risk. Under section 103.2, it is not prohibited to "make funds available" in the circumstance where the "other person" is a "terrorist" but there is no doubt that the funds will not go towards a terrorist activity (for instance, when the collected funds are to be used towards the medical care of the "terrorist" children). The provision of funds towards the commission of a crime that is not a terrorist act does not come under this section either.

One may wonder whether the offence of financing a terrorist is not redundant with the offence of financing an act of terrorism, since both sections indicate that the offences are committed even if a terrorist act does not occur or

64 FATF (2016), para.34, p. 12.

65 Sheller (2006) p. 161.

the funds will not be used to facilitate or engage in a specific terrorist act, or the funds will be used to facilitate or engage in more than one terrorist act. Both offences entail life imprisonment, even for the fault element of recklessness. The Government justified the inclusion of section 103.2 in 2005 by the necessity to have an offence of collecting funds or making funds available *to another person*,[66] rather than just an offence of raising funds in circumstance where the fundraiser is reckless as to whether the funds will be used to facilitate or engage in a terrorist act (s 103.1(b)). This explanation is not convincing. Section 103.2 is redundant and should be deleted.[67]

Section 103.2 sanctions the risk of financing a terrorist act when funds are given to a person while this person, though not a member of a terrorist organisation, could use them towards the commission of an act of terrorism. In this perspective, section 103.2 complements section 102.7 (Providing support to a terrorist organisation). It could have been expected that section 102.6 (Getting funds to, from or for a terrorist organisation) would be a corollary of section 103.2 (Financing a terrorist). This is not the case as the physical elements, though similar, are not the same, and the sanctions differ.

4.4.3 *Financing – Providing Support to – a Terrorist Organisation*

The provisions regarding the financing of a terrorist organisation are found in the Code and in the *Charter of the United Nations Act 1945* (COTUNA) which gives effect to some of the Security Council Resolutions imposing sanctions, in particular UNSCR 1373.

Some terrorist organisations are complex in nature. They are not only involved in terrorism, but they may engage in criminal activities to finance their operations. Some also provide families of deceased terrorists with financial support. Others have charities that aim at alleviating social hardships. Furthermore, it has been observed that the money that does go to terrorist groups is often spent on social welfare programs and not on violent activities.[68] However, a terrorist organisation may spend available funds on an activity other than that for which they were originally intended. Consequently, legislating effectively against terrorism financing is a very difficult task. On one hand, financing terrorism should be prevented wherever possible and providing an incentive to would-be terrorists should be averted. For instance, it may be a strong incentive for some young persons in a poor society with little prospective of employment to know that their families would be looked after financially if they die

---

66 Anti-Terrorism Bill (No.2) 2005, Explanatory Memorandum, p. 13.

67 For a discussion on this issue see Sheller (2006), pp. 160–163.

68 Freeman (2011) p. 472.

TABLE 15 Financing / Providing support (resources) to a terrorist organisation, under the Code and the UNCFT

The Code, s 102.6 Getting funds to, from or for a terrorist organisation	(1) A person commits an offence if: (a) the person *intentionally*: (i) *receives funds* from, or *makes funds available* to, an org (whether directly or indirectly); or (ii) *collects funds* for, or on behalf of, an org (whether directly or indirectly); and (b) the organisation is a terrorist organisation; and (c) the person knows the org is a terrorist org. Penalty: Imprisonment for 25 years. (2) A person commits an offence if: (a) the person *intentionally*: (i) *receives funds* from, or *makes funds available* to, an org (whether directly or indirectly); or (ii) *collects funds* for, or on behalf of, an org (whether directly or indirectly); and (b) the organisation is a terrorist organisation; and (c) the person is reckless as to whether the org is a terry org. Penalty: Imprisonment for 15 years. (3) Subs (1) and (2) do not apply to the person's receipt of funds from the org if the person proves that he or she received the funds solely for the purpose of the provision of: (a) legal representation for a person in proceedings relating to this Division; or (b) assistance to the organisation for it to comply with a law of the Commonwealth or a State or Territory. Note: A defendant bears a legal burden in relation to the matter in sub (3) (see s 13.4).
The Code, s 102.7 Providing support to a terrorist organisation	(1) A person commits an offence if: (a) the person intentionally provides to an organisation support or resources that would help the organisation engage in an activity described in paragraph (a) of the definition of terrorist organisation in this Division; and (b) the organisation is a terrorist organisation; and (c) the person knows the organisation is a terrorist organisation. Penalty: Imprisonment for 25 years. (2) A person commits an offence if: (a) the person intentionally provides to an organisation support or resources that would help the organisation engage in an activity described in paragraph (a) of the definition of terrorist organisation in this Division; and (b) the organisation is a terrorist organisation; and (c) the person is reckless as to whether the organisation is a terrorist organisation. Penalty: Imprisonment for 15 years.

UNCFT Art.2.5

Any person also commits an offence if that person:

(a) Participates as an accomplice in an offence as set forth in paragraph 1 or 4 of this article;

(b) Organizes or directs others to commit an offence as set forth in para.1 or 4 of this article;

(c) Contributes to the commission of one or more offences as set forth in para.1 or 4 of this a group of persons acting with a common purpose. Such contribution shall be intentional and shall either:

(i) Be made with the aim of furthering the criminal activity or criminal purpose of the group, where such activity or purpose involves the commission of an offence as set forth in paragraph 1 of this art; or

(ii) Be made in the knowledge of the intention of the group to commit an offence as set forth in paragraph 1 of this article.

---

in a terrorist attack. On the other hand, well-written CFT legislation should be careful not to restrict funding to mere charitable activities. Not only would this be unfair to their beneficiaries, who rely on these charities, which are usually active in poor societies where the State does not provide adequate services, but also as not to create a ground for terrorism.[69] As Levi remarks,

> [i]rrespective of whose interests one cares most about, it would be ironic if controls over 'terrorist funding' led to a significant widening of the pool of willing suicide bombers, even if the average damage they caused was modest compared with the 'spectaculars' that triggered the 'War on Terrorism'.[70]

However, it seems that these concerns have been largely ignored by the Australian legislature. The Commonwealth CFT legislation is purposely risk-focused. The offence of *getting funds to, from or for a terrorist organisation* under the Code criminalises any financial dealing with a terrorist organisation, even if it is for a charitable purpose or not related to the commission or the facilitation of a terrorist act.

Under section 102.6 of the Code and sections 20 and 21 of COTUNA, any financial dealing with a listed or unlisted terrorist organisation is criminalised, even if it is for charitable purpose or not related to the commission or facilitations of a terrorist act. Hence, the Commonwealth's legislation on the matter lacks consistency. One fails to understand, for instance, why the Code makes an

69 Vlcek (2007), p. 100; Crimm (2008), pp. 619–625.

70 Levi (2010), p. 667.

exception or defence in the case of an association with terrorist organisations provided this "association" is for the purpose of, or for the provision of "aid of a humanitarian nature" (s 102.8(4)(c) Associating with terrorist organisations), but does not allow an exception for giving towards humanitarian activities.

The CFT offences under Division 103 criminalise r*ecklessness as to whether the funds will be used to facilitate or engage in a terrorist act* and recklessness *as to whether another person will use the funds to facilitate or engage in a terrorist act.* However, under section 102.6 (Funding a terrorist organisation), the fault element would only be on the action itself (receiving, making funds available, collecting for a terrorist organisation) not on the use of the funds. The offences pertaining to the financing a terrorist organisation are broken down according to the level of intent and the corresponding penalty. In this regard, the Australian CTF offences are similar to the AML offences of *dealing with proceeds of crime* which focus mainly on the risk that dealing with proceeds of crime entails rather than on the intention to launder money. The offence of financing a terrorist organisation focuses on the funding rather than the act of terrorism, under the premise that any funds given to such an organisation would necessarily be used towards the commission of a terrorist act. Such a presumption is not found in the UNCFT.

The UNCFT criminalises the financing of terrorism when the funding is made with the intention that the funds should be used to commit a terrorist offence; or in the knowledge that they are to be used, in full or in part to fund a terrorist act. The UNCFT appears to be only concerned with the realisation of a terrorist act. Hence, receiving funds that a criminal organisation has collected from donations for charitable purposes and used accordingly would not be illegal. Tappley rightly commented:

> [r]equiring actual knowledge or intention that funds were going to a terrorist organisation would provide greater certainty in the application of the law. Presumably the desire to avoid this uncertainty is one of the reasons why the international instruments have focused on intention. The counter argument to such an approach would be that a person might be wilfully blind to the activities of an organisation and that the use of the fault element of recklessness may capture such behaviour.[71]

In contrast with section 102.6 of the Code, the *provision, support* to the organisation (s 102.7) is linked to a terrorist act. Under the UNCFT, the *provision and collection* of funds, and even the participation, as an accomplice or as another form of participation in a terrorist organisation, require the intent of furthering

71 Tapley (2002), 2001–02. Pieth (2006), p. 1081.

the criminal activity or the criminal purpose of the group, or they must be made in the knowledge of that the group intent to commit a terrorist act. This is stark contrast with the form of participation in a terrorist group under the Code which sanctions participation by imprisonment for 15 years even when the offender is reckless as to whether the organisation is a terrorist organisation (s 102.4). The UNCFT does not preclude Party States from introducing a different fault element in their domestic law. It is important, however, to underline that the Parties' view is that in order to be effective against terrorism, legislation does not need to go beyond the fault elements of knowledge and intention. The justification for section 102.6 (Getting funds to, from or for a terrorist organisation) is not apparent since the conduct is captured in a more satisfying manner under section 103.1 (Financing terrorism). Considering the poor preventive effect of legislation aimed at countering the financing of terrorism in general,[72] one strives, in a society based on the rule of law, to find any justification for watering down the intention to contribute towards the criminal objectives of a terrorist organisation or to facilitate the carrying out of a terrorist attack, whose elements are clearly laid down in the UNCFT.

4.4.4 *Under the COTUNA*

The *Charter of the United Nations Act 1945* (Cth) (COTUNA) gives effect to the Security Council resolutions imposing sanctions against individuals and organisations. Violations of the regulations regarding the freezing of assets belonging to terrorists and terrorist organisations are sanctioned under sections 20 and 21, which were introduced with the *Suppression of the Financing of Terrorism Act 2002*. COTUNA is therefore closely linked with section 103.2 (Financing a terrorist), and Division 102 of the Code (Terrorist organisations) introduced with *Criminal Code Amendment (Terrorism) Act 2003*. It has already been pointed out that neither the Code nor COTUNA defines "a terrorist".

The conduct criminalised under the COTUNA are *dealing with freezable assets* (s 20) and *giving an asset* to a proscribed person or entity (s 21). However, section 21 shows that what is prohibited is not *giving*, which clearly requires an intention, but *making an asset available*. Funds can be made available by mistake or without intention. One can receive something without wanting it. This wording contrasts with section 102.6 of the Code (Financing a terrorist organisation) which specifies that the funding must be done "intentionally". Since COTUNA does not explicitly state that this is a strict or absolute liability offence, or part of an offence, then section 5.6 of the Code applies and section 21, COTUNA is read in as a fault element by default. Nevertheless, such wording

72 Jonsson, Cornell (2007), p. 76; Vlcek (2007), p. 114.

TABLE 16 Sections 20 and 21, COTUNA

Section 20 Offence – dealing with freezable assets	(1) An individual commits an offence if: (a) the individual holds an asset; and (b) the individual: (i) uses or deals with the asset; or (ii) allows the asset to be used or dealt with; or (iii) facilitates the use of the asset or dealing with the asset; and (c) the asset is a freezable asset; and (d) the use or dealing is not in accordance with a notice under section 22. (2) Strict liability applies to the circumstance that the use or dealing with the asset is not in accordance with a notice under section 22. Note: For *strict liability*, see s 6.1 of the *Criminal Code.* (3) It is a defence if the individual proves that the use or dealing was solely for the purpose of preserving the value of the asset. Note: The individual bears a legal burden in relation to a matter in subs (3) (see s 13.4 of the *Criminal Code*)
Section 21 Offence – giving an asset to a proscribed person or entity	(1) An individual commits an offence if: (a) the individual, directly or indirectly, makes an asset available to a person or entity; and (b) the person or entity to whom the asset is made available is a proscribed person or entity; and (c) the making available of the asset is not in accordance with a notice under section 22. (2) Strict liability applies to the circumstance that the making available of the asset is not in accordance with a notice under section 22.

tends to indicate that in the mind of the legislature the fault element was not of such crucial importance that it deserved a mention.[73] This view was shared by Coghlan J,

> on the question of moral culpability, the difference between actual knowledge and recklessness is not all that significant. When choosing to

73 See McSherry (2004) pp. 363–364.

> deal with a particular organisation, the line between awareness of a substantial and unjustifiable risk of proscription and actual knowledge of proscription is a very fine one indeed.[74]

Intention, read into both sections 20 and 21 by default via section 5.6 of the Code, is on the "making available" not in the purpose of facilitating a terrorist act. It is striking that COTUNA does not require that the dealings are in some way connected with a terrorist activity, like the sections under Division 103 of the Code (Financing terrorism). The Act does not require knowledge on the part of the offender that the asset is either frozen (s 20) or the asset or the organisation is listed as terrorist (s 21). On the contrary, strict liability applies to this circumstance. Consequently, and in contrast with section 102.6 (Financing a terrorist organisation) of the Code, the fault elements of the offences of sections 20 and 21 of COTUNA are not broken down according to knowledge and recklessness. According to the Attorney-General, "the application of strict liability is necessary to ensure that a defendant who uses or deals with an asset, which he or she knows to be a freezable asset, cannot escape liability" by demonstrating that he or she was not aware that either making available of the asset or the use or dealing was permissible. The Security Legislation Review Committee (SLRC) was of the opinion that neither the offence nor any element of it should be of strict liability.[75] It is a concern that offences carrying such heavy penalties only require limited criminality.

The offences under COTUNA have been tested in 2010 in a decision of the Supreme Court of Victoria in R *v Vinayagamoorthy & Ors*.[76] The defendants had collected funds (between 2002 and 2005) from the Tamil Australian diaspora during the civil war in Sri Lanka.[77] These funds were sent to the Liberation Tamil Tigers of Eelam (LTTE) to be used for humanitarian aid. The LTTE was not a proscribed organisation under Australian law at the time of the alleged offence, though it was listed under the UN Security Council Resolution (UNSCR) 1373 as a terrorist organisation. The defendants were not prosecuted under section 102 of the Code (Financing a terrorist organisation) for the prosecution would have had to demonstrate that LTTE was a terrorist organisation, which was a complex task. They were also not prosecuted under Division 103 (Financing terrorism) which require the prosecution to prove that the funds

74 *R v Vinayagamoorthy & Ors* [2010] VSC 148, [7].

75 Sheller (2006), p. 165.

76 *R v Vinayagamoorthy & Ors* [2010] VSC 148, 31 March 2010.

77 Between 13 December 2002 and 23 November 2005, *R v Vinayagamoorthy & Ors* [2010] VSC 148 [25].

could be used to facilitate or engage in a terrorist act. They were charged under section 21, COTUNA (Giving an asset to a proscribed person or entity).

The accused were found guilty despite that it was established that their motivation was to assist, in a humanitarian way, the Tamil community and that they did not intend to engage in terrorist activities.[78] The defendants thought that the best way to assist the population in the North of Sri Lanka was to deal with the LTTE. In doing so, they took the risk that the funds could be used inappropriately, "whatever their belief and desire was".[79]

LTTE has not always been considered as a terrorist organisation by the international community. Its status changed with UNSCR 1373 which was prompted by the September attacks against the USA, an event in which the LTTE had no part. The case against Vinayagamoorthy also brought to light that the defendant knew that, at the time, some considered LTTE to be a terrorist organisation but he did not agree with that opinion. Despite the recent endeavours to objectivise the labelling of an organisation as terrorist, it remains an eminently political exercise. This has led Sentas to state that the provisions under COTUNA have been used to criminalise the Tamil diaspora.[80] This case highlights the difficulty of transferring funds for humanitarian purposes into a war torn area. Coghlan J stated that

> the transaction does demonstrate the risk of doing the bidding of others from afar, and does demonstrate how little control you have over how such items are to be used; whether for good on the one hand or for evil on the other. When enthusiasm for the cause overcomes careful judgment, then the risks are high.[81]

This case impacts on humanitarian giving to overseas organisations in troubled areas. Under COTUNA, section 102.6, and *de facto* under section 102.7 of the Code, any financial assistance for charitable purposes through a terrorist organisation has now been ruled out.[82]

Under sections 103.1 and 103.2(b) of the Code, the offences are only committed when there is an awareness of a risk that the asset will be use for terrorism purposes. For some, a population's need could be so great that it would justify

---

78 *R v Vinayagamoorthy & Ors* [2010] VSC 148, [31]. Coghlan J found that the case fell at the lower en of seriousness of offences of this kind at that time.

79 *R v Vinayagamoorthy & Ors* [2010] VSC 148, [27].

80 Sentas (2011) pp. 165–166.

81 *R v Vinayagamoorthy & Ors* [2010] VSC 148, [39].

82 Case of medical assistance construed as material assistance has been discussed by Gani, Urbas (2004), pp. 40–46.

the risk that the funds could be used towards terrorist activities. However, for others, given the present emphasis on the precautionary principle, any risk of terrorism financing is likely to be deemed unacceptable, thus practically preventing any humanitarian or charitable giving to those who live in areas controlled by terrorist organisations. The Independent National Security Legislation Monitor (INSLM) goes even further suggesting that any humanitarian assistance provided by a terrorist organisation eventually only assists the organisation in reaching its objectives.[83] Given that the Code's definitions of terrorism and of a terrorist organisation are both political and ideological, such a reading precludes any financial assistance for humanitarian purposes to medical services of armed forces that do not have the favour of the Australian Government. The provisions of COTUNA and the Code regarding the financing of a terrorist organisation should be harmonised and redrafted to take into account the objective of the funding. This is even more necessary when one considers that the UN listings of terrorist and terrorist organisations are lacking rigorous analysis and rights of appeal.[84]

That there is little evidence that terrorist organisations are funded through charities should lead to a reassessment of the need to maintain recklessness as a fault element. In the absence of knowledge of the actual terrorist destination of the provision and of an intention to facilitate a terrorist activity, gifts that are diverted from charitable donors should be considered as a type of embezzlement, rather than a way of financing terrorism through legitimate means. Such an understanding would be beneficial, both for law enforcement agencies, as it simplifies their task since it is often very difficult to appreciate recklessness, and for the donor who would not be penalised for giving to an organisation whose purposes are concealed.

4.5 Penalties

In Australia, the sanctions for violation of AML/CTF obligations are civil and criminal penalties (fines and imprisonment) imposed by a court. The FATF recommends the imposition of "effective, proportionate and dissuasive" penalties. According to the FATF, the range of fines found in Australia's legislation is sufficiently broad to be viewed as allowing proportionate and dissuasive sanctions.[85]

83 Walker B (2013), pp. 69, 70.

84 See Chapter 5.

85 FATF (2015), p. 26.

The severity of the penalties for terrorism financing under Division 103 (ss 103.1 and 103.2) of the Code, which entail life imprisonment, contrasts with the offences of financing a terrorist organisation (ss 102.6 and 102.7) which entail 25 years imprisonment, or 15 years if the offender has been reckless. In Europe, the view is that offences committed within an organisation are deemed more dangerous than if committed alone and should therefore be sanctioned more severely. It is hence paradoxical that under Commonwealth law, financing a terrorist organisation carries a less severe penalty than financing a terrorist.

It has been noted that the wording of sections 102.6 and 102.7 (Offences of financing or providing resources to a terrorist organisation) does not require that the funds be used towards the commission of a terrorist act (contrary to ss 103.1 and 103.2), because, it is assumed, there is a high risk that they would. However, the Attorney-General's Department explained that under the offences in section 102.7, "the prosecution must prove an intention associated with the planning or financing of a terrorist act. That is, if evidence cannot be adduced demonstrating a link to such a terrorist act, then the offence cannot be made out".[86] Hence, one should conclude that if a person makes funds available to a terrorist organisation with the intention that they should be used towards the commission of a terrorist act, he or she could be charged under section 102.6 (Getting funds to, from or for a terrorist organisation) and not under section 103.1 (Financing terrorism).

Given the assumed link with a terrorist act, imprisonment for life for financing a terrorist or terrorism (ss 103.1 and 103.2) rather than for 25 years for financing or supporting a terrorist organisation appears disproportionate. The Attorney-General explained that the maximum penalty of life imprisonment carried by sections 103.1 and 103.2 was consistent with the penalties applicable to the terrorism offences given that "financing is central to organised terrorist activity and influences both the extent and the seriousness of those activities",[87] but failed to explain why they were more severe than the penalties for financing a terrorist organisation.

Initially, under sections 20 and 21, COTUNA, offences of dealing with freezable assets and of giving an asset to a proscribed person or entity carried up to 5 years imprisonment for an individual. Following recommendations of the Cole report, in 2006, they were increased to 10 years. It is regrettable that for an

86 Attorney-General's Department, supplementary submission to the SLRC in Sheller (2006). See also *Lodhi v R* [2006] NSWCCA 121 [66].

87 Suppression of the Financing of Terrorism Bill 2002, Explanatory Memorandum, p. 5.

offence that carries up to 10 years imprisonment the fault elements have not been clearly laid out.

Hence we observe a gradation. When a person makes an asset available to a proscribed person or organisation under COTUNA, the offender is liable for 10 years imprisonment. This would be the case, for instance, where financial institutions (or their agents) credit an amount to an account without checking if the holder is black listed. If, however, that organisation is not proscribed under COTUNA and the offender is reckless as to whether the organisation is a terrorist organisation, he or she is liable to 15 years imprisonment, 25 years if the offender knows the organisation is a terrorist organisation. Lastly, if the offender does more than make funds available and "provides" them but is reckless as to whether the funds will be used to facilitate or engage in a terrorist act, he or she is liable to life imprisonment.

In addition to a criminal sanction, terrorism financing allows for a confiscation order. One of the purposes of AML/CTF legislation is to permit the confiscation of property used to finance terrorism related activities. Civil asset confiscation orders, which require a lower standard of proof, have been introduced in Australia in 2002. The FATF advocates the implementing of civil forfeiture regimes in situations where criminal liability is not possible, and in particular against legal persons.[88]

4.6 Conclusion

4.6.1 *Contrasting Australia's AML/CTF Legislation with International Treaties*

Australia's CTF legislation bears many similarities with AML legislation and is intertwined with it. Australia's AML legislation criminalises conduct (dealing) when money or property is proceeds of crime, or at *risk of becoming an instrument of crime*, independently of its origin being legitimate or criminal. There is no corresponding provision in the main international treaties dealing with AML. The Australian offence, which goes against the original idea of money laundering which is exclusively concerned with proceeds of crime, fits, however, very well in the new legal CTF landscape which aims at preventing funds of whatever origin, whether legitimate or criminal, from being used to finance a terrorist act. In that sense, Australia's AML legislation can be seen as avant-gardist. This highlights both a difference with, and a lack of coherence with the UNCFT. According to the UNCFT, it is a crime to finance a terrorist organisation,

88 FATF (2016), para 69.

yet even in the UNTOC there is still no specific provision on financing another type of criminal organisation. On that point, Australian legislation appeared much more robust than the international treaties.

Conceptually, Australia's and the international conventions dealing with AML are different. To summarise, Australia's AML legislation looks forward (at the risk which may materialise) while international law looks backwards at the (criminal) origin of the assets. Australia's AML legislation aims to facilitate the administration and enforcement of taxation laws while the international conventions aim at preventing the financial system from being used for money laundering. Although in each case the legislation has a preventive purpose, Australia intervenes at a very early phase of the money laundering process, that is when the illegitimate monies are about to be brought into the financial system that would disguise their illicit origin.

Australia's and the international conventions have also embraced different perspectives since core elements of the offences, as defined by international treaties, are not the principal focus of Commonwealth law. The concealment element in money laundering is not central to the "proceeds of crime" offences of the Code, and the actual purpose of the funding is absent from the offences of financing a terrorist organisation. Australia's CTF legislation focuses on dealing with funds and the potential risk it may entail rather than on the purpose of the funding, which is the commission of a terrorist act. By contrast, the UNCFT focuses on the object of the transaction which is the perpetration of a terrorist act. It does not sanction risk. It is not concerned with the channel, whether it is an organisation, a person or even a terrorist. Furthermore, Australia's legislation conveys the idea that money laundering and acts of terrorism can be prevented by regulating financial transactions, which leads to a false sense of security. Australian legislation fails to take into account that the threat of terrorism and organised crime is fluctuating as terrorists and money launderers adapt their behaviour to the new prescriptive rules.

The fault elements are also vastly different. While the international conventions require knowledge and intent, Australia has broadened the fault elements to include recklessness in terrorism financing, as well as negligence and recklessness in AML legislation.

Commonwealth offences carry more severe penalties than those of States with a civil law tradition. The reason for Australia's very harsh legislation is difficult to comprehend. The mechanism in place seems to suggest that Australia is confronted with a high prevalence of money laundering cases and terrorist attacks. However, contrary to Europe, which has suffered from terrorism for several years, there had been very few terrorist attacks on Australian soil at the time the legislation was enacted, and few afterwards. Furthermore, the use of its financial institutions for funding terrorism is scarce.

1.6.2 *Contrasting AML Legislation with CTF Laws*

There are two main differences between money laundering and terrorism financing. First, AML legislation is designed to tackle large money movements generated by organised criminal activities whereas terrorism can be funded with insignificant money flows. Second, money laundering is, by and large, concerned with the criminal origin of the assets, whereas acts of terrorism are usually financed by legitimate means. The extension of the international AML system to tackle the funding of terrorism has been made without due consideration of the nature of terrorism financing. Since they do not address adequately the way terrorism is funded, they are ineffective to prevent acts of terrorism.

Two situations should be distinguished: the financing of a terrorist act and the financing of a terrorist organisation. There is a consensus that financing a terrorist act does not require large sums of money.[89] For instance, the 19 terrorists who plotted the attacks on the USA in November 2001 spent somewhere between USD 400,000 and USD 500,000 over nearly two years to plan and conduct their attacks – that is about USD 1,000 a month per person. The US government has not been able to determine the origin of the money. The 2002 Bali bombings cost around USD 50,000; the 2005 Madrid attacks about USD 10,000; the London attacks of July 2005 were self–funded and cost less than GBP 8,000.[90] Home-grown terrorism can be paid for by the savings of the persons involved, or by petty crimes. However, funding a terrorist organisation which has training camps and a large infrastructure is expensive. These organisations rely largely on the products of typical organised crime activities, such as drug trafficking, human trafficking, abductions, extortions and maritime piracy.[91] It must be stressed however that, globally, there is little synergy between organised crime and terrorist groups.[92]

Given that before the turn of the 21st century, the methods used by terrorist organisations to transfer funds differed little from those used by traditional

89 AUSTRAC (2014b), p. 2.

90 Home Office (2006), p. 23; Kean, Hamilton (2004), p. 169.

91 Smith, McCusker, Walters (2010), pp. 2–4; Shelley, Picarelli (2005), pp. 52–53.

92 Dandurand, Chin (2004), pp. 6 and 9. See also Grabosky, Stohl (2010), pp. 71,86; Makarenko, Mesquita (2014).

criminal organisations, the FATF was justified in including terrorism, a serious crime, as a predicate offence for money laundering in its legislation against organised crime. Nevertheless, conversely to all other serious crimes targeted by the AML apparatus, terrorism does not generate proceeds. Money is the means of the crime (which is the terrorist act) that is to be seized, not the financial benefit of the crime, which in case of terrorism is non-existent.[93] This is reflected in legislation which contrasts a criminal organisation's objective (obtaining material benefit) with that of a terrorist group which has a "terrorist" objective. Today, considering terrorism and terrorism financing as predicate offences for money laundering is not a satisfactory solution though it is consistent with the occasional funding of terrorist organisations by criminal activities.[94] The reasoning is flawed when the funding originates from legitimate incomes. Hence, Kersten rightly expressed the view that

> [...] it makes no sense to designate the financing of terrorism as a money laundering predicate offence. Rather it should be recognised and distinguished as a separate category. (...) Of course, [... there is a] criminal intent, but it makes no sense to construe the funds used to promote the cause as the 'proceeds' of that criminal intent.[95]

The terrorist acts at which recent legislation is aimed have been funded by legitimate sources, often from the terrorists' own income, petty crimes or by small innocuous transactions.[96] Based on the assumption that some terrorist organisations are funded by donations for charities, SR VIII is the only recommendation that does not pertain to money laundering.[97] It calls for the monitoring of voluntary contributions to NGO's. What complicates the matter is that "in many cases the charities to which donations are given are in fact legitimate in the sense that the charities do carry out some of the work they purport to do".[98] Monitoring the transfer of legitimate assets and not proceeds of crime rests on an *a contrario* scenario which is the basis of the AML legislation.

There is an intrinsic paradox in AML/CTF legislation: Terrorist organisations are clearly criminal groups. However, the financing of terrorism has wrongly

---

93 FATF (2002a), para.12, p. 17.

94 Grabosky, Stohl (2010), pp. 73–86; Makarenko, Mesquita (2014).

95 Kersten (2002), p. 306.

96 Europol (2016), pp. 11–12; See also FATF (2002c), para.18.

97 Now Rec 8, FATF *Recommendations*, 2012.

98 FATF (2002b), point 13.

been construed as a particular aspect of money laundering. From a theoretical perspective, funds from legitimate sources should be excluded from the AML scheme. To remove this theoretical discrepancy, the FATF view is that terrorism financing is a serious crime and therefore subject to the AML/CTF apparatus. However, this reasoning is flawed because terrorism financing does not generate assets, in contrast with the serious crimes which constitute the original predicate offences to money laundering.

The CTF regime has allegedly been set up to prevent the commission of acts of terrorism by detecting financial transactions. However, so far, such pre-emptive detection has not occurred, mainly because the amounts involved are too small and inconspicuous to be detected by a system set up to track large amounts of money. Complex organised terrorist networks, which require large amounts of money, will use financial services. Therefore, those amounts can be detected with "conventional AML regulations" in the same manner as for other organisations. According to the FATF, the principal techniques and mechanisms used by terrorists to transfer funds or conceal connections to their sources vary little from those used by criminal organisations which are estimated to generate large sums of money.[99] Furthermore, this type of financing is not specific to terrorist organisations, given that some criminal organisations are known to fund illegal activities with legitimate assets.[100] This observation explains the use of the existing AML regulations in CTF and in many aspects justifies it. However, the AML scheme was not meant to track down small amounts or legitimate transactions, which SR VIII tries to address. While the money-launderers aim at concealing the criminal origin of the assets, by contrast the terrorists do not attempt to "obscure the money trail". Their "ultimate goal [i]s certainly not to gain wealth or achieve financial respectability".[101] Because they may "want to move money undetected from the source of the fundraising activity to the location of the group or persons that will carry out the terrorist activity",[102] financing terrorism has thus been called "reverse money laundering".[103]

These differences bespeak of the shortcomings of the AML scheme in the fight against terrorism financing. However, such considerations were pushed aside by the desire to be seen to be doing something against terrorism.[104] By

---

99 FATF (2002c), para.15. Bricknell, McCusker, Chadwick, Rees (2012), pp. 14–15.

100 Champeyrache (2000), p. 474.

101 Warde (2007), p. 46.

102 FATF (2010), p. 23.

103 Cassella (2003), p. 11.

104 Warde (2007), p. 36.

extending the AML apparatus to the financing of terrorism, governments may have scored political points with their constituencies, however, the effectiveness of these measures in preventing terrorism financing or terrorist attacks has not been established. The weakness of the CTF legislation is made more apparent by the revelation that, in Australia, federal agencies do not cross-check their database because of the large number of false positives. Hence, for instance, before registering a company, its directors or shareholders, ASIC does not automatically check the Department of Foreign Affairs and Trade's (DFAT) list of terrorist individuals and organisations.[105] Not only does this practice limit the ability to detect terrorist activities but it also misleads the public and undermines its confidence in authorities. One should assume that s/he is not dealing with a proscribed person or business when entering into relation with an officially Australian registered company. In addition, the CTF regime has burdened the financial sector with excessive and inappropriate rules and have impacted negatively on already impoverish societies, making them even more vulnerable to becoming a breeding ground for terrorism.

The inability of the AML model in general, and the Special Recommendations in particular, to satisfactorily tackle the financing of terrorism was already raised by the EU Counter-Terrorism Coordinator. He acknowledged that the CTF system had not been as successful as expected.[106] Since then the financing of terrorist attacks has considerably changed, emphasising even more the inadequacy of the AML/CTF machinery to achieve its promises. An analysis of the financing of 40 jihadi terrorist cells that have plotted attacks in Europe between 1994 to 2013 revealed that terrorists' financial activities are remarkably ordinary.[107] Those jihadists have most commonly relied on funding from the cell members' own salaries and savings. The vast majority of the cells studied (90%) generated their own income, and half of them were entirely self-financed. Only one in four received economic support from international terrorist organisations such as Al-Qaida. Despite the attention Islamic charities have received for their alleged roles in terrorist financing, very few jihadi terrorist plots in Europe have involved money which could be traced to such charities. The 2015 study also found that they were no examples of elaborate schemes involving trade diversion, massive online fraud, or new payment systems such as virtual currencies and non-bank led mobile money services. The flow of remittances generally goes in the opposite direction, from workers in

105 FATF (2015), 4.33–4.35, pp. 75–76.

106 Counter-Terrorism Coordinator (2008), p. 2.

107 Oftedal (2015).

the West to their families in the developing world. Likewise, the hawala system and other informal value transfer systems, appear to have played no direct role in financing operational terrorist cells in Western Europe. Nevertheless, "they may have contributed indirectly, by financing international terrorist organizations that organize training camps and other infrastructure used by the jihadi cells in Europe".[108] Contrary to the assumption that terrorists are turning increasingly to illegal activities and grey markets, the study found little evidence that terrorist involvement in criminal activity had increased over time. However, in 2018, François Molins, procureur de la République de Paris (Prosecutor of the French Republic of Paris) declared that some financial supports sent from France to the Islamic State had come through charities, though he did not provide any figure.[109]

The shortcomings of the AML/CTF regime should be seen as the opportunity to question the validity of CTF measures and call for a review of the strategy against terrorism in general. The fight against terrorism cannot be won on the financing front alone. Fighting terrorism is a multi-dimensional task and many experts and academics advocate a range of coordinated strategies to tackle the problem.[110] As Reuter and Truman observe:

> [T]he most successful operations against terrorist financing have not come through large or suspect transaction reports but rather from sound intelligence work. The anti-money laundering regime in the United States and elsewhere has already been amply criticised yet that same system despite its many failings is advocated to deter terrorist financing.[111]

Focusing on CTF measures has been ineffective to prevent acts of terrorism; it has cost millions to the economies of the countries that have implemented them. They have also diverted law enforcement resources from the organised crime front to a sector that did not yield the expected results. Given public resources are limited, it is essential to reorient law enforcement activities to where they will be the most effective.

Contrary to the initial preventive rhetoric on which the amalgam between TF and ML legislation was built, the purpose of the CFT scheme and data collection are to have a mechanism capable to trace, *a posteriori*, the movement

108 Oftedal (2015), p. 7.
109 Boutry, Decugis (2018).
110 Freeman (2011), pp. 471–473.
111 Reuter, Truman (2004).

of funds. Such a collecting system already existed before 2001. Since 9/11, the rules have been tightened and ways to move assets without leaving an electronic trace are being constantly reduced. Despite its inability to prevent terrorism, the AML/CTF machinery has nevertheless effectively contributed to the understanding, through the analysis of the financial operations of their perpetrators, of how terrorist acts are financed. In cases where the terrorist has not acted alone, it has allowed accomplices to be tracked down.

CHAPTER 5

The Proscription of Terrorist Organisations and the Implementation of CTF UNSCRs

Two of our greatest enemies in the fight against terror are the fear that makes us cheapen our freedoms and the power that makes us cynical of them.[1]

GRAHAM WATSON

5.1 Introduction

Until now, in Australia, most convictions for violations of CTF provisions have been in connection with a terrorist organisation. This highlights the importance of organisations under Australian CTF legislation. The criminalisation of a terrorist organisation is key in Australia's anti-terrorism legislation. Division 102 of the Code lists seven specific offences related to a terrorist organisation. It would seem that from the Code's perspective, it is organisations rather than individuals who mainly perpetrate terrorist acts. The criminalisation of a terrorist organisation is also the base of the proscription regime. Australia's proscriptive regime has two components: under the Code and under *Charter of the United Nations Act 1945* (COTUNA). Under the Code, its purpose is to facilitate the prosecution of offences linked with terrorist organisations under sections 102.2 to 102.8. The proscription does not make an organisation illegal or allow for the confiscation of its assets. It serves as a warning to those linked to the organisation that their activities may be considered as forms of participation in a terrorist organisation. Also, it facilitates the task of those subject to the AML/CTF legislation in identifying the transactions that require enhanced diligence.

COTUNA provides for the prescription of persons and entities pursuant to mandatory UNSCRs that deal with assets. It entails strict observations by financial institutions akin to those imposed by AML legislation. COTUNA serves therefore a dual purpose. Firstly, it enables Australia to comply with its international obligations under the UN Charter, and secondly, it assists financial

1 Watson (2003).

 | DOI:10.1163/9789004359109_006

institutions to comply with the prohibition to deal with the assets of those mentioned in the UN Security Council Resolutions (UNSCRs), or to finance proscribed activities.

This chapter starts by examining the prosecution regimes. It will then focus on listing and delisting procedures. Given that the UNSCRs hold the sanctions regime as an important CTF strategy, a particular attention will be given to the those implemented under (COTUNA).

5.2 Proscription of Terrorist Organisations under the Code

The Code's proscription is based on the UK model. However, over the years the *Terrorism Act* (2000) (UK) has been amended so that now the current provisions differ substantially from the Code's, in particular with regard to the review process, which shall be examined later.

TABLE 17 Terrorist organisation – Section 102.1, the Code

Terrorist organisation means:
(a) an org that is directly or indirectly engaged in, preparing, planning, assisting in or fostering the doing of a terrorist act (whether or not a terrorist act occurs); or
(b) an org that is specified by the regulations for the purposes of this paragraph (see subs.(2), (3) and (4)). (...)
Terrorist organisation regulations:
(2) Before the Governor-General makes a regulation specifying an organisation for the purposes of para. (b) of the definition of terrorist organisation in this section, the Minister must be satisfied on reasonable grounds that the organisation:
(a) is directly or indirectly engaged in, preparing, planning, assisting in or fostering the doing of a terrorist act (whether or not a terrorist act has occurred or will occur); or
(b) advocates the doing of a terrorist act (whether or not a terrorist act has occurred or will occur).

5.2.1 *Terrorist Organisations*

The Code uses the term *organisation* which is defined very loosely as a body corporate or an incorporated body, irrespective of whether it is based outside or inside Australia or consists of persons who are not Australian citizens, or is a part of a larger organisation. The Code's definition is thus quite broad. The threshold at which a collection of individuals becomes a criminal organisation under the Code is low as two persons suffice (s 390.4). It can therefore be a very small group. There is no requirement for a formal structure or leadership. The Code's definition encompasses large organisations such as Al Qaida and ISIS which are thought to be well structured organisations, with a defined leadership, even though such a hierarchic structure within Al Qaida has been disputed.[2] It may also include smaller and transient terrorist groups which may be franchises of larger organisations and claim an ideological affinity in committing terrorist acts. However, according to the Crown, an organisation is understood as a "standing body of people with a particular purpose, not a transient group of conspirators who may come together for a single discrete criminal purpose". This view was also shared by the judiciary in the Benbrika's trials.[3] Not only is such interpretation too narrow compared with the wording of the Code, it also does not capture recent forms of terrorist groups such as the people involved in the truck attack in Nice or the killing of a Catholic priest at St-Eienne-du-Rouvray, near Rouen in July 2016, or the Parramatta, NSW, shooting in 2015.

Under the Code, a terrorist organisation is defined either in reference to specific actions or by regulations, not by the purpose to commit a specific terrorist act. The Code does not require of the organisation a direct engagement in a terrorist act and does not state what kind of connection there must be between the preparatory act and the terrorist act. An indirect engagement is a very vague measure to determine if a terrorist act is being considered, particularly when the Code does not demand that such an act will occur. In the case of advocacy, the Code does not provide any indication on how to gauge when an act committed by a person of a group is to be attributed to the group. Further, there is no definition of "fostering" in the Code. The Victorian Supreme Court held that "[f]ostering can be synonymous with encouraging or something of that nature".[4] Added that there is no requirement of an intention to commit a terrorist act and no requirement that the organisation has a link to Australia, the drafting of section 102.1(2) suggests that any group of people, in which one member could potentially be involved in activities that could be considered as fostering a terrorist act, could be proscribed. The "extremely expansive"[5]

2 Roy (2004), pp. 24–25.

3 *R v Izhar Ul-Haque* (unreported, NSW Supreme Court, 08.02. 2006) Bell J [51]. See also Bongiorno J comments in *R v Benbrika* (Ruling No 35) [2009] VSC 142 [97]-[105] and Benbrika and Ors v The Queen (2010) 29 VR 593 [84].

4 *Benbrika and Ors v The Queen* (2010) 29 VR 593 [101].

5 Federation of Community Legal Centres (2006), p. 27.

definition of a terrorist organisation highlights the preventive aspect of Australia's terrorism legislation. Such a definition is therefore a problem to financial institutions, individuals and companies who want to avoid funding a terrorist organisation. Hence, the proscription scheme may assist in providing a list of those which the Commonwealth consider terrorists.

5.2.2 *Prescription Regime*

The proscription regulation is made *pro forma* by the Governor-General and *de facto* by the Minister through the Attorney-General. The proscription decision under the Code is purely statutory. It is the result of an executive decision, not a judicial process. Initially, only an organisation that had been identified as terrorist by the UN Security Council could be proscribed under section 102. With the enactment of the *Criminal Code Amendment (Terrorist Organisations) Act 2004* (Cth), Australia was enabled to draw its own list, based on its own criteria. The criteria that carry the ministerial decision to proscribe an organisation are not precisely defined. It therefore reflects political considerations, rather than criminality.

Under Australian law, the Minister enjoys a large margin of discretion in making a risk assessment and deciding whom to list and to delist. Given that many organisations may meet the very broad legal definition, and that law enforcement agencies budgets are not unlimited, the Minister must apply some other criteria. Hence, the selection process rests largely on extra-legal requirements. ASIO has revealed six criteria (engagement in terrorism; ideology and links to other terrorist groups or networks; links to Australia; threats to Australian interests; proscription by the UN or like-minded countries and engagement in peace/mediation processes)[6] but fell short of providing the weight to be given to each factor. The Attorney-General's Department indicated that "ultimately, it is about whether listing is in the security interests of this country".[7] However, according to Emerton, "the questions of a link to Australia, or a threat to Australians, seems to have been given very little consideration in most cases, despite the fact that this is the factor that seems to have the greatest relevance to the question of criminalisation". Upon examination of the organisations listed, he concluded that ASIO's criteria "seem to emphasise foreign policy rather than domestic considerations".[8] Overall, some members of Parliamentary Joint

6 PJC on ASIO, ASIS and DSD (2005), p. 15, para.2.24.

7 AGD (2005), p. 14, point 2.19.

8 Emerton (2009).

Committee on Intelligence and Security remain unconvinced as to the robustness of the selection of the listing process.[9]

TABLE 18 Government procedures to list a proscribed organisation under the Code[a]

1. ASIO prepares an unclassified Statement of Reasons, endorsed by DFAT, detailing the case for listing the organisation.
2. Chief General Counsel, provides written confirmation that the Statement of Reasons is sufficient for the Attorney-General to be satisfied on reasonable grounds of the matters required under S 102.1(2) for the listing by regulation of an organisation as a terrorist organisation.
3. The Director-General of Security writes to the Attorney-General outlining the background, training activities, terrorist activities, and relevant statements of the organisation.
4. Having considered the information provided in the submission, the Attorney-General signs a statement confirming that he is satisfied on reasonable grounds.
5. The Attorney-General signs a regulation in relation to the organisation.
6. The Attorney-General write to the Prime Minister advising of his intention to list the organisation as a terrorist organisation.
7. The Attorney-General advises the Leader of the Opposition.
8. The Prime Minister writes to the Premiers of the States and Chief Ministers of the Territories advising them of the decision to list the organisation
9. The Attorney-General writes to the Chairman of the Parliamentary Joint Committee on Intelligence and Security advising of his decision to list the organisation as a terrorist organisation.
10. The Governor-General makes a regulation.
11. The Regulation is lodged with the Federal Register of Legislative Instruments (FRLI).
12. A press release is issued and the Attorney-General's Department's National Security website is updated.

a PJC-IS (2008), 1.10, pp. 2–3.

Under the Code, the consultation process is very limited. The *intergovernmental agreement on counter terrorism Laws* establishes some sort of consultation between the Minister and the states and territory Governments before the final decision is taken but its terms are vague and the consultation seems to be

9 PJC-IS (2007b), para 1.12.

purely formal.[10] No information is given to those concerned prior the decision and not submission can be made. The listing procedures are detailed above.

As an overall strategy against terrorism, the effectiveness of proscribing organisations must be questioned. ASIO admits that it is difficult to measure but believes "that some people had distanced themselves from some of the listed groups".[11]

5.3 Proscription of Terrorist Organisations under COTUNA

COTUNA's purpose is to implement the UN Security Council (thereafter SC) decisions to freeze assets and to prevent those that are owned or controlled by a proscribed person or entity from being made available. Australia implements the UNSCRs relating to the dealings with assets through Regulations issued under COTUNA. In addition, Australia has also established its own independent list under the *Autonomous Sanctions Act 2011* which provides the framework for the implementation of similar sanctions that "like-minded" States have adopted. Not only is the *Autonomous Sanctions Act* modelled on COTUNA, it is also has similar objectives. In some cases, the two lists overlap. The persons and entities listed under the various UNSCRs demanding the freezing of assets and under the *Autonomous Sanctions Act* are found under the *Australian Consolidated List*. At the end of 2018, there were close to 6,000 persons and organisations listed on that List.

The objective of the UNSCRs discussed below is to combat international terrorism and the proliferation of weapons of mass destruction (WMD). They are adopted in accordance with Chapter VII of the UN Charter in order to preserve international peace and security. Different UNSCRs impose different regimes of sanctions. Broadly, UNSCR 1267 pertains to Al Qaida and associates and UNSCR 1373 includes both individuals and terrorist organisations. These two UNSCRS are a major development since they impose economic sanctions on individuals and companies, no longer exclusively on States. UNSCR 1737 imposes sanctions on Iran, UNSCR 1718 on North Korea and UNSCR 2178 on foreign fighters.

To assist the States in implementing the UNSCRs, the Security Council has established corresponding *sanctions committees*. It is mandatory for Member States to proscribe those individuals and entities listed pursuant to UNSCRs. Hence, the 1267 Al Qaida List, the Iran and Korea Lists facilitate the implementation of these international legal obligations. The UN has issued its own *UN Consolidated list*. There is no corresponding list for UNSCR 1373. Instead, each

---

10 PJC-IS (2007a), pp. 49–50.

11 PJC on ASIO, ASIS and DSD (2005), 3.9, p. 29.

TABLE 19 Proscription of terrorist organisation – Part 4, COTUNA

S 14: Definitions	In this part: *Freezable asset* means an asset that: (a) is owned or controlled by a proscribed person or entity; or (b) is a listed asset; or (c) is derived or generated from assets mentioned in paragraph (a) or (b). *Listed asset* means an asset listed by the Minister under section 15. *Proscribed person or entity* means: (a) a person or entity listed by the Minister under section 15; or (b) a person or entity proscribed by regulation under section 18.
S 15: Listing persons, entities and assets	S 15: Listing persons, entities and assets (1) The Minister must list a person or entity under this section if the Minister is satisfied on reasonable grounds of the prescribed matters. (2) The Governor-General may make regulations prescribing the matters of which the Minister must be satisfied before listing a person or entity under subsection (1). (3) The Minister may list an asset, or class of asset, under this section if the Minister is satisfied on reasonable grounds of the prescribed matters. (4) The Governor-General may make regulations prescribing the matters of which the Minister must be satisfied before listing an asset under subsection (3). (5) A matter must not be prescribed under subs(2) or (4) unless the prescription of the matter would give effect to a decision that: (a) the SC has made under Chapter VII of the Charter of the UN; and (b) Art.25 of the Charter requires Australia to carry out; and (c) relates to terrorism and dealings with assets. (6) A person or entity is listed by notice in the Gazette. (7) An asset or class of asset is listed by notice in the Gazette.
S 15A: Duration of listing	(1) A listing under section 15 ceases to have effect on: (a) if no declaration under subsection (2) has been made in relation to the listing—the third anniversary of the day on which the listing took effect; or (b) otherwise—the third anniversary of the making of the most recent declaration under subsection (2) in relation to the listing. (2) The Minister may declare, in writing, that a specified listing under section 15 continues to have effect.

TABLE 19 Proscription of terrorist organisation – part 4, COTUNA (*cont.*)

(3) The Minister must not:
 (a) make a declaration under subsection (2) specifying the listing of a person or entity unless the Minister is satisfied on reasonable grounds of the matters prescribed for the purposes of subsection 15(2); or
 (b) make a declaration under subsection (2) specifying the listing of an asset, or class of asset, unless the Minister is satisfied on reasonable grounds of the matters prescribed for the purposes of subsection 15(4).
(4) The regulations may prescribe a form for a declaration under subsection (2).
(5) A declaration made under subsection (2) is not a legislative instrument.
(6) To avoid doubt, subsection (1) does not prevent:
 (a) the revocation, under section 16, of a listing; or
 (b) the revocation of a listing by operation of section 19; or
 (c) the making of a new listing that is the same in substance as another listing (whether the new listing is made or takes effect before or after the the other listing ceases to have effect because of subsection (1)).

State must maintain its own list. The Counter-Terrorist Committee (CTC), established pursuant to UNSCR 1373, assist States in their obligations to counter terrorism.

The Minister for Foreign Affairs is authorised to allow financial transactions that would contravene the UNSCRs provided, for instance, they pertain to a "basic expense dealing", a "contractual dealing", or an "extraordinary expense dealing", or to humanitarian assistance.[12]

5.3.1 *UNSCR 1267*

Since 1996, the UN SC has ordered sanctions against Afghanistan, the Taliban and Bin Laden.[13] In 1999, with the adoption of UNSCR 1267, it established a Committee (called *1267 Sanctions Committee*) to keep an updated list of individuals

12 See for instance S 30, *Charter of the United Nations (Dealing with Assets) Regulations 2008* and s 14A, Charter of the United Nations (Sanctions—Democratic People's Republic of Korea) Regulations 2008.

13 UNSCR 1076 (1996).

and organisations subjected to travel bans and the freezing of assets.[14] Further, in 2000, the UN Security Council decided to impose a mandatory arms embargo to Afghanistan and ordered the freezing of the assets of Bin Laden and those associated with him.[15] In 2015, the asset freezing requirements were extended to oil, oil products, and cultural property.[16] The measures against Al-Qaida were extended to the Islamic State in Iraq and the Levant (ISIL). Consequently, the name of the *Al-Qaida Sanctions Committee* was changed to the *1267/1989/2253 ISIL (Da'esh) and Al-Qaida Sanctions Committee,*[17] and the Al-Qaida Sanctions List was changed to the *"ISIL (Da'esh) and Al-Qaida Sanctions List"*. For the sake of simplification, the listing under UNSCR 1267 refers here to the list established by the 1267/1989/2253 Sanctions Committee.

UNSCR 1373 (2001) makes it mandatory for UN Member States to take measures to suppress terrorism and to impose targeted financial sanctions in relation to persons and entities, in particular against persons who commit, or attempt to commit, terrorist acts and who participate in or facilitate the commission of terrorist acts, as well as entities owned or controlled directly or indirectly by such persons. Those acting on behalf of, or at the direction of, such persons and entities must also be listed.

With *UNSCR 2178 (2014)*, the UN SC extends the financing prohibitions under UNSCR 1373 to those who go abroad to commit or participate in terrorist acts, or to receive terrorist training. These people and those who support them should be listed on the Al-Qaida list. It also urges enhanced cooperation between the Counter-Terrorism Committee (CTC) established pursuant to UNSCR 1373, the 1540 Committee,[18] and the 1267 Al-Qaida Committee.[19]

5.3.2 *Weapons of Mass Destruction*

Pursuant to its policy against the proliferation of weapons of mass destruction, the UN Security Council expanded its original policy from export controls to financial measures. Also, it issued Resolutions against non-State actors, the Democratic People's Republic of Korea (DPRK) and Iran. They are mentioned

---

14 UNSCR 1363 (2001). See UNSCR 1390 (2002); UNSCR 1822 (2008).

15 UNSCR 1333 (2000). With UNSCR 1988 (2011), the UN Security Council split in two the list created pursuant to UNSCR 1267. UNSCR 1989 (2011) imposed a sanctions regime in relation to Al-Qaida alone. The sanctions regime has subsequently been amended and renewed by UNSCR 2083 (2012) and 2161 (2014). See also Analytical Support and Sanctions Implementation Monitoring Team (2011).

16 UNSCR 2199 (2015).

17 UNSCR 2253 (2015).

18 UNSCR 1810 (2008).

19 UNSCR 2178 (2014).

here because in 2012 the FATF included the proliferation of weapons of mass destruction in its list of predicate offences to money laundering. Specifically, it recommends the implementation of targeted financial sanctions to comply with UNSCRs relating to the prevention, suppression and disruption of proliferation of weapons of mass destruction and its financing. Therefore, the persons and entities listed under those UNSCRs are subject to the AML/CTF machinery.

UNSCR 1540 (2004) requires all states to prevent access by non-State actors to nuclear, chemical, and biological weapons, and their means of delivery. They must take effective measures to prevent proliferation of such items and to establish appropriate controls over related materials. It also established a Committee to oversee its implementation. UNSCR 1540 does not specifically require freezing measures.

5.3.3 *North Korea*

UNSCR 1718 (2006) imposes a sanctions regime in response to the DPRK's nuclear testing. The system has been amended and extended by several UNSCRs. In short, it imposes an embargo on the supply of nuclear material and certain weapons. Moreover, it makes mandatory the freezing of funds that are owned or controlled, directly or indirectly, by the persons or entities designated by the Committee, established to facilitate the implementation of the UNSCR.

To implement this resolution, Australia enacted the *Charter of the United Nations (Sanctions – Democratic People's Republic of Korea) Regulations 2008*, the *Charter of the United Nations (Sanctions – Democratic People's Republic of Korea) List 2014* (the DPRK List) and the *Charter of the United Nations (Sanctions – Democratic People's Republic of Korea) Luxury Goods List 2006*. Violations of the financial prohibitions are sanctioned under sections 6(2), 8(1)(d) and (f), *Charter of the United Nations (Sanctions – Democratic People's Republic of Korea) Regulations* 2008. In addition, Australia imposes an autonomous sanctions regime in relation to the DPRK and has amended the *Customs (Prohibited Exports) Regulations 1958* accordingly.

5.3.4 *Iran*

In 2006, the UN Security Council placed an embargo on Iran in regard to "all items, materials, equipment, goods and technology" which could contribute to Iran's enrichment-related program or the development of Iran's nuclear weapon delivery systems. UNSCR 1737 required States to prevent the supply, sale or transfer directly or indirectly, from their territories or by their nationals, to Iran of the items listed. It also ordered the freezing of funds, other financial assets and economic resources that are owned or controlled by the persons or entities designated in a list, while still allowing for some exceptions. To implement this resolution, Australia enacted the *Charter of the United Nations (Sanctions – Iran) Regulations 2008, the Charter of the United Nations (Sanctions – Iran) Documents List 2014* (the Iran List) and the *Anti-Money Laundering and Counter-Terrorism Financing (Iran Countermeasures) Regulation 2014*. In 2015, UNSCR 2231 terminated previous UN Security Council sanctions for 16 January 2016. The AML/CTF *(Iran Countermeasures) Regulation 2014* was repealed on the 27 February 2016. Hence, financial transactions with Iran of $20,000 or more no longer require authorisation from the Department of Foreign Affairs and Trade (DFAT). However, some of the measures that Australia has implemented under the autonomous sanctions regime in relation to Iran still restrict certain activities.

5.3.5 *Requirements for Listing under COTUNA*

The *Charter of the United Nations (Dealing with Assets) Regulations 2008* (Cth) sets the legal requirements regarding the grounds for listing individuals, entities or assets pursuant to UNSCR 1373.

TABLE 20 Grounds for listing persons, entities or assets

COTUNA (dealing with assets) regulations 2008, Section 20 (Listing for Resolution 1373)
(1) For subsection 15 (2) of the Act, the Minister must list a person or entity if the Minister is satisfied that the person or entity is a person or entity mentioned in paragraph 1 (c) of Resolution 1373. (2) For subsection 15 (4) of the Act, the Minister may list an asset, or class of asset, if the Minister is satisfied that the asset, or class of asset, is owned or controlled by a person or entity mentioned in paragraph 1 (c) of Resolution 1373.

The Regulations makes it mandatory for the Minister to list a *person* or *entity* if she/he is satisfied that the person or entity is mentioned in UNSCR 1373, whereas the Minister may decide to list an *asset* if she/he is satisfied that it is owned or controlled by a person or entity mentioned in UNSCR 1373. In both cases, the criterion for listing is that the Minister "is satisfied". In contrast, under section 15, COTUNA to which UNSCR 1267, for instance, applies, "the Minister must list a person or entity if she/he is satisfied *on reasonable grounds* of the prescribed matters". Given the listing's harsh consequences for individuals and organisations, such a lack of guidelines is astonishing. This contrasts with the requirements under the Code regarding the listing of a terrorist organisation. Hence, under COTUNA, the listing process remains on the whole confidential and the listing decision rests solely on the discretion of the Minister provided that is satisfied that the legal requirements are met. Regulations may be issued to detail these requirements. However, they only specify various prohibitions and offer no guidance regarding the listing process. Reference must therefore be made to COTUNA.

The Minister's discretion is not restricted to the process of the listing but to the listing itself. Section 15 suggests that when the Sanctions Committee lists a person, the Minister is bound to put that name on the Australian list. However, the absence of indication as to what may satisfy the Minister "on reasonable grounds" opens the door to another interpretation. It would suggest that the Minister has the latitude to refuse a listing when it is apparent to him that the person is not involved in terrorism, for instance following a court decision. This is reinforced by section 16 which allows the Minister to revoke a listing under section 15, if he is satisfied that the listing is no longer necessary. It is submitted that had the legislature wanted to remove all autonomy from the Minister in the listing and de-listing process, it would have phrased the sections differently. By insisting that the Minister must be satisfied, it empowers the Minister to decide what constitutes the necessary presence of a name on the list. Further, that the Minister is given latitude is underlined by section 19. The ministerial autonomy in enforcing mandatory UNSCRs on terrorism is indirectly corroborated by Kirby J in *Thomas v Mowbray*.[20] Kirby J went on further to specify that UNSCRs 1267 and 1373 are "binding on Australia as a party to the Charter but subject always, within Australia, to any relevant limitations or restrictions of the *Australian Constitution*".[21] The examination of cases in 5.4.2 should offer some suggestion as to the elements that the Minister should take into consideration when making his/her decision.

5.4 Delisting and Review Procedures

5.4.1 *Under the Code*

The effect of the proscription is limited to 2 years. The purpose of a sunset clause is to force the Minister to review the appropriateness of a listing. Section 102.1(17)(b) provides that anybody may submit a request for de-listing to the Minister, who must consider it.

20 *Thomas v Mowbray* [2007] 233 CLR 307 [281].

21 *Thomas v Mowbray* [2007] 233 CLR 307 [282].

TABLE 21 Terrorist organisation – Section 102.1 (17) and (18), the Code

Terrorist organisation regulations

(17) If:

(a) an organisation (the listed organisation) is specified in regulations made for the purposes of paragraph (b) of the definition of terrorist organisation in this section; and

(b) an individual or an organisation (which may be the listed organisation) makes an application (the de-listing application) to the Minister for a declaration under subsection (4) in relation to the listed organisation; and

(c) the de-listing application is made on the grounds that there is no basis for the Minister to be satisfied that the listed organisation:

(i) is directly or indirectly engaged in, preparing, planning, assisting in or fostering the doing of a terrorist act; or

(ii) advocates the doing of a terrorist act;

as the case requires;

the Minister must consider the de-listing application.

(18) Subsection (17) does not limit the matters that may be considered by the Minister for the purposes of subsection (4).

5.4.1.1 De-listing

The Code does not require that any motivations be given or a statement of reasons be provided to the proscribed organisation, making any appeal difficult. ASIO provides, on its website, the list of the organisations that have been proscribed, and a *statement of reasons*. This "statement" is closer to a list of allegations than an explanation of the grounds of the decision taken by the Governor-General which could be used to launch an appeal. Under Division 102, proscription is an extra judicial decision with the objective of facilitating the prosecution of individuals. The risk of being prosecuted *de facto* as associates, members or directors of the proscribed organisation, precludes those acting on behalf of the organisation from asking directly for a review. The service of a solicitor is thus an implicit requirement for a de-listing application. It follows that in practice, even though the proscription does not *per se* declare the organisation unlawful,[22] the first practical consequence of the proscription is

22 McGarrity (2008), p. 47; Rose, Nestorovska (2007), p. 36.

to push the organisation underground,[23] which complicates detection and the investigation.[24]

The Code does not mention any procedural guarantee in the de-listing stage, or any independent review. There is no indication of the factors or material that must be taken into consideration, and no time frame is given. Since the decision process is opaque, and in absence of the reasons for the decision, there is no guarantee that a considered reflection is given and that the proscription is not just rolled over. The Minister may revoke a listing of his own will, when he is satisfied that the legal criteria are no longer met. In that case, s/he must publish his/her decision in the *Gazette*. The de-listing only operates prospectively. So even if a listing has been found groundless, its effect remains in place for those sentenced for a derivative offence.

5.4.1.2 Parliamentary Review Process

Section 102.1A lays down a parliamentary review process by the Parliamentary Joint Committee on Intelligence and Security (PJC-IS). As with the listing and de-listing procedure, the review process is done in the absence of representatives of the organisation. It is not mandatory to inform the organisation, even by the Gazette, that a review is being conducted. The PJC-IS acts like an ombudsman. Its review is optional and its powers are constricted. It may review the process, including the merit of the decision, and make recommendations to the Parliament, but it has no power to de-list. In the past, full review by the PJC-IS has been precluded given the failure of the Attorney-General to provide timely, comprehensive and accurate information to justify the listings.[25] To date, the PJC-IS has not recommended that an organisation should not be proscribed and neither House of Parliament has ever disallowed a proscription regulation.[26]

5.4.1.3 Administrative Review Process

Apart from the parliamentary review, there is a review under the *Administration Decision (Judicial Review) Act 1977* (Cth), but it cannot invalidate the decision. The review is limited to an assessment of the legality of the Minister's decision.[27] It does not allow a challenge of facts upon which the regulation is based, nor of the reasonableness and proportionality of the decision. This led the SLCL to state that the decisions on proscription are

23 Bronitt (2003a), p. 5.

24 Lloyd of Berwick (1996), p. 57.

25 McGarrity (2008), p. 51.

26 McGarrity, Williams (2018), p. 221.

27 Lynch, McGarrity, Williams (2009), pp. 10, 11.

effectively unreviewable.[28] In 2006, the Sheller Committee concluded that the Attorney-General was under an obligation to observe natural justice in whether or not to put an organisation on the proscription list.[29]

5.4.2 *Delisting under* COTUNA

This section examines the criteria and procedure for listing and reviewing the list under UNSCR 1267 and UNSCR 1373. As an illustration, two landmark decisions taken by the European Court of Justice (ECJ) pursuant to the listing under these UNSCRs will be analysed.

TABLE 22 De-listing – Sections 16 and 17, COTUNA

S 16 Minister may revoke the listing	(1) The Minister may revoke a listing under section 15 if the Minister is satisfied that the listing is no longer necessary to give effect to a decision that: (a) the Security Council has made under Chapter VII of the Charter of the United Nations; and (b) Article 25 of the Charter requires Australia to carry out; and (c) relates to terrorism and dealings with assets. (2) The Minister may revoke the listing either at the Minister's own instigation or on application by the listed person or entity. (3) The listing is revoked by notice in the Gazette. (4) The listing is revoked at the start of the day immediately after the day on which notice is published in the Gazette.
S 17 Listed person or entity may apply to have the listing revoked	(1) A listed person or entity may apply to the Minister to have the listing revoked. (2) The application must: (a) be in writing; and (b) set out the circumstances relied upon to justify the application.

Regarding the de-listing, it must be emphasised that COTUNA does not state the level of satisfaction required. The requirement of being "satisfied on

28 Sheller (2006), pp. 68, 79.

29 Sheller (2006), pp. 82–83. See also Recommendtions 3, 4, 5 and McGarrity (2008), pp. 64–65.

reasonable grounds" is absent in the de-listing decision. Hence the Minister's discretion is greater for de-listing than for listing, suggesting autonomy of the executing powers from the decision of the Sanctions Committee in the de-listing process.

The listing *may* be revoked when the Minister "is satisfied that the listing is no longer necessary" to give effect to a mandatory UNSCR. The Act does not give any indication on the procedure to be followed when listing or delisting. Furthermore, it does not provide any review mechanism. It follows that the principles of Australian administrative law apply.[30] It could be inferred that the Minister's power of appreciation is considerably reduced when implementing a mandatory UNSCR under COTUNA. A reading of Australia's legislation in the light of the case law of the European Court of Justice (ECJ) may suggest a different interpretation. The ECJ's decisions exemplify the role that human rights can play in safeguarding the democratic order that terrorism legislation claims to protect. Thus, they may provide an understanding on how to interpret Australia's current legislation in accordance with internationally held fundamental rights.

Since the EU wanted to ensure a uniform application of UNSCRs 1267 and 1373 by Member States, it adopted several pieces of legislation which were in turn implemented by Regulations which list the names of individuals and organisations. The list is established, reviewed and amended by the Council acting in unanimity. It is regularly updated. The implementation of the EU Regulations has been reviewed by the European Court of Justice (ECJ) in two landmark cases, *Kadi* and *OMPI*. The decisions articulate fundamental rights in the fight against terrorism. They are critical of political authorities that proscribe by *ukase*.[31]

In Australia, apart from the list under section 102.1 of the Code, there are, broadly, two lists which may intersect: one pursuant to UNSCRs and implemented under COTUNA and the *Autonomous Sanctions Act 2011* (Cth). The EU has also two lists: one pursuant to UNSCR 1267 and subsequent resolutions (Al Qaida and associates list) and UNSCR 1373 (terrorists and terrorist organisations list). Member States also have their list which may contain more names than the EU list. In any case, the listing is an administrative matter and not a criminal one. However, its scope and duration has led to considerable hardships and some have seen in them a penal effect.[32]

---

30 Douglas (2012), p. 17. McGarrity (2008), pp. 45–66.

31 Originally, a decree or an edict of the Tsar. By extension, it refers to arbitrary decisions or imperative orders.

32 UN High Commissioner for Human Rights (2009). *Yassin Abdullah Kadi v European Commission, Judgment of the General Court, 30 September 2010, (hereafter Kadi – 3 or Kadi GC II)*, [150].

5.4.2.1 Case Study: UNSCR 1267 – *Kadi & Al Barakaat*

In brief, the facts of *Kadi & Al Barakaat* are as follows: On 19 October 2001, the UN Sanctions Committee put Mr Kadi, a Saudi national, on its list,[33] and did the same on 9 November 2001 with Barakaat International Foundation, registered in Sweden.[34] Consequently, the EU put their names on its list and their assets were frozen under EU legislation. Mr Kadi brought the matter to the court to have the relevant Common Decision and Regulation repealed, alleging breaches of his fundamental rights, that is the right to a fair hearing, the right to respect for property and of the principle of proportionality, and the right to effective judicial review.[35] Al Barakaat had similar requests.[36] The Court of First Instance (CFI, later renamed General Court) rejected their requests (*Kadi – 1 or Kadi GC 1*) and both cases were joined in appeal to the Grand Chamber (ECJ) which granted the appellants' requests (*Kadi – 2 or Kadi CJEU 1*).[37]

In its 2005 Decision, the CFI asserted the prominence of international law above the EU legal order. It held that the impugned legislation was a direct enactment of UNSCR and it had no authority to review, even indirectly, the UNSCR. The Court, however, opened the door for a review of the "disputable" basis[38] of the *jus cogens*, "understood as a body of higher rules of public international law binding on all subjects of international law, including the bodies of the United Nations, and from which no derogation is possible".[39] It nevertheless concluded that there was no violation of fundamental rights,[40] which suggests that *jus cogens* does not offer the same standard of review as the general principles on which EU legislation is based.[41]

In reviewing the CFI decision, the ECJ took a different approach. It did not examine the issue at hand by reference to *jus cogens* nor did it dispute the

33 *Yassin Abdullah Kadi v Council of the European Union and Commission of the European Communities, Case T-315/01, Judgment of the Court of First Instance, 21 September 2005, (hereater Kadi – 1 or Kadi GC 1)* [23].

34 *Ahmed Ali Yusuf and Al Barakaat International Foundation* v *Council of the European Union and Commission of the European Communities*, [24] and [25].

35 *Kadi* – 1 (*Kadi GC 1*) [59].

36 *Yusuf and Al Barakaat* [42].

37 *Yassin Abdullah Kadi, Al Barakaat v Council of the European Union*, Case C-415/05 P, Judgment of the Court (Grand Chamber) of 03.09.2008 (hereafter Kadi – 2 / *Kadi CJEU 1*).

38 Eeckhout (2007), p. 197.

39 *Kadi* – 1 (*Kadi GC 1*) [226].

40 *Yusuf and Al Barakaat* 2005, [344]; Kadi – 1 (*Kadi GC 1*) [288].

41 Eeckhout (2007), p. 187. Tzanakopoulos (2010), p. 258.

prominence of international law above the EU legal order. Rather, it took a very "EU stance". The ECJ made two fundamental observations. First,

> it must […] be noted that the Charter of the United Nations does not impose the choice of a particular model for the implementation of resolutions adopted by the Security Council under Chapter VII of the Charter, since they are to be given effect in accordance with the procedure applicable in that respect in the domestic legal order of each Member of the United Nations. The Charter of the United Nations leaves the Members of the United Nations a free choice among the various possible models for transposition of those resolutions into their domestic legal order.[42]

Consequently, the contested regulation cannot be considered an act directly attributable to the UN. It is rather an internal matter. Hence, the ECJ has jurisdiction to review the validity of Community measures in the light of fundamental rights.[43]

Secondly, the ECJ observed that the UNSCR in question does not make the absence of judicial review mandatory or oppose the respect of fundamental freedoms in general. In other words, the absence, in the UNSCR, of provisions regarding mechanisms which guarantee fundamental rights (such as the rights of the defence, the rights to effective judicial review of those rights) does not imply that they should be forgone in the implementation stage at the national level.[44] Consequently, the ECJ annulled, on account of several infringements of the EU legal order, the impugned legislation, insofar as it concerned the two appellants.

Some academics have acclaimed the ECJ's ruling as a victory for human rights, vindicating criticisms that have been voiced about the lack of judicial review for the listing under the UNSCR.[45] Others have been very critical of the ECJ's decision for indirectly reviewing the UNSCR,[46] and seeing it as weakening EU's commitment to international law and institutions, even naming its reasoning as "chauvinist".[47] These criticisms are an overreaction. Even if it has

---

42 *Kadi* – 1 (*Kadi GC I*) [298].

43 *Kadi* – 1 (*Kadi GC I*) [314] [317].

44 *Kadi* – 1 (*Kadi GC I*) [299] [337] [348] [370].

45 Cameron (2003b), pp. 225–256; Michaelsen (2010a), p. 459; Michaelsen (2010b).

46 Michaelsen (2009), p. 343; Tzanakopoulos (2010), p. 257.

47 De Búrca (2010), p. 4. Burca's view is quite ironical given that the author admits that US courts hold similar views, which are based on the Americans' conviction about the "merits of US-style democracy" and the "power of the US in the international realm" (p. 45). Further, as Eeckhout points out, one cannot see what is chauvinist and parochial about

indirectly exposed the failing of the UN listing mechanism in regard to fundamental rights, the ECJ decision does not depart from the international order, for two reasons. First, the responsibility of listing and de-listing rests technically with the Sanctions Committee and not the Security Council. Although the Security Council is engaged, for practical reasons, it stays at arm's length. This distance makes room for criticisms and improvement of the listing procedure. In fact, the Sanctions Committee has reviewed its listing procedure and established an *ombudsperson* to whom de-listing requests are to be addressed for examination by the Sanctions Committee.[48]

Secondly, though the CFI's ruling affirms the autonomy of the EU's legislation implementing the UNSCR 1267,[49] it is only partial and cannot be construed as a departure from the international order. The ECJ's annulment of a regulation does not free Member States of their obligation under international law.[50] Since, in the EU, respect for human rights is fundamental to its legal order,[51] the *Common Position* and Regulations should have included provisions regarding effective judicial protection. In short, there is an autonomy of the EU legal order when implementing international legislation on the internal level. The ECJ does not get into the issue of a hierarchy of legal norms.[52]

The autonomy of EU law was further asserted in *Kadi – 3* (or *Kadi GC II*). The General Court interpreted *Kadi – 2* (*Kadi CJEU I*) as stating that so far as "the principles of liberty, democracy and respect for human rights and fundamental freedoms, enshrined in article 6(1) EU as a foundation of the Union" are at stake, "the constitutional framework created by the EC Treaty" is a "wholly autonomous legal order, not subject to the higher rules of international law – in this case the law deriving from the Charter of the United Nations".[53]

The ECJ's ruling did not remove the names of the appellant from the list. The effects of the impugned regulation were maintained for a maximum period of three months to allow the Council to take a new decision in accordance with the ECJ decision.[54] Following the ECJ's decision, the Council has issued a new regulation, amending the contested one and indicating the redress

the court applying fundamental rights norms which are so similar to the ICCPR and which the UN itself promotes and seeks to enforce (Eeckhout (2010), pp. 1504–1505.) See also Gowlland-Debbas (2009).

48 UNSCR 1822 (2008) and 1904 (2009). *Kadi – 3* (*Kadi GC II*) [24–27].

49 Robert (2012), p. 38.

50 Eeckhout (2007), pp. 191, 192.

51 *Kadi – 1* (*Kadi GC I*) [335].

52 Eckes (2009a), p. 377.

53 *Kadi – 3* (*Kadi GC II*) [119].

54 *Kadi – 2* (*Kadi CJEU I*) [372–376].

procedure.[55] On this basis, the Commission issued a new Regulation which still mentioned Mr Kadi's name, copying the motives given by the Sanction Committee, without having received any evidence.[56] The Commission alleged that its power of review was limited to "wholly manifest errors of fact or assessment, such as an error as to the identity of the person designated",[57] and it could not review the UN decision. COTUNA holds a similar deference. Mr Kadi appealed against the new Regulation. The General Court found that if the intensity and extent of judicial review were limited in the way advocated by the Commission, "there would be no effective judicial review of the kind required by the Court of Justice in *Kadi* but rather a simulacrum thereof". (*Kadi – 3* or *Kadi GC II*)[58] *Kadi – 3* (*Kadi GC II*) is an even stronger indictment that the impugned UNSCR are breaching fundamental rights.

Consequently, Mr Kadi's request was granted in 2010 (*Kadi – 3* / *Kadi GC II*). The Commission and the Council, supported by a large number of EU Member States, appealed against *Kadi – 3* (*Kadi GC II*).[59] In its decision on 18 July 2013, the Grand Chamber of the CJEU dismissed the appeals (*Kadi – 4 or Kadi CJEU II*).[60] Although it upheld the precedent decision in *Kadi – 3* (*Kadi GC II*), stating that the presented evidence did not substantiate maintaining Mr Kadi's name on the EU sanctions list, it gave the Court the opportunity to clarify the standard of review that should be applied in checking the implementation of measures that are designed to give effect to resolutions adopted by the Security Council under Chapter VII of the UN Charter and the type of judicial protection that should be afforded when fundamental rights are at stake.

Reiterating the statement by the General Court in its previous decision, the Court emphasised that the EU Courts must ensure in principle the full review of the lawfulness of all Union acts in the light of the fundamental rights forming an integral part of the EU legal order. In particular, respect for the rights of the defence and the right to effective judicial protection requires that the competent EU authority must disclose to the individual concerned the specific and concrete reasons why the competent authorities consider that the individual

55 Council Regulation (EU) N°1286/2009 of 22 December 2009, pp. 42–46.

56 *Kadi* – 3 (*Kadi GC II*) [95]. Gautier (2008), p. 4 called it a "twin list".

57 *Kadi* – 3 (*Kadi GC II*) [96].

58 *Kadi* – 3 (*Kadi GC II*) [123].

59 See *Opinion* of Avocate General Bot, Joined Cases C-584/10 P, C-593/10 P and C-595/10 P, *European Commission Council of the European Union, United Kingdom of Great Britain and Northern Ireland v Yassin Abdullah Kadi*, 19.03.2013.

60 *European Commission, United Kingdom of Great Britain and Northern Ireland, and the Council of the European Union v. Yassin Abdullah Kadi*, Joined Cases C-584/10 P, C-593/10 P and C-595/10 P, Judgment of the Court (Grand Chamber), 18.07.2013 (*Kadi* – 4 or *Kadi CJEU II*).

concerned must be subject to restrictive measures, including the evidence upon which the basis of the impugned decision rests.[61] It is the task of the competent EU authority to establish that these reasons are well founded. It is not the task of that person to adduce evidence of the negative, that those reasons are not well founded.[62]

Overriding considerations pertaining to the security of the EU, the ECJ stated that undisclosed information cannot under any circumstances constitute a ground for any claim of secrecy, confidentiality of information or of evidence which may prevent the EU Courts from considering it.[63] In Mr Kadi's case, the EU authorities had disclosed all the information they had received from the UN Sanctions Committee, that is the summary of reasons, but they could not justify them by any evidence.

This standard of review is to be applied as long as the UN cannot grand full judicial protection, hereby stating that any *ex officio* review set up with the UN Sanctions Committee or the newly established UN Ombudsperson procedure is not sufficient. According to the Court,

> [t]he essence of effective judicial protection must be that it should enable the person concerned to obtain a declaration from a court, by means of a judgment ordering annulment whereby the contested measure is retroactively erased from the legal order and is deemed never to have existed, that the listing of his name, or the continued listing of his name, on the list concerned was vitiated by illegality, the recognition of which may re-establish the reputation of that person or constitute for him a form of reparation for the non-material harm he has suffered.[64]

Eventually, the UN Sanctions Committee deleted Al Barakaat's Swedish branch from the list,[65] and all other Al Barakaat branches on 21 February 2012.[66] In October 2012, it removed Mr Kadi's name from its list.[67] The judicial challenges to the implementation to UNSCR 1267 have certainly played a role in the changes that the Sanctions Committee has implemented to its own listing and

61 *Kadi – 4* (*Kadi CJEU II*) [97] [111] [116].

62 *Kadi – 4* (*Kadi CJEU II*)[121].

63 *Kadi – 4* (*Kadi CJEU II*)[125].

64 *Kadi – 4* (*Kadi CJEU II*) [134].

65 Öhlén (2009).

66 UN Press Release (2012).

67 Analytical Support and Sanctions Implementation Monitoring Team (2012), Annex I, p. 31.

de-listing procedure. However, much still needs to be done before fundamental rights, as defined in the EU legal order, are respected by the UN Sanctions Committee.[68]

5.4.2.1.1 *Other Jurisdictions*

Canada: Other national jurisdictions have followed the approach taken by the European Court of Justice. They have declared themselves competent to review national laws implementing UNSCR 1267.[69] They have held the Sanctions Committee's system of listing to be incompatible with the fundamental right to effective review before an independent and impartial court.[70] This is reflected in the case of the Canadian Federal Court in *Abdelrazik v Canada*.[71]

The UK courts have been more cautious. The England and Wales High Court annulled several assets freezing decisions of HM Treasury.[72] They were found to be *ultra vires*, mainly because the Treasury took its decisions on the basis of the *United Nations Act 1946* which according to the majority was never intended by Parliament to impose such draconian measures.[73] It suggests that were a decision by the Australian Minister to be brought before a court, a similar decision would not be warranted given the recent Parliamentary scrutiny before the adoption of the amended version of COTUNA. However the High Court also held that the principle of legality requires that general or ambiguous statutory words should not be interpreted in a manner that infringes fundamental rights.[74] A similar view is held by Finn J.[75] Consequently, unless the Act clearly states that natural justice should not be observed, the principle of fair trial should prevail.

68 See also the comments of Andersson, Cameron, Nordback (2003).

69 *R. v. Khawaja* [2006] O.J. N°4245; 2006 ON.C. LEXIS 4158, Judgment of 24 October 2006.

70 *A, K, M, Q & G v. HM Treasury* [2008] EWCA Civ 1187 [152]. For a discussion of court cases, see Tzanakopoulos (2011) especially pp. 131–137.

71 *Abdelrazik v The Minister of Foreign Affairs* [2009] FC 580 [51]. Judgment of the Federal Court of Canada, 04.06.2009.

72 For instance in *A, K, M, Q & G v. HM Treasury* [2008] EWHC 869 (Admin) (24 April 2008); *A, K, M, Q & G v. HM Treasury* [2008] EWCA Civ 1187 (30 October 2008). Confirmed on appeal *A, K and M v HM Treasury* [2010] UKSC 2. *Hay v HM Treasury* [2009] EWHC 1677 (Admin) (10.07.2009). *HM Treasury v Mohammed Jabar Ahmed and others (FC); HM Treasury v Mohammed al-Ghabra (FC); R (Hani El Sayed Sabaei Youssef) v HM Treasury* [2010] UKSC 2 (SC). For a discussion of these cases see Hooper (2012). Johnston, Nanopoulos (2010), pp. 217–220.

73 *A, K and M v HM Treasury* [2010] UKSC 2 [183–186].

74 A & Ors v HM Treasury [2008] EWCA Civ 1187 (30.10.2008) [45] and [46].

75 In *State of South Australia v Slipper* (2004) 136 FCR 259 [279–280].

5.4.2.1.2 *Under the ICCPR*

In *Nabil Sayadi and Patricia Vinck v Belgium*,[76] the UN Human Rights Committee (UNHRC) held that it was competent to rule on communications from individuals who claim to be victims of a violation of any of the rights set forth in the Covenant, and who are subject to the jurisdiction of a State party, even when it regards the compatibility with the Covenant of the national measures taken to implement a UNSCR.[77]

The facts of the case are as follows: On October 2002, the Global Relief Foundation, an American Muslim charity, was put on the UN sanctions list. Sayadi and Vinck (the authors), both Belgian nationals, were the director and secretary of the European branch of the American association. In November 2002, the Belgian authorities communicated this information to the Sanctions Committee. The authors' names were put on the UN Consolidated List in January 2003, and subsequently on the EU list. A Belgian criminal investigation against them was eventually discontinued but their names remained listed. The UNHRC also noted that other States had branches of the American association on their territory, and they did not report the administrators' names to the Sanctions Committee. The UNHRC concluded that

> Article 103 of the Charter does not override the illegality of violations of the Covenant. Article 103 does not exempt a State that gives Charter obligations precedence over other international obligations from its international responsibilities, and it is not a ground for precluding the wrongfulness of an act in the form of a violation of an obligation not contained in the Charter.[78]

It was the first time that a UN Committee, specially set up to overview the implementation by Member States of human rights obligations, found that national law taken pursuant to UNSCR was in breach of the Covenant. It indirectly put in the limelight the legitimacy of Security Council sanctions in regard to human rights. The UNHRC established the responsibility of the State for putting the authors on the Consolidated list on the basis of incorrect information. The Committee declared that the authors' rights to travel freely

76 *Nabil Sayadi and Patricia Vinck v Belgium*, Communication N°1472/2006, U.N. Doc. CCPR/C/94/D/1472/2006, 22 October 2008.

77 *Nabil Sayadi and Patricia Vinck v Belgium*, 10.6.

78 *Nabil Sayadi and Patricia Vinck v Belgium*, 5.8.

had been breached and their honour and reputation unlawfully attacked by the dissemination of personal information following their listing by the Sanctions Committee, given the negative association that can been inferred from it.[79]

In July 2009, Sayadi and Vinck's names were removed from the Consolidated list and the EU list. The Belgian authorities, arguing a lack of legal basis, declined Sayadi and Vinck's request for compensation.[80] This should not be the case under COTUNA.

By deciding to refer their case to the UNHRC rather than the European Court of Human Rights (ECtHR), Sayadi and Vinck undoubtedly contributed significantly towards the cause of human rights within the Sanctions Committee, considering that a ruling of the UNHRC arguably carries more weight in the UN than a ruling by the ECtHR or the ECJ. Nevertheless, this exercise could have been prevented had the Sanctions Committee taken anti-terrorism measures consistent with human rights, from the onset, and ensured that its decisions were based on correct information.[81]

Mansour Leghaei et al. v Australia: This decision is sure to set a precedent, particularly for those who cannot access the ECJ or the ECtHR to seek redress. Non-European residents of States who are Party to the ICCPR, such as Australia, may now be inclined to petition the UN Human Rights Committee. Such was the case in a related issue. Mansour Leghaei, an Iranian Australian resident had his request for permanent residency declined on security grounds but was never given the reason for the decision. On appeal, the Federal Court noted that whereas Australian citizens (or permanent residents) who are the subject of an adverse security assessment are ordinarily entitled to notification of that fact and to a statement of reasons, the other residents have no right to receive such a statement, nor indeed any statutory right to be notified of the assessment; further, national security concerns override any duty to afford procedural fairness. In any case, the court found that, in the main, courts are "ill-equipped to evaluate intelligence".[82]

In April 2015, the UNHRC found that Australia's procedure lacked due process of law.[83] It found that Australia had breached its obligation under the

---

79 *Nabil Sayadi and Patricia Vinck v Belgium*, 10.7, 10.12.

80 Wille (2009). However, Cameron held that under the then EC Treaty, the Council would be liable for compensation. See Cameron (2003a), p. 213, and note 140.

81 Flauss (2010), pp. 378 and 382.

82 *Leghaei v. Director General of Security* [2005] FCA 1576, [70] and [84].

83 *Mansour Leghaei et al. v Australia*, Communication N°1937/2010, U.N. Doc. CCPR/C113/D/1937/2010, 28 April 2015.

ICCPR and arbitrarily interfered with Leghaei's family life by forcing him to leave the country after having lived there legally for 16 years. It concluded that Australia must "provide the author with an effective and appropriate remedy, including a meaningful opportunity to challenge the refusal to grant him a permanent visa; and compensation". Australia is also under an obligation to prevent similar violations in the future.

5.4.2.2 Case Study: UNSCR 1373 – *OMPI / PMOI*

UNSCR 1373 makes it mandatory to Member States to draw their own list of terrorists and terrorist organisations in order to freeze their assets. To ensure Member States' compliance, the UN Security Council established the Counter-Terrorism Committee (CTC). In order to implement UNSCR 1373, the EU has issued a list under Regulation 2580 (2001).[84] This list contains the name of persons who commit, or attempt to commit, terrorist acts or who participate in, or facilitate, the commission of terrorist acts, as well as groups and entities owned or controlled directly or indirectly by such persons, but not the names of those in the Al Qaida and associates list. In the EU, it is incumbent on the Member States to establish their own list of organisations and individuals that must be subject to the freezing requirements. Consequently, the EU list cohabits with the list of each EU Member State. In contrast with COTUNA and the Code, the EU list is not based on the sole appreciation of one person but follows a specified procedure:

> The list (…) shall be drawn up on the basis of precise information or material in the relevant file which indicates that a decision has been taken by a competent authority in respect of the persons, groups and entities concerned (…) based on serious and credible evidence or clues, or condemnation for such deeds. (…).
>
> For the purposes of this paragraph "competent authority" shall mean a judicial authority, or, where judicial authorities have no competence in the area covered by this paragraph, an equivalent competent authority in that area.[85]

84 Council Regulation (EC) No.2580/2001 of 27 December 2001 on specific restrictive measures directed against certain persons and entities with a view to combating terrorism, p. 70.

85 Art.1.4, Common Position 2001/931/PESC.

The names of persons and entities on the EU list are added on proposals by Member States and are reviewed at least every 6 months.[86] This list has an intra-European ("internal use") dimension.[87] It is meant to facilitate the work of the financial sector to identify which assets to freeze. It prohibits financial services with those listed. In a similar way to COTUNA, it is not restricted to terrorist organisations but also includes individuals. At national level, the administrative side of the "black list" may be coupled with measures of a criminal nature, and be used as a base for a proscription regime. The EU procedure has been scrutinised by the ECJ in *OMPI/PMOI*.

5.4.2.2.1. *OMPI* (*Organisation des Modjahedines du peuple d'Iran*)

In brief, the facts of *OMPI* (Organisation des Modjahedines du peuple d'Iran) are as follows: the People's Mojahedin Organisation of Iran (PMOI), founded in 1965, is an Iranian opposition movement. It aimed at replacing the Shah of Iran and subsequently the Mullahs' regime by democracy. It had several branches, including the National Council of Resistance of Iran (NCRI), a body defining itself as the "parliament in exile of the Iranian resistance" and a military wing operating inside Iran. The PMOI alleged that it has expressly renounced all military activity since June 2001. On 28 March 2001, the UK put the PMOI on its list of organisations proscribed under the *Terrorism Act* 2000. The PMOI was not on the EU's initial list pursuant to UNSCR 1371, but was added on 2 May 2002 and maintained in the subsequent lists. In Australia, the Minister for Foreign Affairs has listed the PMOI on 21 December 2001 (Consolidated list). It has never been listed as a terrorist organisation under the Code.

In 2001, the PMOI asked the Home Secretary to remove its name from the proscribed organisations list but he refused. The PMOI then lodged an appeal to the Proscribed Organisations Appeal Commission (POAC), which was dismissed in 2002, on the ground that "there was no requirement to hear the applicant's views beforehand, such a hearing being impractical or undesirable in the context of legislation directed against terrorist organisations".[88]

The PMOI brought its case to the European Court of Justice (ECJ) to have its name removed from the EU list. The Court of First Instance (CFI) found that the contested decision was adopted in the course of a procedure during which the applicants' right to a fair hearing was not observed. Further, the decision did not contain a sufficient statement of reasons which precluded the Court

---

86 For more about the listing process within the Council see Cameron (2003 b), pp. 225–256.

87 *European Parliament v Council of the European Union*, 19.07.2012, points 17 and 20.

88 *Organisation des Modjahedines du peuple d'Iran* v. *Council*, Case T-228/02, Judgment of the Court of First Instance (Second Chamber), 12 December 2006 (thereafter *OMPI CFI – 1*) [16].

from reviewing the lawfulness of that decision. Consequently the decision was annulled in December 2006 (*OMPI CFI – 1*).[89]

In 2006, the PMOI lodged another appeal to the POAC. A year after *OMPI CFI – 1*, the POAC ordered the Home Secretary to remove the PMOI from the proscribed terrorist organisations list.[90] It gave its decision after having conducted a thorough review and had access to classified information. It found that the Home Secretary's decision was "properly characterised as perverse".[91] His subsequent appeal was denied[92] and the PMOI's name was removed from the list on 23 June 2008, with the approval of both Houses of Parliament.

After *OMPI CFI – 1*, the EU took a new decision and maintained the PMOI on its subsequent listings, alleging new elements. On 16 July 2007, the PMOI appealed and the CFI annulled the contested EU decision on 27 December 2008 (*PMOI CF1 – 2*).[93] France's appeal against this decision was rejected (*PMOI GC – 3*).[94] The PMOI's name was removed from the EU's list in January 2009. The USA did the same in 2012.[95] Eventually, the Council issued new guidelines regarding the listing procedure. The listing of PMOI's name was fraught with controversy amidst political and diplomatic considerations in the context of negotiations with Iran regarding its nuclear development. It was alleged that France left the name on the EU list to give the Americans a bargaining chip in their negotiations with Iran, as they wanted the PMOI to remain listed. However, the POAC and the CFI found that these allegations were not supported by objective evidence.[96]

The PMOI cases highlight some important procedural points. The Council must observe the right to a fair hearing of the parties concerned when they act with a view to giving effect to UNSCR 1373.[97] The CFI noted that the Regulation

89 *OMPI CFI – 1* [2], [12], [16], [18], [173], [174].

90 *Lord Alton of Liverpool & Others (In the Matter of The People's Mojahadeen Organisation of Iran) v Secretary of State for the Home Department,* Proscribed Organisations Appeal Commission (POAC), Appeal No: PC/02/2006, 30th November 2007, (PMOI POAC-1) [362].

91 PMOI-POAC [360].

92 *Secretary of State for the Home Department v Lord Alton of Liverpool & Others (In the Matter of The People's Mojahadeen Organisation of Iran),* The supreme court of judicature Court of Appeal, [2008] EWCA Civ 443, 07.05.2008 (PMOI-POAC-2).

93 *People's Mojahedin Organization of Iran* v *Council of the European Union,* Case T-256/ 07, Judgment of the Court of First Instance (Seventh Chamber), 23.10.2008, (*PMOI CFI – 2*).

94 *French Republic v People's Mojahedin Organization of Iran,* Case C-27/09 P, Judgment of the Court (Grand Chamber) of 21.12.2011, (PMOI GC-3).

95 Lemonde.fr with AFP (2009). Lemonde.fr with AFP (2012).

96 *PMOI CFI – 2* [152]. Conference Internationale des Juristes (2004), p. 5. See also Casaca (2002), Question Écrite E-2531/02 posée par Paulo Casaca (PSE) au Conseil (11 September 2002) (2003/C 155 E/031).

97 *OMPI CFI – 1* [170].

did not provide for any procedure for notification of the evidence adduced or for a hearing of the parties concerned. In *OMPI CFI – 1*, the CFI made fundamental distinctions between the initial listing and the subsequent ones. It also made some important comments regarding the statement of reasons.

(a) The CFI made a marked distinction between the initial decision to list and the subsequent decision to maintain the listing. When the initial decision is taken, it is essential to ensure a surprise effect to preclude the prior disposal of funds. Hence the competent authority is under no obligation to give prior information about its intention to freeze funds. However, after the adoption of the initial decision to freeze funds, notification, including evidence, must be given either concurrently or as soon as possible. The notification must state the reasons for the Council's decision, in particular why it considers, in the exercise of its discretion, that such a measure had to be adopted in respect of the party concerned. Once the funds are frozen, it is no longer necessary to ensure a surprise effect in order to guarantee the effectiveness of the sanctions. It follows that any subsequent decision must be preceded by the possibility of a further hearing and, where appropriate, notification of any new evidence. The party must be heard in any case even if he has not expressly requested it.[98]

(b) The Court of First Instance clearly stated the paramount importance of Community institutions giving comprehensive reasons for decisions so that first, the persons concerned are correctly informed and can ascertain whether or not the decision is well founded; secondly to enable the Community judicature to exercise its power to review the lawfulness of the decision.[99]

When the EU's decision is based on a national decision (in this case the UK), it is essential that it has been taken by a competent authority after a fair hearing where the applicant can *effectively* make known his view.[100] The ECJ recognises that there are instances when some information may be withheld, such as in matters of public policy, public security or the maintenance of international relations. However, in the particular case of the freezing of assets, the CFI held that

> review is all the more imperative because it constitutes the only procedural safeguard ensuring that a fair balance is struck between the need to combat international terrorism and the protection of fundamental rights. [...] The Community Courts must be able to review the lawfulness and merits of the measures to freeze funds without it being possible to

98 *OMPI CFI – 1* [120], [126], [129], [131], [132], [139], [146].

99 *OMPI CFI – 1* [89].

100 *OMPI CFI – 1* [119]. See also *OMPI CFI – 2* [145].

raise objections that the evidence and information used by the Council is secret or confidential.[101]

The CFI specified that statements of reasons must be specific and reflect a sufficient level of scrutiny to allow the CFI to assess if the rule of law has been observed. A subsequent decision to freeze funds may not consist merely of a general, stereotypical formulation. A failure to state the reasons cannot be remedied by the fact that the person concerned learns the reasons for the act during the proceedings before the Community Courts.[102]

The UK removed the PMOI from its list in 2008. In January 2009, the PMOI was the first organisation to be removed from the EU list. The USA did the same on 21 September 2012, followed by Canada on 20 December 2012. In Australia, MPs have called for its delisting.[103] The PMOI was removed from Australia's *Consolidated List* after 25 November 2016.

5.4.3 Lessons from *Kadi* and *OMPI/PMOI*

The listing/de-listing process under EU legislation contrasts significantly with the Code's, which is characterised by the absence of representatives of the organisations concerned in the process and the lack of procedural fairness in general. In Australia, whether under the Code or COTUNA,[104] the listing/proscription process remains on the whole confidential and rests solely on the executive's discretion provided that the very broad legal requirements are met. This opens the door to considerable uncertainty, inconsistent application,[105] and possible discrimination. Several academics have criticised the present focus of law enforcement agencies on Islamic organisations, calling it discriminatory.[106] However, the laws do not target the Islamic community. Nevertheless, these comments highlight the effect of the legislation's breadth as well as the large margin of appreciation bestowed on law enforcement

101 *OMPI CFI – 1* [155]. This is supported by ECtHR in *A. and Others v. The United Kingdom*, Application n°3455/05, Judgment of 19 February 2009, [224] and *Kadi* – 3 (*Kadi GC II*), [174]. See also*OMPI CFI – 1* [159].

102 *OMPI CFI – 1* [139], [143], [151]; See *Kadi* – 3 (*Kadi GC II*) [176].

103 Thomson (2010), p. 1727. Thomson (2012), p. 943. See British Senate (Notice Paper N°153 [Senate Notice Papers] General Business, Notice given 21.06.2004).

104 The *Autonomous Sanctions Act* 2011 is not discussed here for it is not directly part of the anti-terrorism apparatus, but the remarks made here regarding COTUNA would apply *mutatis mutandis*.

105 Federation of Community Legal Centres (2006), p. 24.

106 Sheller (2006), point 8.23. Carne (2008), p. 41. Lynch, McGarrity, Williams (2009), p. 14.

agencies which are inclined to target the group that is today perceived, rightly or not, to constitute the biggest threat to the security of Australia. In the past, the group was the communist party. Today, it is the Islamic fundamentalists. Given that the FBI has recently declared that cyber attacks have supplanted Islamic terrorism as the top security threat and the close relationship between Australia's and US' agencies, in the future it could be the hackers,[107] or nationalist movements.

The lack of proper review contrasts with the European law. Furthermore, the PJC-IS's and SLRC's proposals for improving the present review process, though going a long way to remedy the unfairness of the system, fall below the ECJ benchmark for a process respectful of fundamental rights.[108] Such large powers bestowed on one person require a transparent decision process and a fair review mechanism. In 2008, the then Minister for Immigration, Chris Evans, called for a change:

> I have formed the view that I have too much power, in terms of the power given to the minister to make decisions about individual cases. (…) I'm uncomfortable with that, not just because of concern about playing God, but also because of the lack of transparency and accountability for those decisions.[109]

To remedy this situation, lessons could be drawn from the jurisprudence of *OMPI*. In order to ensure the surprise effect of the freezing order and its worldwide application, the Minister remains obliged pursuant to UNSCR 1267 to list that person in Australia, at least unless he knows that the listing is unjustified. Once the listing has been made, the Minister has the latitude to delist when he considers that it is no more necessary. Arguably, it is no more necessary when the person's name has been removed from the UN Consolidated List. It is also no more necessary, it is submitted, when the person is not involved in terrorist activities, or in other words, when the listing is found to be unjustified following a review or judicial process.

COTUNA does not make allowance for such a process. It even does not provide for the person concerned to be heard, either before the decision is taken (which is in line with *Kadi*) or afterwards, nor even to be informed. This contrasts with the recommendations of the Federal Court of Australia (FCA)

---

107 See Hosenball, Zengerle (2013). Bussard (2013).

108 Sheller (2006), pp. 85–86 and 99–100. SS 4, 5 and 6. For a discussion of the greater intensity of judicial review in the UK, see Roos, Hayward, Morss (2010–2011), p. 106.

109 Evans (2008).

which require that the owner of the assets be heard as early as possible when a freezing order is issued.[110] It is the FCA's view that a freezing order is a serious measure because it can restrict the right to deal with assets, and is commonly granted without notice. Consequently, it should be viewed as an extraordinary interim remedy, and a proper review of the Minister's decision should be conducted as early as possible.

COTUNA provides that a listed person or entity may ask the Minister to revoke the Australian listing. Giving the power to de-list to the one who took the initial decision undermines the objectivity of both the listing and de-listing process.[111] The only available recourse for review is under the *Administrative Decisions (Judicial Review) Act 1977* (Cth) (ADJR Act) which is limited to the legality of the procedure. Under COTUNA, there is no procedure laid down for an independent review on merit that would go near satisfying the requirements spelt out in *Kadi*. The pre-eminence of the executive power under Australia's anti-terrorism legislation weakens the democratic mechanism underlying the principle of the separation of powers.[112]

Finally, it is worth noting that Australia's legislature recognises that assets may be frozen "wrongly". Under COTUNA, owners of assets, or their holders, who suffered a loss as a result of their assets being wrongly frozen may seek compensation from the Commonwealth. For example, if a bank freezes the funds in a person's account in the mistaken but honest belief that the person is a proscribed person or entity, that person may be entitled to compensation from the Commonwealth for any loss he or she suffers as a result. In any case, this provision intends to protect the financial institutions when they act in compliance, or purported compliance, with UNSCR 1373. It does not suggest that a listing could be unwarranted. No indication is provided as to what constitute "wrongly" except that it excludes action done in good faith and without negligence. Under COTUNA, there is no compensation for damage to reputation for a "wrong" listing.

The severity and the lasting effect of the administrative nature of the ministerial decision under COTUNA make it akin to a penal decision. It is therefore proposed that regulations be made to ensure not only that procedural fairness be guaranteed,[113] but also that an effective review of its merit be undertaken, at least before the listing is subject to renewal.

110 Federal Court of Australia, *Practice Note CM 9*, Freezing Orders (Also known as "Mareva Orders" or "Asset Preservation Orders").

111 McGarrity (2008), p. 49.

112 See Eckes (2011).

113 Tully (2010), p. 58.

5.5 Effects of the Listings

The consequences of being listed or proscribed are severe. Once an organisation or an individual has been listed, their assets are frozen and it becomes a criminal offence to deal with their assets or to make assets available to them. These measures are meant to restrict the flow of funds to and from the organisations and individuals listed. The social stigma attached to being listed is compounded by social isolation imposed in practice by proscription.[114] This social exclusion is meant to prevent the organisation from spreading and hence reduces its capabilities. However, when these measures are not warranted, they besmirch one's reputation by implying that the individual or entity in question is associated with terrorists or worse is a terrorist.[115]

In addition, in Australia, once proscribed, individuals connected with that organisation become liable to prosecution for one of the derivative offences. The mere presence of an organisation on the proscription list carries the irrefragable presumption that it is a terrorist organisation. For instance, a person's involvement with a terrorist organisation (whether it has been listed, proscribed or found to be so by a court) entitles the Minister of Immigration to refuse him or her a visa, even if that person has not taken part in any terrorist activities.[116] This was the case of Dr Haneef who saw his Australian visa cancelled after he was charged with assisting an organisation, reckless to the fact that it was a terrorist organisation. The criminal charge was dropped after it was discovered that it was groundless. The decision of the Minister for Immigration was found invalid,[117] which was confirmed on appeal.[118] Spender J held that there should be a nexus between the defendant and the criminal activity of the other person, group or organisation.[119]

Given the harsh and enduring consequences of the listing, some have equalled the so-called precautionary measures to penal sanctions.[120] The ECJ has questioned their preventative and temporary aspect, particularly when they are imposed for a long period of time,[121] and so has the UN High

114 *Nada v Switzerland* (Application 1059/08), Judgment of Grand Chamber, 12.09.2012 [38].

115 Marty (2007), point 26. See also Cameron (2006a), pp. 10, 11.

116 Ss 501.1(a) and 6(b), *Migration Act 1958*. See Harris Rimmer (2008), pp. 12, 13.

117 *Haneef v Minister for Immigration and Citizenship* [2007] FCA 1273. See also Clarke (2008).

118 *Minister for Immigration & Citizenship v Haneef* [2007] FCAFC 203.

119 *Haneef v Minister for Immigration and Citizenship* [2007] FCA 1273 [188].

120 See also Analytical Support and Sanctions Implementation Monitoring Team (2009), point 34. See also *Kadi* – 3 [60] and [192].

121 *Kadi* – 3 [149,150].

Commissioner for Human Rights.[122] The Australian Government does admit that freezing of assets under the *Autonomous Sanctions Act 2011* is of penal character[123] though it may serve a preventative design. The same may be said for the listing under COTUNA. COTUNA provides for some exceptions to this hardship. This contrasts with the Code, under which disallowments are for the payment of legal representation in proceedings relating a terrorist organisations offence and for assistance for the organisation to comply with a law of the Commonwealth or a State or Territory.

Under anti-terrorism legislation, the Ministers have been vested with considerable powers that have serious impact, not only on corporations, but also on individuals. This impact may be financial, when assets are frozen, or social, as people who usually associate with them refrain from contact for fear of criminal punishment. Given the penal effect of listing under a UNSCRs or proscription under the Code, a judicial review process respectful of fundamental rights is needed. Scrutiny by Parliament or votes cast by the electorate after a ministerial decision does little, if anything, to correct the wrong suffered by those unjustly subjected to these measures.

5.6 Conclusion

5.6.1 *Focus on Organisations*

Australia's anti-terrorism legislation was initially designed to target Al-Qaida and other large jihadist extremist organisations, their structures, financial capacities, then their fighters returning home to commit attacks on Australian soil. However, since the laws were passed, the terrorists' profile has changed. The AFP acknowledges that in Western countries the terrorist threat has increased, changing from primarily large-scale operations involving substantial, organised networks to smaller-scale lone actor style attacks.[124] Although jihadist extremist attacks account for the most serious forms of terrorist activities resulting in nearly all reported fatalities in Australia and Europe, there are more attacks carried out by separatists in Europe than jihadists.[125] There, according to Europol, the largest number of attacks in which a terrorist affiliation can be identified were carried out by left-wing and anarchist activists, with right-wing attacks, including xenophobic attacks (cf. London, 19 June 2017),

122 UN High Commissioner for Human Rights (2009), point 42.

123 Autonomous Sanctions Bill 2010, Explanatory Memorandum, p. 1.

124 AFP (2017).

125 EUROPOL (2016); EUROPOL (2017a).

attacks against refugees, asylum seekers and ethnic minorities are also steadily on the increase.[126]

In Australia, the present threat comes from lone wolves and home-grown activists, radicalised individuals claiming to act on behalf of a terrorist group, and less from persons coming back from overseas battle-fields. Similarly, a recent study analysing all "jihadist attacks" that took place in the US and Europe between June 2014 and June 2017.[127] It found that only 18% of the attackers were known to have previously been foreign terrorist fighters (FTFs) and that only 8% of the attacks were carried out by individuals acting under direct orders from the "Islamic State" leadership. It is expected that "individual jihad" would remain a strategic weapon at the hands of terrorist organisations to strike in "enemy land". Figures show that nearly two-thirds of those arrested in the EU under suspicion of terrorism were EU citizens (63%) with the majority born in the EU (58%).[128] Of the known "jihadist terrorists", only 5% were refugees and 6% were illegal immigrants. In Australia, the latest terrorist attacks were also committed predominantly by individuals who have made Australia their home. In New Zealand, the 2019 Christchurch massacre was perpetrated by an Australian holding white-supremacist views.

The change of the perpetrators' profile signals a change of terrorism funding with self-financing becoming more common over time. In contrast with large attacks planned by organisations, small cells and individual terrorists have relatively minor financial requirements. FTFs and their facilitation networks are predominantly self-funding (they tend to rely on their employment income, the support from family and friends, social welfare and/or bank loans). An analysis of the financing of 40 jihadi terrorist cells that have plotted attacks in Europe between 1994 to 2013 found that smaller cells are more likely to be self-financed, cells with FTFs are more likely to receive support from terrorist organizations abroad, and self-financed cells are more likely to execute attacks.[129] This results in the current trends that terror attacks are increasingly likely to be led by single or a few individuals rather than by a large organisation. The new radicalised terrorist cannot be detected with CTF legislation. Hence, the Code's emphasis on terrorist organisations may appear too restrictive. Furthermore, proscription may not facilitate the detection of terrorist activities, because it pushes the organisation underground. However, it does simplify the work of the prosecution. Once proscribed, the prosecution does not need to prove that the organisation is terrorist in nature. In addition, the grounds for proscription

126 EUROPOL (2017a), p. 10.

127 Vidino, Marone, Entenmann (2017).

128 EUROPOL (2016), pp. 31, 11.

129 Oftedal (2015), pp. 19–20.

cannot be challenged at trial. Under the Code, proscription is the starting point for a number of derivative offences, couched in very broad terms "to allow law enforcement agencies to address terrorism activity before substantive crimes are committed", eluding the requirements of inchoate offences.[130] Consequently, in jurisdictions where proscription has been introduced, there are increased calls for "de-proscription".[131]

5.6.2 *Breadth of Legislation*

The breadth of Australia's anti-terrorism legislation may provide the needed flexibility to adapt to changes. On the other hand, its reliance on considerable discretionary powers, first to list or proscribe terrorist organisations and then to prosecute,[132] is a cause of concern. By criminalising conduct that is very remotely associated with the commission of a terrorist act, the legislation does not prevent individuals who have no terrorist intent from being investigated and prosecuted. The fact that the way the courts have applied the legislation has alleviated the concerns of some[133] does not remove its intrinsic feature.

Although there is a clear need to act preventively against terrorism, the legislation's breadth is such that it does not offer sufficient guarantee of targeting the right individuals,[134] which in the long run could prove excessively costly to the tax-payers and inefficient in terms of security. Australia's terrorism strategy bestows on law enforcement officers unprecedented powers of appreciation in deciding what to investigate and what to ignore. The lack of strict legal criteria suggests that even a strong suspicion would be enough to warrant a listing under COTUNA or the Code. There is a danger of arbitrary profiling based on law enforcement's appreciation of the risk, which might be done on religious, national or even political lines.[135] In Saul's view, this risk is minimal because the officers focus on the violence and not the motive.[136] Unfortunately, this is not always the case.[137] Every now and then, cases do come to light where officers, because of prejudices, focused on certain types of extremists while ignoring others, with dire consequences. For instance, the German security authorities

130 Submission of the Commonwealth DPP (2006), quoted in the Sheller (2006), pp. 44, 45.
131 Walker (2018), p. 250.
132 See the opinion of Lord Hoffmann in *Home Secretary v AF* (N°3) [2009] UKHL 28 [70].
133 McGarrity (2010), p. 127.
134 Federation of Community Legal Centres (2006), p. 15.
135 Chadwick (1997), p. 330; Emerton (2007).
136 Saul (2007), pp. 34, 35.
137 De Schutter (2002), pp. 147, 148.

failed to investigate assassinations committed by a neo-Nazi group, allegedly because they were too focused on Islamism extremism.[138]

5.6.3 *Restricted Judicial Review*

The UN listing procedure is not transparent and offers no guarantee of impartiality. Names are listed on Member States' request and are only delisted by consensus. Initially, the individuals and organisations listed were not informed of the reasons for the listing and could not request a review or a delisting.[139] The many criticisms about the lack of judicial review for the listing under the UNSCRs prompted the creation of a working group focused on the human rights implications of counter-terrorism in 2008. Despite some changes, such as the service of an *ombudsperson*, the process remains an exclusively governmental and diplomatic procedure.[140] Tzanakopoulos argues that it is incumbent first and foremost on the Member States to ensure that legislation which implements the UNSCRs guarantees the rule of law.[141] The absence of due process at the UN level has been reflected in the domestic listing of UN Member States.

The lack of transparency and natural justice is the hallmark of the Australian proscription regimes under the Code and COTUNA. McGarrity and Williams argue in favour of executive proscription on the basis that "the executive branch of government is significantly more experienced than the judiciary in making policy-based decisions involving such a mix of political considerations",[142] highlighting thereby the political and subjective aspect of proscription regime, which contrasts with the appreciation of a judicial decision. However, lack of experience does not mean lack of competence. Furthermore, the point is not about the nature of policy-based decisions but about the decisions' compliance with fundamental rights and freedoms which a democratic government should uphold. Restricting judicial review is a door open to abuse of powers. In Europe, the judges of Strasbourg (ECtHR) and Luxembourg (ECJ) have reviewed AML/CTF laws and done it remarkably well despite those political and ideological considerations. They have set the frame in which security legislation can co-exist without infringement on fundamental rights. In Australia, when legislation allows the courts to review decisions, the judges also do so in a satisfactory manner, in the very limited legislative competence granted

138 Lemonde.fr with AFP & Reuters (2011), Lemonde.fr with Reuters (2011), Caldini (2011).

139 Fassbender (2006), pp. 3–32.

140 *Kadi – 1 or Kadi GC 1* [267]; *Kadi* – 3 [128].

141 Tzanakopoulos (2011).

142 McGarrity, Williams (2018), p. 219.

to them.[143] Given that the implementation of Australia's AML/CTF legislation may lead to substantial violations of fundamental rights and freedoms, Australian laws should also simultaneously offset this risk by the strengthening of the democratic state which the said legislation is allegedly meant to protect, and to minimise the risk associated with arbitrary decisions.

Some remarked that much of the material which led to the Australian Attorney-General's proscription decision is based on material that would be inadmissible in courts. In any event, they conclude that "the courts are not sufficiently resourced or experienced in intelligence-gathering to undertake this role".[144] This view contrasts with the one expressed by the PJC-IS. After examining Australian reviewing and delisting procedures, and the decisions of the ECJ, the Committee recommended that an external merit review of a decision to list a person, entity or asset under s15 of COTUNA should be made available in the Administrative Appeal Tribunal (AAT).[145] Currently, the AAT, in reviewing the nature of merits, is not to decide whether the decision was the correct or preferable one on the material before the decision-maker, but, rather, to determine whether the decision was the correct or preferable one on the material before the Tribunal.[146] Nevertheless, as part of its review, the AAT can access classified information, as ASIO deems appropriate, on a confidential basis, to make its decisions. The examination of the case law regarding the listing and de-listing process of organisations and individuals pursuant to UNSCRS 1267 and 1373 has shown that many have seen their assets frozen and have suffered travel restrictions without reason. To-date, legislation directed to Australia's security does not give the AAT leeway to consider the effect of the decisions on an individual's personal life.[147] Greater transparency – or rather, less opacity – in the decision making process to list a person or an organisation as well as larger review powers, are thus needed.

It should not be underestimated that uncertainty regarding the respect of principles of legality and the presumption of innocence may also restrain some States from granting mutual assistance and extradition to Australia. Arguably, the greatest concern lies with Australia's proscription regime as set in Division 102. There cannot be a fair trial if the material element of the offence, i.e. the

---

143 *CMHV and Director-General of Security and Minister for Foreign Affairs* [2017] AATA 1547 (22 September 2017).

144 McGarrity, Williams (2018), p. 220.

145 PJC-IS (2006), Rec 22.

146 *Drake v Minister for Immigration and Ethnic Affairs* (1979) 46 FLR 409 [589]; see also *CMHV and Director-General of Security and Minister for Foreign Affairs*, para.37.

147 *CMHV and Director-General of Security and Minister for Foreign Affairs*, para.43.

organisation is a terrorist organisation, cannot be challenged in court.[148] This is particularly concerning for offences that do not require an intention to facilitate, in one way or another, a terrorist act. Hence it would be advisable to either abolish the proscription regime or at least to amend the provisions so to allow the proscription to be challenged either in court during a trial, or before the trial. It is suggested that Australia's listing and delisting procedures should draw on the case law of the ECJ and the ECtHR.

5.6.4 *A Way Ahead*

The lack of due judicial process displays a blatant disregard for individuals and entities listed, a weak commitment to the democratic principles that anti-terrorism legislation is supposed to uphold and a poor management of resources towards an effective response to terrorist activities. Dick Marty, Council of Europe Committee on Legal Affairs and Human Rights rapporteur and former Swiss prosecutor observed:

> It is not the very principle of black lists which is in question: this may be a useful instrument in certain circumstances and, in any event, for a limited period of time. But it is unacceptable that no clear procedure is foreseen and the most elementary rights are thus violated. If one adds to this picture the practice of abductions ("extraordinary renditions"), of secret detention centres and the trivialisation of torture, this provides a worrying, devastating message: principles that are as fundamental as the rule of law and the protection of human rights are optional accessories applicable only in fair weather. Such an approach means nothing more and nothing less than handing the terrorists their first victory – to criminals who precisely wish to put into question the validity of our free and democratic societies and who intend to destroy the system.[149]

Putting individuals under such hardships, resulting from being put on a list on the basis of untested allegations, not only pays a disservice to the cause it is supposed to serve, it is also a great waste of resources. Keeping a large pool of suspects distracts law enforcement agents from pursuing the real terrorists, burdens the resources and eventually undermines the credibility of security agencies.[150] It is therefore essential, not only for human rights considerations, that allegations be fully tested in a process that upholds natural justice but also

148 Sheller (2006), point 10.32.

149 Marty (2007), point 93.

150 Marty (2008), point 17.

not to give grounds to terrorism. De Kerchove has observed that Al Qaida affiliates do not refer to the terrorists responsible of the 2005 Madrid bombing for they have been duly tried and sentenced, but they exalt the brothers in arms that are still detained by the USA in places such as Guantanamo, Abou Graib and Bagram prisons. In his view, it the lack of natural justice of the US regime that feeds Al Qaida's rhetoric and fight.[151]

It has been stated that the fight against terrorism should strike a right balance between the need for security and human rights.[152] In this perspective, fundamental rights often tend to be perceived as hindering the work of law enforcement agencies.[153] Others have argued that in order to strengthen the fight against terrorism which aims at bringing down a democratic society, it is imperative that the rule of law, on which basis our society is built, be upheld.[154] It is submitted further that respecting fundamental rights should be seen as essential to an effective management of resources in the struggle against terrorism, and any crimes, for that matter.[155] Upholding human rights in the face of serious danger is not an easy task. Serious danger is however no excuse for compromising the foundations of our democracies, particularly when the danger is about the survival of democracy itself, as the rhetoric goes. Therefore the way the ECJ has tackled the issues, after an initial somewhat tepid start, can be considered a very positive development. A Bill of Rights may contribute to address and reduce any reservations or objections regarding the breadth of Australia's terrorism legislation and the possible breach of fundamental principles such as legality, presumption of innocence and fair trial. Its absence actually compounds the concerns regarding Australia's anti-terrorism provisions.

151 De Kerchove (2012), p. 85.

152 Garrigos-Kerjan (2006), pp. 189–192. For a discussion on this issue see Zeldner (2005), pp. 507–533.

153 De Schutter (2002), p. 90.

154 Calamandrei (1981), Gil-Robles (2005).

155 Bronitt (2003b), p. 82.

CHAPTER 6

Appraising AML/CTF Legislation in the International Context

> Democracy secretes in itself forces that threaten it, and what is new today is that these forces are superior to those that attack it from outside. To fight and neutralise them is made even more difficult as they lay claim to the spirit of democracy and therefore appear to be legitimate.[1]
>
> TZVETAN TODOROV

6.1 Introduction

AML/CTF legislation illustrates a paradigm shift of enormous proportion. Fox commented that the implementation of AML legislation had triggered an extraordinary expansion of federal criminal law despite the Commonwealth not having plenary power of the criminal law of the nation.[2] AML/CTF legislation redefines the contours of criminality by redrawing the traditional understanding of crime and serious crime, in two ways in particular: by emphasising financial crime as being one of the most severe forms of criminality; and by criminalising under specific offences, which make a large use of recklessness as the mental element, conduct that was previously considered to be inchoate offences. Ashworth and Zedner have highlighted the preventative justice elements of the new provisions in an attempt to eliminate or mitigate risks of criminal behaviours.[3] This shift has challenged the traditional reactive paradigm of criminal law based on investigation and prosecution of past offences.

1 Todorov (2012), p. 13. "La démocratie sécrète en elle-même des forces qui la menacent, et la nouveauté de notre temps est que ces forces sont supérieures à celles qui l'attaquent du dehors. Les combattre et les neutraliser est d'autant plus difficile qu'elles se réclament à leur tour de l'esprit démocratique et possèdent donc l'apparence de la légitimité".

2 Fox (1998), p. 11.

3 Ashworth, Zedner (2012).

 | DOI:10.1163/9789004359109_007

In addition, AML/CTF legislation innovates new ways of enforcing legislation by bestowing unprecedented power to agencies and making the private sector a pivot in the fight against crime while restricting the appeal process and the rights of individuals, especially in the areas of property and privacy.

These changes appear to have been carried by a wave of political convenience but have rarely been questioned in terms of efficacy and their impact on democracy. This chapter therefore examines the rationale of extending AML apparatus to CTF and reflects on the meaning of theses changes for our present democratic system.

6.2 Questioning the Rationale of the AML/CTF Apparatus

6.2.1 *From Carpet-Bombing Legislation to Risk-Based Supervision*

The criminalisation of money laundering marks the shift from prosecuting individual members of a criminal organisation to attempting to deprive the organisation of its assets. The prevailing view of governments of industrial nations was that organised crime was a global threat not only to the development and stability of their own countries but to society as a whole. The AML regulations have been regarded as the "the most effective way of combating organised crime and transnational organised crime".[4] Making money laundering a criminal offence led to the confiscation of the profits of criminal organisations, a measure that was seen as having two effects: hampering the financing of these organisations' activities and preventing their stranglehold on the legal economies. Confiscation also diminishes the financial rewards of crime. As Stessens remarked, "this trend has led to the criminalisation of money laundering being seen as an instrument that can be used against any type of acquisitive crime".[5] The AML legislation which was designed initially against drug trafficking has been transposed first against organised crime, then against terrorism and weapons of mass destruction (WMD), and lately against economic warfare, arguably giving it its true justification.

Stessens rightly observed that "most legislators have opted for what could be described as the legal equivalent of carpet bombing: (almost) every activity that may be construed as being for the purpose of money laundering has been criminalised".[6] The more FATF's Recommendations were adapted to various methods of concealing the origin of ill-gotten assets, and extended to CTF and

4 Bassiouni, Vetere (1998), p. xlviii.

5 Stessens (2000), p. 117.

6 Stessens (2000), p. 126.

more recently to the financing of WMD, the more financial and non-financial institutions, and individuals alike were subjected to the AML/CTF regime. The extension of the AML scheme to the financing of terrorism and of the proliferation of WMD appears to have been done on the premise of political convenience rather than because it is an appropriate way to prevent these activities from occurring. The apparatus has not yielded the expected results and is very costly to maintain.

6.2.1.1 The Machinery Produces Poor Results

When AML legislation was introduced, it was considered the panacea to bring heads of criminal organisations to justice and hamper criminal activities. It was expected that a large number of heads of criminal groups and professional money launderers would be brought to justice. This has hardly been the case.[7] Few prosecutions have occurred as a direct result of a suspected transaction report. Despite AML having been implemented for nearly 30 years, organised crime is still flourishing. It has even diversified from drug trafficking to more lucrative activities like trafficking of human beings, which is now considered the fastest growing criminal business in the world. It is even considered that money laundering is increasing rather than declining.[8] In Australia, the money launderer is usually the predicate offender and not a professional money launderer.[9] This tends to indicate that those prosecuted were not involved in large criminal organisations. Commonwealth AML has not been effective in catching the "big fish" of organised crime. It appears that the historical case of Al Capone was the exception rather than the rule. Similarly, CTF regulations were to be the silver bullet against terrorism,[10] but the result has been disappointing. In 2017, it was revealed that since 2011 the Commonwealth Bank of Australia (CBA) had been in breached of the AML/CTF regulations, failing to monitor transactions on 778,370 accounts, failing to provide over 50,000 threshold transaction reports, failing to report suspicious transactions pertaining to money laundering, and allowing approximately $9.1m suspicious funds to be transferred to Hong Kong.[11] Further, it was alleged that the CBA failed to act even after a warning from the Australian federal police (AFP). The Australian Commonwealth Bank scandal begs the question of just how much oversight of the financial industry is actually taking place in practice.

---

7 Gurule (2008), p. 373; Warde (2007).

8 Unger (2013), p. 673.

9 FATF (2005b), 83, p. 28.

10 Jonsson, Cornell (2007), p. 76.

11 Theguardian.com (2017a); Theguardian.com (2017b); Letts (2017).

6.2.1.2 Two Strategies

The examination of the initial AML regulations reveals two different strategies: the first one, rooted in a mistrust towards financial institutions, does not give a large appreciation margin in its implementation; it leads to the systematic reporting of transactions over AUD 10,000. It has led to the creation of huge banks of data, which are both costly to analyse and in which it is almost impossible to find a substantial case of interest. According to Lindsey, principal economic adviser of candidate George W Bush, reports that banks had to fill out have a ratio of 25,000 reports to one case brought, and with 0.2 percent convictions.[12] Furthermore, prescriptive legislation must be constantly adapted to new money laundering techniques devised by criminals to defeating the system. The second strategy relies on the relevant industries' expertise in detecting whether a transaction or a service could be part of a money laundering scheme; it favours the reporting of suspicious transactions. It is more efficient than the threshold reporting model. Pieth and Aiolfi observed that

> [s]tatistics indicate that whilst there are relatively fewer notifications of suspicious transactions, they typically result in a criminal prosecution. An unusual transaction notification system would generate probably less than 5 per cent of criminal investigations, whereas the corresponding figure for a suspicion-based system could be well over 50 per cent.[13]

This regime however has two main drawbacks. Firstly, law enforcement tasks are extended to the private sector; and therefore it relies heavily on the ethics and training of the financial institutions' personnel. Consequently, great attention must be paid to the supervision of financial institutions to ensure that they comply with the regulations issued by the prudential supervisory authority. Secondly, the costs for these institutions are passed on to customers.

From the outset, Australia has adopted a dual reporting system of mandatory reporting of transactions above AUD 10,000 and of suspicious matter report / suspect transaction report (SMRS/SUSTRS) which leads to the production of a colossal amount of reports, over 44 million in 2010–11, of which less than 45,000 were reports on suspicious transactions.[14] In 2013–14, AUSTRAC received 90 million financial transactions and SMRS/SUSTRS, representing an increase of 360% from 2009. They resulted in 14 cases leading to terms of imprisonment.[15]

---

12 Lindsey (1999). Vlcek (2008), pp. 26–27.

13 Pieth, Aiolfi (2004), pp. xix and 18.

14 AUSTRAC (2011); Summary.

15 AUSTRAC (2014a), p. 8; AUSTRAC (2014c).

Regarding terrorism financing, in 2014–2015, there has been a 300% increase in SMRs/SUSTRs identifying suspicion of terrorism financing (118 reports) but no convictions.[16] In 2017–18, AUSTRAC received 136,225,100 reports from industry, among those were 4,087,000 SMRs/SUSTRs. Yet, despite this increase, there are still comparatively few convictions reported.[17] Of all reports transmitted, only a handful lead to a prosecution and even less to a conviction, which indicates that the system is not efficient in accurately detecting money laundering cases.[18] Australian authorities appear never to have questioned the cogency of its model.

6.2.1.3 Risk Minimisation

A balance should be kept between the burdens imposed on financial institutions and individuals and the real risk of money laundering. Monitoring should be done according to the principle of proportionality:[19] "The fact that pizzerias were involved in a well known money laundering case does not justify a requirement for the identification of all pizzerias' customers".[20] Although nearly twenty years ago Australian academics advocated some form of risk management,[21] the concept has only been introduced recently in Australian legislation. AUSTRAC defines risk management as the process of recognising risk and developing methods to both minimise and manage the risk.[22] Spurred on by the FATF, the Commonwealth Government introduced, in 2006, a risk-based approach to AML/CTF under which businesses are obliged to develop their own risk assessment and their own risk management strategy. In addition, enforcement still remains tainted with a prescriptive approach.[23] However, such assessment is "problematic when it comes to the threat of terrorism that is extremely difficult to quantify for individual financial institutions".[24] A 2012 Australian survey showed that the large majority of businesses estimated the risk of money laundering and terrorism financing (97.8% and 99.5% respectively) to be very low or non-existent.[25] In 2017, AUSTRAC estimated the risk overall as "medium" and "major" in the NPO sector.[26]

16 AUSTRAC (2015).
17 AUSTRAC (2018), p. 34.
18 FATF (2005b), 27–31, pp. 6, 8; FATF (2015), para.3.45. AUSTRAC (2018), p. 34. AUSTRAC's annual reports 2016–17 and 2017–18 do not provide figures on convictions.
19 European Economic and Social Committee (2006), 3.3.1. See also European Central Bank (2005), p. 113.
20 European Commission (1995), *Report*, point 4, p. 8.
21 Braithwaite (1993), p. 668; Fisse (1994), pp. 181; Fisse, Leonard (1997), pp. 22–25.
22 Austrac (undated).
23 FATF (2005b), para.18, 315 to 320.
24 Bures (2015), p. 226.
25 Walters, Smith, Davis, Choo, Chadwick (2012), pp. 70–71.
26 Austrac – ACNC (2017), pp. 9, 11.

To respect the essence of the new legislation, one would expect that the costs incurred by reporting entities in implementing the new legislation would be proportional to the risk within their industry of money laundering and terrorism financing. This appears not to be the case. For small entities, or those dealing with non-financial transactions, the initial risk assessment can be very costly.[27] Concerns have been raised that the government is underestimating the expected economic and practical cost of implementing the compliance programme.[28] McNeil rightly stated that "to be truly risk-based, the various requirements should be elective requirements applicable when circumstances warrant it".[29] However, recent Australian AML/CTF legislation is not seen as a revamp of previous policies but rather as an add-on of a new international principle.[30] It is still therefore predominantly prescriptive. Furthermore, the expected reduction of expenses which should have followed the introduction of a risk-based approach has been counteracted by a further extension of the AML/CTF apparatus. It is also presumed that most actors rely on a wide understanding of the precautionary principle and tend to over-report to avoid sanctions. This view was shared by the Council of Bars and Law Societies of Europe (CCBE). It expressed the concern that increasing the lists of detailed examples in the risk-based approach (RBA) guidelines was counter-productive as the "lists of examples will result in more reports, not because the transaction involved actually has a ML/TF risk, but merely because one is afraid that in retrospect it could be argued that a mistake has been made". Eventually, this would defeat the advantages of the RBA and bring back the rule-based "*ticking the box*" practice that the RBA was meant to replace.[31] Some have noted that the justification for imposing penalties on reporting entities for lack of compliance has not been substantiated by evidence showing that the lack of compliance facilitated money laundering.[32] Nevertheless, Australian legislation contains very harsh penalties, even for recklessness. Australian AML/CTF regime is amongst the most severe in the world.[33] Moreover, a lower civil standard of proof applies to some of these penalties. Under those circumstances, designated entities would be less inclined to take a risk of using the reduced procedures offered in the new scheme, for fear of being found later of not having been fully

27 Geary (2009b), pp. 15, 16.
28 Mark (2008), p. 6. LCA (2011).
29 McNeil (2007), p. 341.
30 McNeil (2007), p. 342.
31 CCBE (2011), para 7, p. 3.
32 McNeil (2007), p. 343; Geary (2009b), p. 13.
33 Allens Arthur Robinson (2006).

compliant with the law.[34] It follows that the paper flow may not be reduced. To make matters even more uncomfortable for these reporting entities, the AUSTRAC rules that permit a risk-based approach are expressed in mandatory language. As Geary puts it, "in essence, a risk-based approach must be used where permitted",[35] prompting Bures to comment that this had "further diminished the already dubious effectiveness of the CTF regime".[36]

Moving from lip-service to effective implementation of risk management would require a fundamental change of perspective. The examination of Commonwealth AML/CTF legislation has shown that Australia's Government is averse to taking risks. This is exemplified by the Code's criminalisation of dealing with money when there is a risk that the assets could have a criminal origin, or be used for the commission of a crime, a concept absent from the international money laundering definitions. AUSTRAC has defined risk as "the combination of the probability of an event and its consequences. In simple terms, risk can be seen as a combination of the chance that something may happen and the degree of damage or loss that may result if it does occur".[37] There is no weight given to any of these factors. Under these terms, the probability, though minimal, is never zero. Such a philosophy leads to an over-controlling society.[38] Based on ASIO's statement that "a terrorist attack is feasible and could well occur",[39] the precautionary principle requires Australia to establish, and maintain, an expensive CTF apparatus, even if by all accounts the probability of identifying, and preventing a fund transfer to finance terrorism is virtually nil. To sum up, too much emphasis has been put on the ability of the AML/CTF regime to prevent and prosecute criminal organisations and terrorists. So far there is no evidence that the data collected does more than confirm already on-going investigations. Traditional law enforcement has been arguably more effective in catching criminals than the AML/CTF regime. Budget allocation of security agencies should reflect this.

6.2.2 *A Costly Machinery*

The AML/CTF apparatus is expensive. The costs of implementation fall on private institutions whose costs are passed down to consumers, eventually affecting the overall economy.[40] It is also costly for security agencies.

34 Deloitte (2011), p. 286; Simonova (2011), p. 356; Unger, Van Waarden (2009), pp. 977–978.
35 Geary (2009a), p. 216.
36 Bures (2015), p. 226.
37 AUSTRAC (undated).
38 Dubuis (2011).
39 O'Sullivan (2007).
40 Sathye (2008).

AML/CTF requirements generate two types of costs for the private sector: First, the costs to those subjected to the legislation of complying with the AML/CTF regulations, including training the personnel, and secondly, the reporting costs. In 2006, a study prepared for the British Financial Services Authority (FSA) estimated the total cost of the administrative burdens imposed on the UK financial services industry by the rules in the FSA Handbook between GBP 440 and 660 million.[41] These costs impact on the domestic economy as they are passed on to consumers by way of increased borrowing costs and higher taxes.[42] From an early stage, the entities subjected to AML/CTF legislation have consistently voiced their objection to the regime given the high costs they have incurred. Whereas the Australian Government does not seem to have conducted even a simple cost-benefit analysis before introducing the new measures, the FSA commissioned a report to identify the cost/benefit implications of certain proposed changes, before deciding on what type of risk assessment and management to adopt.[43] Some hold the view that Australia does not give enough consideration to the costs of the new regulation to the regulated entities.[44] These concerns have been dismissed on the ground of public interest.[45] It seems that the costs of compliance are seen as a just impost for businesses that are perceived to make profits through conducting financial transactions.

In addition, there are the law enforcement agencies' costs of analysing the data. To analyse the data contained in the reports requires a large workforce. When introducing the suppression of the *Financing of Terrorism Bill 2002*, the government said there would be no direct financial impacts. However, it expected "a positive revenue outcome for the Commonwealth" with the enactment of the AML/CTF 2006.[46] Contrary to what was promised, confiscated assets that go into the State coffers are not sufficient to compensate the sums involved in running the AML/CTF machinery. In addition, the figures put forward can be misleading. The "street value" of the seized drug which is reported by official media may give a false sense of success. For instance, a drug trafficker was arrested and charged for importing 13 kilos of cocaine (street value close to AUD 1,3 million). However, he had to pay his overseas suppliers.

41 Real Assurance Risk Management Limited (2006), p. 5.

42 Sathye (2008), p. 349; Vlcek (2008), p. 28.

43 Pricewaterhouse Coopers LLP (2003).

44 Geary (2009b), p. 15; Sathye (2008).

45 Jack (1993), pp. x, xi; Sherman (1991), 4.133, p. 82.

46 *Anti-Money Laundering and Counter-Terrorism Financial Act 2006* / replacement Explanatory Memorandum, p. 3.

He was selling the drug for AUD 60 per gram to street sellers who resold it for AUD 100 per gram. The trafficker made a profit estimated to be AUD 240,000 between 2004 and 2011, which equates to a yearly income of about AUD 35,000, a far cry from the income generally attributed to illegal drug importers.[47] Consequently, after having initially underestimated its own costs of dealing with the system it was setting up, the Commonwealth Government decided to tackle the increased costs of running the AML/ACT apparatus by introducing the *Australian Transaction Reports and Analysis Centre Supervisory Cost Recovery Levy Act 2011* (AUSTRAC Levy Act), an "Act to impose a levy on persons regulated by the AUSTRAC". Its rationale is the following; since reporting entities provide services that are vulnerable to exploitation for money laundering and terrorism financing purposes, they have created the need for regulation by AUSTRAC. It is therefore "appropriate that industry meet the costs of regulatory systems that ensure the integrity of their operating environment". The objective of the levy is to ensure that AUSTRAC will recover the costs it incurs as a supervisory authority, its costs of supporting small business compliance, its legal costs for enforcing its decisions, as well as other administration costs. To maximise the income generated by the levy, the *AUSTRAC Supervisory Cost Recovery Levy (Consequential Amendments) Act* amended the AML/CTF Act and introduced compulsory enrolment for all reporting entities regulated by AUSTRAC. It was expected that the introduction of this legislative package would collect AUD 118.3 million over the period 2011–15.[48] Since 2016, AUSTRAC's activities as AML/CTF regulator and FIU are funded in full through by the industry contribution. Nevertheless, during the 2015–16 and 2016–17 financial years, AUSTRAC has produced a deficit of AUD 21.6 million in 2015–16 (total expenses AUD 85,639) and of AUD 8.7 million in 2016–17 (total expenses AUD 70,851).[49] The Australian Government's policy could not be more out of step with the conclusion of a European study on the benefits and costs of AML regulations which stated that

47 Maspoli (2012).

48 Australian Transaction Reports and Analysis Centre Supervisory Cost Recovery Levy Bill 2011, Australian Transaction Reports and Analysis Centre Supervisory Cost Recovery Levy (Collection) Bill 2011, Australian Transaction Reports and Analysis Centre Supervisory Cost Recovery Levy (Consequential Amendments) Bill 2011, Explanatory Memorandum.

49 AUSTRAC (2017), p. 71. For the first time, in 2017–18, AUSTRAC produced a net operating surplus of $2.2 million due to $4.9 million of unfunded depreciation and amortisation expenses (AUSTRAC (2018), p. 57).

> combating the ML must be beneficial at all the various levels that are potentially involved in the rather complex operation of dirty money. Designing incentive-compatible regulations – both at national and international levels – represent the future challenge in order to increase the economic and political feasibility of the proposed cost and benefit analysis.[50]

Under the Australian Government's perspective, financial institutions are not considered victims of criminals. By a strange twist, the need for AML/CTF legislation is laid on the reporting entities and no longer on the money launderers. Now, those who were previously considered to be "vulnerable" are to pay even if there is no evidence that their industry has been used for the purpose of money laundering or terrorism financing, and even if they do not directly benefit from the regulation. Fisse queried why financial institutions had to bear AML compliance costs and why they should not be spread:

> It is unclear why the social cost of improving suspect transaction controls against money laundering should be imposed mainly on financial institutions rather than spread more through general taxes in the same way as many countries spread the costs of improving stolen vehicle tracking systems or enhancing surveillance technology for detecting terrorists or plane hijackers.[51]

6.2.3 *Terrorism Financing, a Type of Money Laundering?*

Looking at the AML measures against organised crime, it is clear that the CTF provisions follow the same pattern. Money laundering was a new crime. Financing terrorism is a new criminalisation to the extent that terrorism is a new offence. The apparatus to track it down is not new since it is built into the AML system. Given the fundamental differences between money laundering and terrorism financing, it should not have been the case. The reason for the convergence may be found in the strong influence of the 2001 terror attacks on political authorities.

Before the events of 11 September 2001, experts were already examining the ways terrorist groups moved or concealed their funds in order to support their operations. The FATF had tried to establish if there were significant differences between the methods used by terrorists and those used by organised crime

50 Barone, Masciandaro (2008), p. 260.

51 Fisse (1994), p. 187.

groups. At the eve of the 11 September terrorist attacks, differences, if any, were not considered significant.

> Material discussed by the experts appeared to indicate that there is little difference, first, in the source of funding for both types of groups. Terrorists generate proceeds to support their activities through criminal activity (and sometimes from contributions or donations) in virtually the same way that organised crime does. The methods used for laundering funds in both cases are also virtually the same. Moreover, many countries consider that terrorist acts or even affiliations with such groups constitute a serious crime. There is no agreement on whether anti-money laundering laws could (or should) play a direct role in the fight against terrorism. Some countries, for example, are not able to use anti-money laundering legislation for tracking or restraining suspected terrorist money if the source of the funds was a voluntary contribution and not a criminal act. There are also differences between jurisdictions as to which groups are classified as terrorist organisations. Certain of the FATF experts were of the opinion that terrorist related money laundering is a distinct subcategory of money laundering. Others held the opposite view and believed that terrorism can be adequately targeted under existing laws.[52]

Considering that money laundering legislation does not appear to have managed to hamper the activities of organised crime significantly, it is astonishing that the AML measures should have been chosen as a blueprint for CTF. In their perceived need to be seen to be doing something substantial against terrorism, political authorities chose to quickly adopt what were considered to be persuasive measures the effects of which could not be disputed, at least by the non-experts. These measures include the freezing of assets controlled by alleged terrorist suspects. As Warde points out "[t]he financial terrain is particularly inviting to punitive warfare. It is impenetrable to most observers and in particular to the media, casualties are largely invisible, and political consequences only manifest themselves in the long term".[53]

The effects of the blacklisting of individuals and entities suspected of having a link with terrorist organisations has fallen short of the expectations raised by the politicians' rhetoric used to introduce them. So far, there has been "no independent evidence whatsoever that the black listing technique has any

52 FATF (2001), para.86, p. 28.

53 Warde (2007), p. xxii.

significance effect on limiting terrorist financing".[54] Some of those listed had no connection with the organisation to which they were allegedly connected, which led to the wrong assets being frozen and human rights violations for those thus deprived of their property. In cases where a review was possible, the (judicial) scrutiny has allowed shortening of the list of suspects by removing names of innocent parties. However, it is the task of law enforcement agents to ensure that only the right suspects are blacklisted in order to avoid overloading the machinery. Blacklisting is not an easy task. There are various factors which contribute for listing the wrong names. First, the authorities have relied on tips i.e. on unverified information or not immediately verifiable allegations to draw the blacklists. Secondly, given the transnational aspects of terrorism, foreign names, sometimes with multiple spellings must be transposed into English. For instance, in Australia and Europe, Al-Qaida is spelt usually with an i, while the US and the UN, it is spelt mainly with an e (Al-Qaeda). Also there is the occurrence of homonymy or erroneous transliteration of names. Hence, targeted individuals and entities might escape the controls due to minor variations in the names while others are wrongly listed or detained. All these shortcomings suggest that black listing is a political statement rather than an effective way to counter terrorism.[55]

The US Commission of inquiry on the September 2001 attacks concluded that in about every respect the funding of the attacks differed from the widely believed assertions. "No rogue states were involved. No charities, hawalas, Islamic banks, front companies, or rich Saudi merchants were involved. The amounts were small".[56] The two principal financial facilitators (a Pakistani and a Saudi) were identified as having wired most of the funds from the United Arab Emirates. The UNSC Recommendations regarding Bin Laden and Al Qaeda taken before 9/11 did not allow identifying any suspicious transactions. Furthermore, the allegations that Al-Qaida used gems to finance its activities or transport assets were never substantiated.[57]

> Ultimately, although the intelligence community devoted more resources to the issue and produced somewhat more intelligence, it remained difficult to distinguish al Qaeda's financial transactions among the vast

54 Cameron (2006), p. 80; Legrand (2018).
55 Legrand (2018), p. 363.
56 Warde (2007), pp. 169, 170.
57 Passas (2006), p. 286.

> sums moving in the international financial system. The CIA was not able to find or disrupt al Qaeda's money flows.[58]

Had the FATF Special Recommendations been enforced before 2000, they would not have red-flagged any of the hijackers' transactions.[59] Someone aptly commented that the "laws that target 100% of the population to control the behaviours of 0.001% are also seldom productive, not least because they tell the 0.001% how not to get caught".[60]

In the last 10 years or so, there has been a shift towards low-cost attacks. For instance, in the preparatory phases of the terrorist attacks in Paris in January, costs are estimated at EUR 25,000 and those on 13 November 2015 at about EUR 80,000.[61] The use of prepaid cards, electronic, online payment methods,[62] make these transactions difficult to trace with the result that the CTF scheme has been ineffective to prevent terror attacks. The FATF special Recommendations seem to have been engineered for a bygone type of terrorist organisation, if they were ever able to prevent the financing of terrorism. Moreover, in recent years different types of terrorists and terrorist attacks have emerged. Some of the perpetrators appear to only have an ideological link with a terrorist organisation. They have very little training, if any. They are radicalised very quickly, often through the internet. Many of them are not known by law enforcement authorities and are moving, "under the radar" so to speak. The current threat is posed by home-grown terrorists, franchisees, "lone wolves", and small cells, which require little financial means and, in many cases, are self-funding. No cross-border transactions are needed. Also in Australia, the FATF estimates the risk to be small-scale collection of funds, including legitimate assets, to either support Australians travelling abroad go the conflict zones or to finance domestic terrorist acts.[63] Consequently, it is not surprising that CTF measures have been so ineffective. Pre-emptive detection of terrorist activities through the CTF scheme has not occurred primarily because the funding of terrorism typically involves small and inconspicuous transactions and CTF relies on the AML mechanism which was set up to track large amounts of money. The lack of success of CTF measures is mostly due to the fact that they were not designed specifically against terrorism but were tailored for organised crime.

58 Kean, Hamilton (2004), p. 186.

59 Passas (2006), p. 283.

60 Warde (2007), p. 23.

61 Lemonde.Fr with AFP (2018).

62 EUROPOL (2016), p. 11.

63 FATF (2015), 4.5, p. 70.

It is suggested that not only is the "one size fits all" concept not very effective, it also proved to be a very expensive way of trying to address the terrorism threat.

To prevent the development of WMD, the UN SC had recommended initially border controls and the monitoring of shipments. The recent addition of the control of financial transactions may not yield better results than for CTF. Considering that trade is currently an opaque activity,[64] focusing on practical ways to make it more transparent is may be a far better way to identify and prevent suspicious shipments and transactions than the AML regime.

6.2.4 *A Different Approach Is Needed*

Not only has focusing on CTF measures been ineffective to prevent acts of terrorism, it is also very expensive. Considering that counter-terrorism activities have diverted law enforcement resources from the organised crime front to a sector that did not yield the expected results,[65] and that public resources are limited, a complete rethinking of the anti-terrorism strategy is required. In any case, the new strategies would need to be scrutinised so that their efficacy and cost-effectiveness can be objectively assessed. Hence, it would be advisable to develop AML/CTF system whose effects are measurable.[66] To that end, reliable data are needed. Strategies should be regularly assessed by independent bodies so as to ensure correct implementation and not the mere perpetuation of an ineffective system.

Criticisms of CTF legislation pertain to the incorrect underlying rationale and methodology which resulted in the extension of the AML machinery to CTF, as well as to the presumption that CTF would prevent acts of terrorism; they do not pertain to the rules regarding customers' identification (KYC) and data recording. Already in 2002, the FATF had warned that "it should be acknowledged [...] that financial institutions will probably be unable to detect terrorist financing as such". Consequently, "[i]t is the competent enforcement authority or the financial intelligence unit (FIU) [...] that is in a position to determine whether the transaction relates to a particular type of criminal or terrorist activity and decide on a course of action", not the financial institutions.[67]

Complex organised terrorist networks which require large amounts of money may use financial services. Those amounts should be detected with conventional AML regulations in the same manner as for other organisations. It follows that the transactions should be traceable to the payer. However, large

64 Passas (2006), p. 286.
65 Shelley, Picarelli (2005), p. 54.
66 Magnusson (2009), p. 111.
67 FATF (2002c), point 9, p. 3.

organisations like Al Qaida are likely to find means to finance the new type of terrorist attacks which require little financial means.[68] As Charles Calomiris points out: If an organisation can recruit "30 people willing to die on its behalf, it will have no problem getting 100 non-terrorists living in the US or in Europe to open a bank account on behalf of a terrorist friend".[69] In all likelihood, a State which wants to circumvent the UN SC financial sanctions to acquire or develop WMD will also have the means to do so. Therefore, the question that needs to be asked is what conceptual model is needed to ensure a correct "risk assessment" and "risk management" to prevent and detect money laundering, and if such a model would be applicable to terrorism and proliferation financing. Galland outlines an answer based on a study of various models.[70] Taking into account that criminals, whether money launderers or terrorists, have an ability to adapt themselves continuously to their enemy,[71] anticipative imagination is a better preventive tool than prescriptive rules.[72] Galland advocates that front line operators should be granted greater control and initiative, rather than being compelled to follow a set of rigid rules. Peretti-Watel concurs.[73] In order to be efficient, AML/CTF techniques must put human competence in the centre of the apparatus.[74] This requires time and the right to make mistakes as part of the learning process, which is precisely what Australian AML/CTF legislation tends to avoid. The best way to develop the capability to detect money laundering, or terrorist schemes, as well as their perpetrators, is not solely by increasing computer analysis, but also by giving a leeway to front line operators to fulfil their tasks. Fitzgerald even suggested that "in a risk-based controls system, businesses should not expect to face an enforcement action for every failure to identify or block a transaction with blacklisted party".[75]

Data recording should be used, not for analysing every single transaction, but to randomly monitor transactions,[76] and institutions. It has been suggested that moving away from mandatory thresholds for reporting transactions and focusing on mandatory reporting of *suspicious* transactions would allow resources of prosecution agencies to be used more effectively against money laundering. In addition, it might be judicious to concentrate on "high risk

68 Kean, Hamilton (2004), p. 172.

69 The Economist (2001).

70 Galland (2006), pp. 359–381.

71 Caneppele, Calderoni, Martocchia (2009), pp. 151–172; Harvey (2009), p. 98.

72 Galland (2006), pp. 372, 374.

73 Peretti-Watel (2006).

74 Galland (2006), pp. 359–381; Vlcek (2007), pp. 111, 112.

75 Fitzgerald (2007), p. 44.

76 Fisse, Leonard (1997).

professions" that are likely to be targeted for money laundering, while ensuring a sporadic monitoring of non-traditional financial institutions or professions.[77]

The emphasis on AML/CTF legislation, versus traditional law enforcement activities, may not only be due to a trend towards new technologies, but as Naylor suggests a shift to prosecute market-based crimes rather than predatory offences.[78] It could possibly also be explained by a more general inclination to value clerical work rather than hands-on jobs and paperwork rather than field work. As a result, the traditional work of law enforcement has been put aside. Nevertheless, it is through this painstaking and dangerous work in the field that Italy has scored its great successes against various criminal organisations.[79] It appears that the AML regime has played a very marginal role, at best, in the arrest of the heads of these organisations. In a similar way, it is the close cooperation between French and Spanish police that has brought about major successes against the Basque separatist movement (ETA), not the CTF regulations.[80] In Australia, drug trafficking has been curbed by the increasing amount of drugs seized, not by information provided from financial transaction reporting.[81] There is a risk that AML/CTF regime may have become a lazy and inefficient way out of the hard and effective work of law enforcement. If the dangers posed by organised crime are as claimed, then it is imperative that a fair assessment of crime policy be conducted, and, if found wanting, a more effective one embraced, even if it means having to admit that the present machinery is deficient.

6.2.5 *Beyond Crime Control*

AML legislation was set up initially to fight drug trafficking, and then serious organised crime. Despite its enactment, organised crime has risen, both internationally and domestically. Since CTF legislation has been enacted, more terrorist attacks have taken place than during the previous decade. Further, it would appear that none of the cases that have been brought to court have indicated that the AMF/CTF machinery has been useful in helping to identify terrorist attacks in preparation.[82] The promises that these regulations would prevent acts of terrorism have not materialised. CTF legislation seems to be

77 Stessens (2000), p. 136. See also Braithwaite (1993), p. 666.

78 Naylor (2003b).

79 Bozonnet, Decamps (2007); RTS.ch (2012).

80 Chambraud (2007b); Lemonde.Fr with AFP (2007b); Canellas (2009); Lemonde.Fr with AFP (2010); Lemonde.Fr with AFP (2011a); Lemonde.Fr with AFP (2011b).

81 Walker J (2004), p. v.

82 Bures (2015), pp. 227, 229; Lynch, McGarrity, Williams (2015), pp. 64–74.

even less effective than AML legislation. This may be indicative of some strategic errors: First, the criminal policymakers have been too confident in their expectation of the results of their "wars" against organised crime and terrorism; secondly, they have withdrawn troops from the front-line of traditional law enforcement.

Since the more AML/CTF apparatus is pushed forward, the more costly it becomes, one would expect it to be reassessed and ultimately changed. To date, there is no sign of a fundamental rethink in governmental circles.[83] A close look reveals that behind the initial rhetoric accompanying the adoption of AML legislation, there were other purposes of an economic and fiscal nature. These hidden objectives may plead in favour of maintaining the present system. Given that in Australia, Commonwealth AML legislation is based on the head of power on fiscal matters, it may thus be reconciled with its true nature.

6.2.5.1 Prevention and Repression

From its inception, AML legislation had a dual purpose of prevention and repression. The preventive dimension seeks to make the use of legal financial services more risky and costly for traffickers of all kinds and therefore less attractive to them. It is the view shared by the EU, the US and the FATF that the objective of the AML/CTF regime is to ensure the integrity of the financial system. Repression serves a different purpose. It aims at sanctioning any prohibited financial transaction and at providing for the confiscation of the assets of criminal and terrorist organisations. This dual purpose of prevention-repression still exists today making a proper assessment of AML/CTF legislation difficult if not contradictory. FATF's methodology does not provide sufficient clarification as the "expected results" are not objectively defined, leaving the assessment by and large an "opportunistic" exercise, plagued with political and economic considerations.[84]

Depending on the point of view, the small number of court cases can be seen as a success or a failure. From a preventive perspective, the small number of prosecutions and convictions may illustrate the effectiveness of AML procedures, as the financial system is sound and free of assets of criminal origin. Alternatively, from a repressive point of view, the few number of court cases may display that legislation, law enforcement and the criminal justice system are not able to deal effectively with this type of crime. Either way, the number of court cases is not a reliable indicator. Some have tried to track suspicious

83 Tyre (2010), p. 80. This contrasts with academics' researches. For instance, Reuter, Truman (2005); Harvey (2005); Crimm (2008), p. 626.

84 Romaniuk, Keatinge (2018).

transaction reports (STRs) from their filing to criminal convictions in order to identify the rates between the STRs sent, the number of investigations opened, the number of convictions and the confiscations ordered. These data would be helpful in assessing the AML regime and in allowing a sound cost/benefit analysis of AML provisions which could be used for political decision making and operational matters. However, this is nearly an impossible task given the lack of reliable and comparable data.[85] Nevertheless, Europol admitted recently that in 2014, the EU Financial Intelligence Units received almost 1 million reports and that, on average, just 10% of suspicious transaction reports were further investigated.[86]

Confiscation is an underlying purpose of AML legislation. The number of confiscation orders for money laundering is not a better guide either. On one hand, if the legislation has a primarily preventive effect, a small number of confiscation orders would indicate that there are few assets to confiscate and that large criminal organisations are not operating in this jurisdiction.[87] On the other, if the main objective is to confiscate illegal assets belonging to criminal organisations, the meagre results (less than 1%) can only be disappointing. The introduction of civil forfeiture in 1977 and the unexplained wealth laws in 2010 have not altered this. Between 1999 and 2004, in Australia, only 37% of the value seized was eventually forfeited. In 2013–2014, this figure went down to 22.77%. The confiscated amounts increased, reaching 57.4 million in 2015–2016.[88] However, simultaneously with this increase, the authorities also raised their estimate of the value of the proceeds of crime in Australia. In 2006, the Government estimated the proceeds of crime to have a value of approximately AUD 11.5 billion per year. In 2012, it had risen to 15 billion.[89] The rise could be explained by the broadening of the predicate offences which led to an increase of estimated illegally acquired assets. However, over the past years the figures have been in keeping overall with the United Nations Office on Drugs and

85 Tavares, Thomas, Roudaut (2011); EUROPOL (2017b), p. 39; Levi, Reuter, Halliday (2018), pp. 317, 322–324.

86 EUROPOL (2017c).

87 Mitsilegas (2003), p. 153.

88 Orders for a value of AUD 154.7m were made and AUD 41.3m were recovered. Walker J. (2004), p. 42; FATF (2015), p. 64; Australian National Audit Office (2017), p. 18.

89 Anti-Money Laundering and Counter-Terrorism Financing Bill 2006, Explanatory Memorandum. In 2011, AUSTRAC's estimate was between AUD 10 to 15 billion; Lawler (2012). John Lawler was the Australian Crime Commission Chief Executive Officer. Today, there is no official current estimate of the proceeds of crime in Australia; see FATF (2015), p. 30.

Crime's (UNODC) figures. It estimates that less than 1% of global illicit financial flows are seized and frozen.[90] Assessing the deterrent effect, if any, of the AML/CTF legislation is a challenging task, even more so when comprehensive data are lacking.

Conversely, terrorism *financing* legislation is eminently preventive. The success of the AML/CTF laws cannot be measured in terms of pecuniary value but, possibly, by the number of prosecutions for terrorism financing. In any event, the true measure of the success of anti-terrorism legislation is by the number of thwarted activities.[91] Thirteen terror attacks have been prevented in Australia between September 2014 and August 2017.[92] However, there is no evidence that this was made possible because of CTF legislation. It is difficult, if not impossible, to assess its effectiveness independently since terrorism information is rarely available to the public and counter-terrorism data are classified documents. This has been underlined with the controversy regarding the Terrorism Finance Tracking Programme (TFTP) set up by the USA in the aftermath of the 9/11 terrorist attacks. The TFTP allows US agencies to access the Brussels-based banking consortium SWIFT (Society for Worldwide Interbank Financial Telecommunication) data.[93] Concerns were raised in the EU regarding the possible breach of privacy laws and both the Ombudsperson and courts have sought clarification on the issue. They were not given access to all the requested information allegedly on the basis that the potential combination with other elements known about SWIFT's business and a specific set of analyses that terrorists might potentially undertake could possibly lead them to understand what information was held by security agencies.[94] Consequently, the secrecy surrounding the TFTP prohibits not only an assessment of whether the protections set out in the TFTP Treaty, introduced upon the EU's request, are implemented correctly, if at all, but also whether the TFTP has any effectiveness.

It cannot be excluded that the size of the proceeds of crime and terrorist finances may be exaggerated in order to mobilise public support for broader

90 UNODC (2011), p. 5; UNODC (2014), p. 14.

91 Reuter, Truman (2005) submit that money laundering in general should be measured by the reduction of criminal activities that generates the laundering, p. 57.

92 ASIO (2017), p. 3.

93 SWIFT provided electronic instructions on how to transfer money among 7,800 financial institutions worldwide in 2006. The cooperative is owned by more than 2,200 organisations, and virtually every major commercial bank, as well as brokerage houses, fund managers and stock exchanges, use its services. SWIFT routes more than 11 million transactions each day, most of them across borders. See Lichtblau, Risen (2006).

94 Pozen (2005); De Goede, Wesseling (2017), p. 263.

legislation, and pro-active enforcement methods.[95] Political and law enforcement authorities seem to be ever calling for broader powers and more means. Such calls are built on two main underlying assumptions: First, that the amount of money laundered is huge and is getting bigger; second, that good legislation would automatically lead to substantial court cases. Few have questioned the cogency of the machinery.[96] The 2005 FATF assessment of Australia's legislation exemplified the paradox of the premises on which the AML/CTF regime is built. The FATF team praised Australia's AML legislation and in the same breath implied that it is not effective.[97] In 2015, Australia has been criticised for the limited use of AUSTRAC information as a trigger to commence AML/CTF investigations.[98] The FATF has concluded that the Australian convictions for money laundering and terrorism financing should be higher given "the nature and the scale of the risks",[99] but loses sight that not every risk eventuate. In 2013, to clarify the "marking keys", the FATF issued a *Methodology for assessing technical compliance with the FATF Recommendations and the Effectiveness of AML/CFT systems*, detailing ten "immediate outcomes" which mainly focus on the thorough implementation of the Recommendations. It is expected that adequate compliance with the Recommendations will "ultimately" lead to a reduction in money laundering and terrorist financing activity. As Levi, Reuter, Halliday point out,

> it is clear that there are many countries that have very weak AML/CFT systems but represent a minimal threat to the global system. The very weakness of the legal system that helps lead Uganda to the 4th lowest position of the Basel Institute's ML rankings also makes that country an unattractive country in which to place financial assets, stolen or otherwise, for the medium or long term, especially not for funds from crimes elsewhere.[100]

The push for more repression relies mainly on the figures of assumed organised crime turnovers. Those estimates vary, depending who brought them forward. For instance, upon the introduction of legislation, the Attorney-General's

95 Stessens (2000), p. 89.

96 Most Academics have focused mainly on the costs/benefits analysis to question the system; see Alvesalo, Tombs (2005), p. 13. Vlcek (2008).

97 FATF (2005b), point 82, p. 28. See also Harvey (2009).

98 FATF (2015), p. 5.

99 FATF (2015), pp. 8, 77.

100 Levi, Reuter, Halliday (2018), p. 324.

Department estimated that approximately AUD 11.5 billion was being laundered in Australia per year. However, Walker's study suggested that, for the same period, crime in Australia generated between AUD 2.8 billion and AUD 6.3 billion, with the most likely figure being in the vicinity of AUD 4.5 billion.[101] The UNODC estimates that money laundering assets have a value of between 2 and 5% of the GDP.[102] Given its underground nature, even the most thorough study has to rely on figures provided by law enforcement agents, which at best can be considered an educated guess.[103] Since there are no reliable figures, it makes the whole issue of the appraisal of the AML/CTF susceptible to many different interpretations. Moreover, considering that there is no objective benchmark to assess the risk and the scope of organised crime and terrorism financing, the FATF's mutual evaluation exercise on the efficiency of AML/CTF mechanism in curbing money laundering, terrorism and proliferation financing has become open to foreign policy considerations. This is particularity clear with the cases of the Democratic People's Republic of Korea (DPRK) and Iran. Given their economic markers, one may wonder why these two countries would be put on the top of the list of those who are seen as posing "a real threat" to the integrity of the international *financial* system.[104]

It is puzzling that the balance between the costs, the benefit, the fairness of the system and the public interest should not have led to a thorough reappraisal of the system. The present situation is a stalemate. On one hand, if AML legislation is declared ineffective, it is feared that it would discourage financial institutions from cooperating with the law enforcement authorities or make them question the usefulness and the costs of the efforts they are required to make.[105] On the other hand, enacting even more repressive legislation, with more severe penalties and an extension of the list of offences, will not yield the expected results. More rules may not only be more difficult to implement and justify. In addition, according to risk management experts, the new measures may be counter-productive in the way that they generate more reports, making detection even more difficult and costly.[106] Unfortunately, the

101 *Anti-Money Laundering and Counter-Terrorism Financing Bill* 2006, Explanatory Memorandum; Walker J (2004).

102 UNODC (2015), p. 55.

103 Walker J (1995), p. 37; Walker J (2004), p. 68; Harvey (2008). Most estimates assume that criminals have a rational behaviour regarding their expenditures. FERWERDA (2009), p. 904. Pieth, Aiolfi (2003) have compared the effectiveness of transactions in the two systems in selected States. Also Pieth, Aiolfi (2004), p. 5.

104 FATF – LEWIS (2016).

105 Stessens (2000), p. 422.

106 European Commission (2011), p. 3.

present trend is not towards fundamental reform but rather towards more legislation, and more control.[107] The emphasis on the precautionary principle generates a fear of what could happen were ineffective measures to be lifted.[108] Also, some may not want to be labelled as not doing their part to the AML/CTF fight. Furthermore, it could also be that it is more convenient to perpetuate the system than to question it. After having recommended tougher legislation, developed risk-prevention policies, the latest focus seems to be on widening and speeding information sharing.[109] Maintaining and developing the machinery also provide jobs; extending it creates new ones. Consequently, it is most likely, given the present terrorism context, that the system would not be questioned. It could even be diverted from its initial objective to serve other purposes.

6.2.5.2 The Control of Financial Markets

On the background of an increasingly globalised financial community and a looming economic crisis, we observe an international strengthening of the FATF standards as well as an extension of the scope of the Recommendations. The momentum thus created may be used to capitalise on the paper trail generated by the AML/CTF legislation and to use it at international level against organised financial crime and tax related offences, with a view to increasing State revenue. Pieth acknowledges that the FATF 40 Recommendations had a secondary goal, if not a hidden agenda, which was "to reduce drastically the use of cash world-wide in order to establish a paper trail wherever possible".[110] This long-term objective has been echoed by the Commonwealth Secretariat which advocates for a progressive move towards a cashless society.[111] The mid-term objective is the adoption of international regulations for financial markets, allegedly seen as the only way to prevent international crime operators from holding hostage legitimate business all over the world.[112] In this perspective, whether the CFT measures are appropriate or not appears irrelevant.

Since the late 1990s, there has been a growing trend among the strongest economies to impose their own standards using AML regulations, in particular, against organised crime, in order to limit the competitive edge of foreign international institutions. This move coincided with the implementation of costs and risk minimalisation policy. Three examples are worth mentioning. The first is the FATF's efforts in the 1990s to bring non-compliant countries into

107 Gurule (2008), pp. 381–393; Warde (2007) p. 187.
108 See Braithwaite (1993), pp. 661, 668; Michaelsen (2010c), p. 262.
109 EUROPOL (2017b), p. 39.
110 Pieth (2002), pp. 366–367.
111 Commonwealth Secretariat (2006), p. 59.
112 Pieth (1998), pp. 161 and 168.

line with its AML policy. Officially, the FATF's action was motivated by the perceived flight of black money from regulated financial centres to non-regulated ones. These non-compliant countries and territories (NCCT) are often offshore jurisdictions that are known to offer advantageous fiscal regimes, which are competing against the services provided by the main international financial centres. In its "world wide mobilisation against money laundering", the FATF threatened the NCCT with a financial embargo, a move that could potentially have suffocated these fragile economies. Doyle called it "a policy redolent of extraterritorial bullying".[113] The second is the US AML legislation: The *International Money Laundering Abatement and Financial Anti-terrorism Act 2001* (IMLAFA), which is part of the PATRIOT Act, extends US jurisdiction over any foreign financial institution that has a correspondent relationship with a US bank. It allows the courts to seize funds in USD deposited in an interbank account. Officially, the objective is to reduce the exposure of the US dollars being used for illicit purposes.[114] Practically, it is a powerful tool for extraterritorial financial policy. The third example is the introduction by the EU of exceptions to the KYC rule. To dispense with the paper work, and the increasing costs generated by complying with the AML requirements, the EU introduced in 2001 an exception to the identification obligation. Only approved financial institutions can benefit from this exception, thus creating an incentive for non-EU financial institutions to comply with European legislation in order to establish a preferred business relationship.[115] This was strengthened in 2015 with the adoption of the fourth money laundering Directive (4AMLD).[116] EU's exceptions to identification rules can be regarded as a tool to fight off competition from institutions which did not incur the high compliance costs associated with the EU legislation. Limiting the non-Member States competitors' margins in order to level the playing field of the Member State industries has become a compelling argument,[117] which won over the International Monetary Fund (IMF) and AUSTRAC.[118]

> There is no conflict between free, competitive markets and anti-money laundering regulations. On the contrary, there is considerable synergism between the two. The same oversight and supervision mechanisms that

113 Doyle (2002), p. 281.

114 Canestri (2015), pp. 224, 5.

115 European Commission (1995), p. 10, point 3.

116 European Parliament and the Council (2015), Directive 2015/849 of 20 May 2015, OJ L141, pp. 73–20, 06.06.2015.

117 Stessens (2006), pp. 202–203.

118 Jensen (2008), p. 93.

> operate to ensure the smooth functioning of the market-orientated financial system make a strong contribution to the information base and the general environment of integrity.[119]

These policies are revealing of the power that strong economies are ready to exert to impose their agenda and to fight off competition. The examples point to the risk that measures taken in the context of an internationally approved criminal policy can be construed as pursuing mere economic national interests. The inclusion of tax crimes in the list of predicate offences to money laundering may illustrate this even further.

6.2.5.3 Fiscal Offences as Predicate Offences to Money Laundering

Technically, money laundering is a subsidiary offence. Originally, only offences that generated monetary gain were subject to the AML apparatus. Terrorism financing and then proliferation financing are built on an a-contrario scenario because the origin of the funds may be legitimate even if the purpose of the transaction is not. This is also the case of tax offences committed by individuals who fail to declare their legally earned income in full to the tax authorities. Recent AML/CTF legislation appears to make an amalgam between organised financial crimes and fiscal offences, including tax evasion and money laundering. This rationale needs to be questioned given their differences. Masciandaro warns that

> [t]he specificity of money laundering and financing terrorism must always be borne in mind, since the definition of policies for preventing and combating them must not passively follow the schemes of action devised for combating tax evasion.[120]

Money laundering does not generate any direct victim, contrary to the predicate offence.[121] Money laundering thus contrasts with financial fraud and fiscal offences which deprive the State of revenue, reduce the income of share-holders, force workers out of their jobs, deter potential investors and distort competition. Fraud cases against public funds are a notable exception because "the false document is at the same time the instrument by which monetary advantage is acquired *and* the tool to disguise the illegality of the act".[122]

---

119 Camdessus (1998), pp. 40–41.

120 Masciandaro (2006), p. 370.

121 There are potentially indirect victims if the proceeds are re-invested in criminal activities.

122 Van Duyne (2003), pp. 77, 78.

In Australia, the majority of illegal proceeds are derived from fraud-related offences,[123] hence tracking the predicate offence and the subsidiary offence is one and the same task.

Organised financial crime is an aspect of organised crime. Its threat to society is described in the same terms as organised crime. It can be defined as "activities of organised crime groups which abuse financial or payment systems with a view to financial gain".[124] It includes *inter ali*a fraud, counterfeiting and VAT fraud. Financial crime is also broader than tax evasion offences and tax fraud.

Fiscal offences are more often committed by an individual, whether a person or a company, rather than by a criminal organisation. While a tax-payer may aim at minimising taxation or even at avoiding it, typical money launderers have no objection to paying taxes on their income as it legitimises them. Paying tax is the supreme achievement for the money launderer: the assets have been recognised by the State as legitimate income; they have been made tax worthy (vs object of a confiscation order); they have lost their criminal smell; they have been properly laundered. It can be expected that large criminal organisations will keep laundering money as long as the profits of the criminal activities cannot be declared for fear of prosecution and confiscation.

In the last twenty years, following the economic turndown, tax evasion has steadily moved towards the top list of priorities of the global community. The distinction between tax minimisation and tax avoidance is not always easily established and leaves room for interpretation. In short, as the ATO puts it, the difference between tax minimalisation (tax planning) and tax avoidance largely comes down to intent. Tax planning is organising tax in the most effective way within the intent of the law. In contrast, tax avoidance schemes involve the deliberate exploitation of the tax system to reduce tax. It is therefore considered as eroding the integrity of the tax apparatus.[125] Aggressive tax planning, understood as stretching the interpretation of what is "legal" as far as possible to the limit, has now come under scrutiny and is considered as steps towards tax avoidance.[126]

The scandal surrounding the Panama Papers was the opportunity for the FATF to press for more transparency regarding beneficial ownership of companies, trusts and other corporate vehicles. Interestingly, when the

123 FATF (2005b), pp. 5 and 15; Walker J (2004), p. 68; AUSTRAC (2011), 68.

124 Commission of the European Communities (2004), p. 3.

125 ATO website, <https://www.ato.gov.au/General/Tax-planning/Tax-planning-vs-tax-avoidance/>, last viewed March 2019.

126 See Cachia (2017).

scandal happened, Panama had just been removed from the NCCT list. The FATF argued that the Papers referred to a period prior the affair where Panama was not compliant with the international benchmark.[127] The FATF's present position contrasts with its initial policy. From the outset, the FATF had decided to deal exclusively with criminal offences and not tax offences, which are traditionally excluded from international mutual assistance in penal matters. This exclusion stems from a traditional concept of State sovereignty by which taxation is viewed as part of the State's financial domestic policy, whose economic interests may conflict with other States.[128] In this perspective States are seen as economic competitors. A change was initiated by the EU, which was concerned with the emergence of a single economic market. It observed that money launderers would sometimes declare that their transactions pertained to tax matters (the so called "fiscal excuse") to deter financial institutions from reporting the transaction, even if it was suspicious. Information exchange between agencies was advocated. The EU concern that tax fraud, particularly VAT fraud, was depriving them from substantial resources,[129] was later shared by the FATF. Eventually, in 1998, the FATF recommended the scrapping of the fiscal exception and its 2012 revised FATF Recommendations include "tax crimes" in the list of recommended predicate offences. Other international organisations followed suite: The 1999 UNCFT abrogated the fiscal offence exception. In 2010, the Council of Europe introduced a Protocol to its *Convention on Mutual Administrative Assistance in Tax Matters* to which Australia is a Party.[130] The EU has introduced tax crimes as a predicate offence in the 4AMLD when they are punishable by deprivation of liberty or a detention order for a maximum of more than one year or by deprivation of liberty or a detention order for a minimum of more than six months.

The international process towards the inclusion of tax offences in its AML regime contrasts with Australia's position. From the outset, fiscal considerations have been at the heart of the Commonwealth's AML apparatus. Basing its initial legislation on the head of power pertaining to taxation was not just a convenient move. It stems from a fundamental understanding that permeates the whole system. In contrast with international treaties, the Commonwealth's has a broad understanding of the predicate offence which is defined as some

127 FATF – LEWIS (2016).

128 Stessens (2000), p. 299; Vlcek (2004), pp. 227–242.

129 VAT (GST). VAT constitutes for some the most important source of fiscal revenue, and Member States VAT own resources contribute up to 25% of the Community budget. Australia has conducted a study on this problem: see Sullivan, Smith (2012).

130 *Convention on Mutual Administrative Assistance in Tax Matters* (ETS 127); *Protocol amending the Convention on Mutual Administrative Assistance in Tax Matters* (ETS 208).

sort of illegal activity and not just a serious crime. The international trend to focus on tax offences seems to have only strengthened Australia's resolve. In Australia, financial crimes attract some of the harshest penalties. For instance, the penalty for trafficking in persons is 12 years imprisonment, and 20 years for an aggravated offence. The maximum penalty for dealing with proceeds of crime is 25 years imprisonment. One wonders if the more severe penalties imposed to protect the State financial interests rather than to sanction offences against life and freedom truly reflect Australian values. Considering that predicate offences are also defined according to the severity of the sanctions the offence bear, it would not be surprising that in order to make fiscal offences "fit" into the AML machinery, the major world economic powers will press for increased penalties for financial crimes to reflect on the conduct's seriousness. If so, Australia may again be considered as a forerunner. Although justified by the 2001 terrorist attacks, AML/CTF provisions are designed more for economic warfare rather than the fight against terrorism or the proliferation of WMD. Considering that in Australia, federal AML/CTF legislation is based on the legislative power relating to fiscal matters, it may, at last, have come into its own.

6.3 Money Laundering and Terrorism Financing (Legislation) as a Threat to Democracy?

Legislation to counter organised crime and terrorism has been justified in order to protect peace and security, public and legal order in general, and democracy in particular. However, the legislative process leading to its adoption has been marred by the unprecedented influence of non-democratically elected bodies such as the UN Security Council and the FATF. Furthermore, law enforcement tasks and security assessment have been subcontracted to the private sector. An added concern is that some substantive provisions do not meet the basic principles of criminal law held traditionally by democratic States.

6.3.1 *The Influence of Soft Law in the Legislative Process*

As Georges Abi-Saab noted, "the term "*soft law*" refers to the lack of justiciability of the instruments in which the rules are enshrined (*instrumentum*) rather than to the content of the rules themselves (*negotium*)".[131] This section looks at the unprecedented influence on legislation of non-elected bodies such as the FATF, the UN Security Council and private actors, which warp the normal democratic legislative process and undermine the foundations of democratic

131 Abi-Saab (1993), pp. 62–63.

societies and their legal order. Related concerns regarding the erosion of democratic principles are also highlighted.

The role of soft law in AML/CTF legislation has been explained by various factors such as the absence of formal international legislator or the traditional influence of international financial law in global economic affairs.[132] Soft law can be used by powerful States as a means to influence international and national legislation. The influence of soft law, which has permeated organised crime and terrorism legislation at the international level, has impacted not only Australian AML/CTF laws, but also Australia's definition of a terrorist organisation under the proscription process.

6.3.1.1 The FATF

The FATF initial mandate focused exclusively on money laundering. It now includes the financing of terrorism and the proliferation of weapons of mass destruction. The FATF 40 Recommendations have been described as the "crown jewel of soft law".[133] The FATF has emerged as an indispensable player in shaping legislation with its influence being felt widely beyond its Member States. Indeed, the FATF considers itself a "policy-making body". The action of the FATF has undoubtedly contributed significantly to a better understanding of money laundering and the measures that need to be put in place to tackle it. Its major achievement is to have rallied governments to adopt the principles it established. This worldwide influence could be the expression of the FATF's foresight in defining measures that the international community needed to take to curb organised crime. Such an achievement may make the FATF legitimate for some but it does not make it compliant with democratic values and accountability.[134]

Despite being called "recommendations", the FATF 40 Recommendations are morally binding on Member States. In case of non-compliance, the FATF can apply pressure and sanctions, even on non-member States. However, the assessment process was found lacking in methodological coherence, standardisation, and partiality.[135] For instance, whereas the Task Force took measures against Turkey and Austria, it did nothing to compel the USA to remedy to its serious lack of compliance. Some small economic Member States' poor compliance has come under close scrutiny while that of the more powerful Members has been ignored. These criticisms led the FATF in 2002 to issue a

132 Stessens (2000), p. 16; Brummer (2010).

133 Stessens (2000), p. 17.

134 Black, Rouch (2008), pp. 225–227.

135 Pieth, Aiolfi (2004), p. 20; Gilmore (2004), p. 94.

Methodology for Assessing Compliance with Anti-Money Laundering and Combating the Financing of Terrorism Standards. Given that there is no regulated recognised independent enforcement system, there is also no proper means to monitor the use by the FATF of its "counter-measures" outside the G-7, which is not an independent authority. The FATF's influence can be seen as another manifestation of the hegemony of the most powerful economies harnessing their political influence to pursue their own agenda. The FATF's approach displays blatant disregard of the rule of law by those States which are often most prone to rebuke those that do not abide by it. Levi and Gilmore rightly warned,

> if the economic activities of independent states are defined as illegitimate facilitators of 'the enemy' that 'require' disablement in the 'Wars' on organised crime and terrorism, this poses obvious dangers for the traditional rights of minority nations who are cajoled or threatened into submission.[136]

6.3.1.1.1 *Reduced Margin of National Parliaments*

The advantage of the involvement of bodies such the FATF in AML/CTF is to create soft law regulations that are made by experts in a non-confrontational manner and can be issued very quickly. The disadvantage is that the FATF acts outside any parliamentary mandate. Further, its eminence puts pressure on elected representatives, narrowing the leeway given to national parliaments when adopting legislation.[137] The Australian Government has been motivated to pass recent revisions by the need to comply with the updated FATF Recommendations. It is concerning that the FATF Recommendations and the UNSCRs are placed on the same footing as international treaties to which Australia is a Party. For instance, section 3(3)(a) of the AML/CTF Act makes it legally binding to address the FATF recommendations as part of "matters of international concern". Further, the AML/CTF Act 2006 includes not only the FATF Recommendations at the time the Act was adopted but also the subsequent FATF amendments, which amounts to giving a "blank cheque" to a non democratically-elected body to impose its views upon the Australian legislature. It is submitted that demonstrating the merit and the necessity of the proposed provisions is essential, and even more so when the foreseen laws infringe on fundamental principles and rights of individuals. Governments should demonstrate to national parliaments the way in which soft law regulations are effective and beneficial.

---

136 Levi, Gilmore (2002), p. 360.

137 Pieth, Aiolfi (2004), p. 12.

6.3.1.2 The UN Security Council

When in 2001 the UN Security Council took the unprecedented step to "decide that all States [should] prevent and suppress the financing of terrorist acts", it overstepped their sovereign freedom to decide whether or not to become party to the 1999 *Convention for the Suppression of the Financing of Terrorism*. By issuing specific instructions, the UNSCR 1373 curbed national parliaments' prerogative to legislate freely on the matter.

Traditionally, legislative powers rest, within the UN, with the General Assembly. Rosand has justified the Security Council's move by the General Assembly's inability to adopt a Convention against terrorism.[138] This argument ignores that a Convention against terrorism financing had already been adopted. Moreover, the UNSCR does not provide for a definition of terrorism, which is the stumbling block in the adoption of a general convention against terrorism. Therefore Pieth and Aiolfi rightly noted that

> the inability or unwillingness of international bodies and supervisors to define terrorism (beyond the empty formula used in the UN Convention) is most unfortunate because the formula "combating the financing of terrorism" threatens to extend the use of AML-mechanisms to all sorts of unrest world-wide. To put it another way, there is a danger that AML efforts could themselves be perceived as an instrument of oppression, rather than the emancipatory tool that it has been so far.[139]

The powers of the Security Council's monitoring body have rightly been criticised for their discretionary character.[140] The violation of accepted principles of the rule of law in terrorism financing matters and the repressive use of the UN apparatus and influence are particularly well exemplified in the black listing of individuals and organisations.

Given that the authority of the UN Security Council rests on the UN Charter, UNSCRs should be implemented in ways that respect human rights and freedoms, as defined in the article 1 and the ICCPR, so as to ensure cohesion within the UN legislative texts.

6.3.2 *A Different Type of Law Enforcement*

The emphasis on the financial aspects of organised crime and terrorism resulted in the adoption of innovative ways of enforcing criminal legislation which

138 Rosand (2005), p. 576.

139 Pieth, Aiolfi (2004), p. 35.

140 Michaelsen (2010b), p. 85.

would have been previously inconceivable. The private sector has become an indispensable law enforcement agent and the transmission of personal and commercial data is done on a confidential basis, escaping the scrutiny of the judiciary.

6.3.2.1 The Financial Intelligence Units (FIUS)

In order to facilitate the transmission of the mandatory information from those entities subjected to AML/CTF regulations, States have set up FIUS. Often, they have a dual role: they specialise in the analysis of financial transactions reports, offer advice to those subject to the AML/CTF regulations; also, they transmit relevant information either to a domestic law enforcement agency or to prosecutorial authorities, or to another FIU. Given its processing and analytical role, AUSTRAC is a central cog in the AML/CTF machinery, however it is not a law enforcement agency for the purpose of the *Freedom of Information Act 1982* (FOI Act). In Australia, AUSTRAC is more than a Financial Intelligence Unit. It has also been granted legislative authority, a role which may conflict with its law enforcement tasks.

6.3.2.1.1 *Legislative Tasks*

With the introduction of the AML/CTF Act, AUSTRAC has been bestowed with the responsibility of issuing AML/CTF Rules that are binding to implement the AML/CTF Act. AUSTRAC is allowed to issue regulations, and list exceptions to the due diligence principle. Hence, the perceived necessity to comply with the FATF is also felt in the way legislation is being implemented, with the setting up of agencies whose decisions are not subject to judicial review. As an enforcement authority, AUSTRAC has also the authority to issue fines. These various roles conflict with each other. Furthermore, AUSTRAC's Chief Executive Officer (CEO) can exempt services from the legal obligations laid down in the AML/CTF Act or modify its application. Since 2017, the AML/CTF Act provides for a review mechanism of AUSTRAC CEO's decisions. The Administrative Appeals Tribunal (AAT) may review certain decisions taken by the AUSTRAC CEO (see Part 17A, AML/CTF Act). However not all decisions are reviewable by an independent authority. The AUSTRAC CEO enjoys a large margin of discretion in his/her decisions. He is under the administrative authority of the Minister for Justice and Customs (within the Attorney-General's portfolio) who is not entitled to give him instructions on specific cases (s 228). Despite the fact that AUSTRAC considered AUSTRAC CEO's capacity as the rule-maker of legislative instrument compatible with the human rights and freedoms,[141] it is suggested

141 AUSTRAC (2014d), pp. 3 and 16.

that the same agency should not be both in charge of issuing regulations and enforcing them without its decisions being subject to proper review by an independent authority.

6.3.2.1.2 *Law Enforcement*

AUSTRAC oversees the implementation of AML/CTF legislation by the reporting entities. It provides advise to stakeholders on how to understand their ML/TF risks and how to comply with their obligations. However, according to designated entities, this advisory role should be increased.[142] AUSTRAC seems to favour consultation with the reporting entities.[143] A confidential remediation approach is the preferred way of dealing with cases of breach, an approach which may preserve the businesses' reputations but lacks transparency.[144] When AUSTRAC discovers a breach of the provisions of the AML/CTF Act, it may accept an *enforceable undertaking*, which, once publicised, "becomes a benchmark against which other regulated entities can measure themselves".[145] In case of a reporting entity's failure to take remedial action and persistent non-compliance, AUSTRAC may choose to apply to the Federal Court for a *civil penalty order* (s 175). It may also issue *infringement notices* (s 184) and order the payment of a fine.[146] It may also *cancel the registration* of businesses. Despite its broad prerogatives, AUSTRAC's oversight has been called into question by the CBA scandal.

6.3.2.1.3 *Transmission of Information*

The information collected by AUSTRAC is shared, under specific conditions, with a number of agencies on national and international levels, and also with the private sector. The aim of the dissemination of financial data is to assist the detection of illegal transfers and thus to disrupt serious and organised crime, and terrorism. In practice, however, the results are disappointing. AML/CTF legislation presupposes that confidential data are transmitted by various parties whose confidential handling may be questionable.

6.3.2.1.3.1 National Level

In January 2018, AUSTRAC had 46 partner agencies within Australia such as the AFP (Australian Federal Police), Australian Criminal Intelligence Commission,

142 AGD (2016), p. 4.
143 Grabosky, Braithwaite (1986), p. 1.
144 Geary (2009b), p. 13.
145 For further discussion, see Geary (2009b).
146 Mcneil (2007), p. 341.

Australia Security Intelligence Organisation (ASIO), Office of National Assessments, Australian Prudential Regulation Authority (APRA), and the Australian Taxation Office (ATO). Information provided to AUSTRAC is intended to assist them in their tasks of revenue collection, law enforcement and national security measures.

Access and use of the information depends on various factors such as the function and status of the agency, whether the agency is a Commonwealth one or not, and the purpose for which the information will be used. The issue of information sharing is therefore complex and somewhat discrepant. The shortcomings of the AML/CTF Act have been recently highlighted during the 2016 review as inhibiting the sharing of AUSTRAC information across agencies involved in national operations and task forces.[147] Some steps have already been taken with the adoption of the 2016 amendment of POCA to remedy this situation. Another concern brought up by the Review is that the legislative protections and controls laid out in Part 11 of the AML/CTF Act, which outlines secrecy and access provisions regarding information, do not adequately safeguard all information that is collected under the AML/CTF Act, particularly when it is collected by other agencies or even AUSTRAC under section 49 (requesting further information relating to SMRS, TTRS or IFTIS from reporting entities or another person). It is expected that the Government will act upon the Recommendations brought forward by the report to grant a comprehensive protection to all these sensitive data.

The transmission of information is subject to the final decision of the heads of various Australian agencies. There is no legal mechanism in place to supervise the process or to appeal against it. Only in the limited case of remedial decision made by the AUSTRAC Chief Executive Officer (COE) can the matter be reviewed by the Administrative Appeals Tribunal. The tip-off offence makes monitoring the proper transmission of the information virtually impossible. To protect the identity of an informer or to prevent the person concerned being made aware that a suspicious transaction report (STR) has been issued, the Act sanctions the disclosure that a suspicion has been made or that a STR has been submitted to AUSTRAC (the tip-off offence). The penalty may reach 2 year imprisonment or 120 penalty units, or both. Furthermore, information provided to AUSTRAC may not normally be shared to a court or tribunal if it relates to a suspicious matter report. Suspicious transactions reports are not admissible in evidence. However, the courts may obtain the relevant information in order to carry into effect the provisions of the AML/CTF Act or the FTRA. Hence it appears that the information can be used to prosecute an offence but not to oversee the correct handling of information.

---

147 AGD (2016), p. 119.

6.3.2.1.3.2 International Level

The FIUs communicate between each other and transmit information often by-passing the strict rules of mutual assistance in criminal matters.[148] In AML/CTF matters, the FIUs exchange information between themselves informally, directly and often spontaneously. The UN Security Council and the FATF have repeatedly urged their member states to improve the information flow, remove obstacles and speed up the transmission process. In April 2018, AUSTRAC had agreements with over 90 countries to exchange information and financial intelligence, including Cambodia, China, Panama, Russia and Turkey. The 2016 amendment of POCA made national foreign law enforcement agencies, as well as the 2 international law enforcement agencies (INTERPOL and Europol) designated agencies.

Shared information may include tip-offs from informers or confidential bank documents.[149] The informal character of the transmission does not mean however that the AML/CTF Act does not specify conditions for communication. Protections and controls over the use of AUSTRAC information, including prohibitions on some disclosures are specified in Part 11 of the AML/CTF Act. Nevertheless, the transmission basically relies on trust since there is no procedure in place to monitor how the information is handled by a foreign State. In case of violations of the "appropriate undertakings" given by the government of the foreign State coming to the knowledge of the FIU, the only sanction may be to refuse to collaborate further, which might be difficult given the political and economic weight of some States. Moreover, sensitive and confidential information received by AUSTRAC (or another Commonwealth agency or authority) from another FIU does not have the protections given to sensitive and confidential AUSTRAC information. This information is therefore admissible in court and tribunal proceedings conducted in Australia. The Attorney-General is of the opinion that foreign agencies and foreign governments may be reluctant to share sensitive and confidential information with AUSTRAC and has recommended the Act be amended.[150]

Since these transmissions are informal, it is impossible for the person concerned to make an appeal or ask for a review. Furthermore, because the information is confidential, it cannot be verified, hence there is no guarantee that it is reliable or relevant, or does not unduly violate the right of privacy of the persons or business concerned. In 2006, on the eve of the introduction of the AML/CTF Act, concerns were voiced that "personal information of some

148 Stessens (2000), p. 258, 9.

149 Chaikin (2011).

150 AGD (2016), p. 120.

citizens will through the conduit of Suspicious Matters reports be available to a broad range of Australian and foreign authorities".[151] Studies have shown that the internal procedure put in place by the FIUs to monitor the flow of information does not offer sufficient guarantee of the correct use of information. Black and Rouch have found that the "transnational regulators do not (yet) operate within a constitutional framework. The usual panoply of constitutional mechanisms of accountability and legitimacy which characterises liberal democratic constitutional systems is not necessarily available".[152] It has been suggested that in order to protect all of AUSTRAC's sensitive information from being publicly disclosed was for AUSTRAC to be classified as a "law enforcement agency" for the purposes of the FOI Act.[153] However, this would not address the protection of sensitive information in the hands of the private sector.

6.3.2.2 The Private Sector

The involvement of private organisations and businesses can be seen in two separate stages of the AML/CTF mechanism: in the negotiation of the soft law provisions and in the implementation of its regulations.

6.3.2.2.1 *Negotiating the Soft Law Provisions*

The input of the Basel Committee on Banking Supervision (BCBS) and the Wolfsberg Group of Private Banks in the shaping of the FATF Recommendations is well known. The involvement of the private sector combined the financial interests of their members with the one of the public in fighting money laundering. For instance, the Wolfsberg Group of Private Banks, which was concerned with the disparate application of the AML rules, developed their own rules which they applied to all their operations at home and abroad, including in offshore centres. Assuming "that the Group members make up more than 60 per cent of the work market in private banking, with perhaps 50 per cent of the market share in each key offshore destination, in practical terms these rules have great potential for becoming the leading principles throughout the industry"[154] which they did. In addition, the Wolfsberg Group succeeded in convincing the FATF to follow a risk-based approach. A more recent example is the influence of the Committee on Payments and Market Infrastructures (CPMI) on the change of policy regarding correspondent banking relationships. Banks had been closing down accounts of financial institutions

151 Harris Rimmer, Jaggers (2006), p. 13.

152 Black, Rouch (2008), p. 224.

153 AGD (2016), p. 121.

154 Pieth, Aiolfi (2003b), p. 362.

which were deemed poorly compliant with FATF standards (in what is called a *de-risking* process) or for which the due diligence process costs were too high. This pushed the payments underground. It also had an impact on the international trade, growth, and financial inclusion. To remedy this situation, the CPMI, in partnership with the BCBS and Financial Stability Board (FSB), made recommendations to the FATF which were accepted in the form of new guidelines.[155] Such influence has been criticised by those who hold the view that the risk-based approach gives too much power to private companies.[156] However, as Tom Sherman AO explains, the reliance on individuals or corporations to abide by regulations or codes of ethics, including auditing by regulators as a checking mechanism, follows the deregulation of the Australian financial system in the 1980s,[157] and hence may be considered as unavoidable.

The involvement of the private sector in the drafting of soft law can be understood as an attempt to increase the participation of civil society in what is largely considered an undemocratic process. As Tham correctly observes, democratic principles require that the interests of others affected by the legislation be treated with equal respect, namely consumers and staff of financial institutions, which has not been the case so far.[158] The participation of the financial sector however carries a broader scope as it may reinforce the compliance of the private actors. Pieth and Aiolfi draw the attention to

> [o]ne of the key lessons learned by supervisors since 1990 [...] that "empowerment" of co-operative entities in the private sector is the most effective way to secure business integrity. This explains why defining due diligence is currently done in a triangle involving inter-governmental organizations/government agencies – members of the private sector – and civil society.[159]

6.3.2.2.2 *Private Sector as Law Enforcement Agent*

A great innovation, and of more significant concern, is the involvement of the private sector in the implementation of the AML/CTF apparatus in two different ways, firstly as an informer and secondly as a law enforcement agent.

---

155 FATF (2018). See also Vlcek (2018).

156 Tham (2007) pp. 143, 144.

157 Sherman (1991), p. 17, para.2.46.

158 Tham (2007) pp. 143. For a discussion of legal cross-pollination between money laundering criminalisation and rules such as the banks' private Code of Conduct (CDB), the supervision practice of the Swiss Banking Commission and the case law of the Swiss Federal Court, see Stessens (2000), pp. 104–108.

159 Pieth, Aiolfi (2004), p. 33.

There is a growing reliance of the authorities on the designated businesses to perform law enforcement tasks. Recent legislation has enlarged the participation against money laundering to other actors including those involved in non-financial services and even individuals. The addition of CTF to the AML regime has led to a substantial increase in responsibilities for those subjected to the AML/CTF regulations. Implementing AML/CTF legislation is a difficult and complex task, given that the ways of concealing illegal transfers of assets vary over time as criminals seek to evade the system. Moreover, the transjurisdictional aspects, which are inherent to transnational crime, compound the complexity because the legal requirements differ in practice from one State to another. In order to avoid the sanctions prescribed by AML/CTF legislation, those subject to it tend to over-report. This trend is inevitable under the present strategy.

Complying with AML/CTF legislation can be burdensome and time consuming for an institution, which may wish to rely on third parties to perform some of its obligations. It may appoint an agent to fulfil the customer due diligence requirements. Also, the risk-based approach has increased the reliance of designated businesses on other parties to carry out intelligence work, such as determining what are risky transactions, businesses and customers. In addition, the sheer volume of daily transactions requires financial institutions to rely on software to identify and analyse suspicious transfers in order to comply with the legal reporting requirements (threshold transactions reports (TTRs), suspicious matters reports (SMRs), and international funds transfer instructions (IFTIs)). These software packages need to be regularly updated to take into account the legislative changes, including the international and national black lists, which are essential for those institutions active on the international scene. Given that law enforcement authorities do not provide such software, financial institutions rely on private firms which develop and maintain software. Hence, the AML/CTF has created a double delegation: from law enforcement agencies to institutions and individuals subjected to the legislation, and further to the private companies which produce software. It follows that the private sector has now been become a national security agent, as Wesseling explains:

> In daily practice, it means that a range of private professionals (developers of detection software, compliance officers within banks, legal experts...) are responsible for the filtering and pre-selection of the risky profiles and transactions through an accumulation of individual and fragmented decisions. Subsequently, these decisions structure the investigations led by FIUs and eventually the prosecution of terrorism financers. Hence, by charging banks with the responsibility to combat terrorism financing, a

> shift has taken place as banks are now involved in national security questions and are even the first to make certain security decisions.[160]

According to Liss and Sharman, there are two main firms active in this market: World-Check and ACAMS (Association of Certified Anti Money Laundering Specialists).[161] A 2011 survey showed that 61% of European banks and 55% of US banks rely exclusively on such commercial risk-assessment software, the remainder combine them with internal procedures.[162] Researchers observed that "the upshot is that by a logic of delegation and default, World-Check sets the specific content of AML policy for many of the world's most important private financial institutions".[163] The dependence of the private sector on a few profit-orientated companies to carry their law-enforcement tasks is concerning.

Many of World-Check's staff are recruited directly from law enforcement agencies. To make matters worse, many law enforcement agents, particularly in the US, seek an accreditation by World-Check to further their employment prospects. It follows that the AML/CTF apparatus has created a situation where law enforcement officers are trained to implement AML/CTF regulations and identify suspicious transactions by those who produce the software, or, to put it differently they are trained to identify what the software producer company considers suspicious or problematic, and by extension what is not suggestive of money laundering or terrorism financing. In other words, enforcement agents are told where to look and not where to look. Liss and Sharman have concluded that "AML firms have become de facto rule-makers".[164] Given the influence which US authorities, in general, and US agencies, in particular, have over national FIUs and the AML/CTF machinery, this is a worrying issue.

Considering that both financial institutions and software producers are profit-driven and share a common purpose which is to reduce both their costs and the businesses' legal exposure to the AML/CTF regulations, it is reasonable to expect that they would support one another to clear themselves of any potential lack of conformity. It is in the interest of software producers to guarantee to their clients that they will be able wipe out any foreseeable problems. Training law enforcement agents is an ideal opportunity for software contractors to strengthen their position. This blatant conflict of interests between the

160 Wesseling (2013), p. 209.

161 Liss, Sharman (2014), pp. 10, 16.

162 KPMG (2011), p. 19.

163 Liss, Sharman (2014), p. 11.

164 Liss, Sharman (2014), p. 20.

law enforcement tasks bestowed on the private sector and its profit-driven objective raises doubt as to whether the AML/CTF regulations are correctly implemented, not in the letter of the law but in the spirit and intent of the legislature.

The increased reliance of the authorities on the private sector has led to growing calls for legislation changes so that relevant information may be transmitted more widely within institutions and also to selected third parties. In 2016, based on the practice of free flow of information between designated businesses, their branches and contractors in the UK and US, the Attorney-General's Office recommended expanding the circle of persons and institutions holding suspicious or confidential information, to allow multinational companies to share their data to develop their AML/CTF policies, subject to appropriate privacy restrictions.[165] However, it is of concern that the practical implementation of the AML/CTF legislation requires collection of sensitive private data some of which may fall outside the scope of the *Privacy Act 1988* (Cth). Upon the examination of the AML/CTF Bill 2006, the Office of the Privacy Commissioner had advocated a restricted circle of agencies handing personal information:

> ...[an] individual's personal information collected for the purpose of enforcing serious crime, such as money laundering and terrorism financing, should generally only be used for such purposes. Collecting and sharing personal financial information for matters of lesser gravity than AML/CTF and other similarly major crime may not align with community expectations concerning how this information should be handled.
>
> The Office reiterates its previous view that the access to personal information held by AUSTRAC should be narrowly restricted to those agencies and other bodies that require such information as a necessary part of responding to major crimes.[166]

Considering that, even within FIUs, the correct handling of information cannot be guaranteed, expanding further the circle of persons entitled to these data to private companies exposes the clients of financial institutions to a higher risk of having their business's confidential information (clients, contract amounts, financial arrangements) breached, accidently or not. This risk is compounded by a lengthy retention period of 7 years under the Australian AML/CFT scheme, in contrast with the 5 years recommended by the FATF. Any disclosure to competitors opens the door to potential serious harms (market loss, closure

165 AGD (2016), p. 123.

166 Harris Rimmer, Jaggers (2006), p. 14.

of business, jobs losses). Therefore, the lack of oversight over these companies is worrying. It is compounded by the opacity of security decisions taken within banks which are rather opaque and can be controversial, for example when different banks or bank employees treat similar cases differently.[167] Liss and Sharman found that though they may act in line with basic State interests, they often escape the control of particular government institutions because of "overlapping sovereignty claims, delegation and the relative novelty of this kind of actor".[168]

Not only are these law enforcement tasks carried out without financial compensation, in Australia, services and persons regulated by the AUSTRAC are furthermore hit by a levy.[169] Masciandaro has pointed out that sanctioning and burdening the economic agents is not the road to follow. "Rather, to increase the active collaboration from the economic agents involved, the path to take with decision is that of incentives and mutually agreed regulations".[170] However, the designated businesses subject to the AML/CTF regulations may have found ways to alleviate their legal burdens. For instance, they may use the data collected as part of their KYC requirements to refine their customer profile in order to improve their marketing strategy,[171] or even sell them further if anonymised.

The increasing reliance of the authorities on private unpaid contractors to enforce security legislation is confounding. Their compliance is ensured by an armada of heavy penal and financial sanctions. Under AML/CTF legislation, private institutions and individuals were compelled to report transactions and suspicious activities and clients, violating a long held tradition of duty of confidentiality, at a time when the reporting of serious crimes was not mandatory. Even today in Australia, outside AML/CTF legislation, mandatory crime reporting is limited. It includes child sexual abuse, elder abuse and HIV matters. It is most disturbing that financial crime has been given such prominence so as to trigger rules and sanctions that do not even exist when crimes against life are committed.

The Australian AML/CTF scheme rests on a paradox: The reporting entities act as law enforcement agents but their competence is not recognised: They are deemed competent enough to assess the suspicious or risky character of a transaction or a business, yet if they fail by "recklessly" making a wrong

167 Wesseling (2013), p. 211.

168 Liss, Sharman (2014), p. 21.

169 *Australian Transaction Reports and Analysis Centre Supervisory Cost Recovery Levy Act 2011* (AUSTRAC Levy Act).

170 Masciandaro (2006), p. 370.

171 Wesseling (2013), p. 208.

assessment, they are liable for prosecution.[172] These entities face a dilemma. The imposition of strong penalties on the private sector is moderated by their overwhelming influence on the definition of the regulations implementation and on the reliance of the authorities to perform law enforcement tasks.

It is therefore suggested that law enforcement agencies should regain better ownership of the AML/CTF apparatus. Ideally, detection software should have been produced by the FIUs. In any case, detection software should at least be produced under the responsibility of law enforcement agencies. This would also guarantee the secure handling of sensitive data and a better supervision of those private companies acting as law enforcement agents. It would contribute in overcoming transjuridictional variations in legislation and promote a uniform treatment. Oversight should not be limited to the correct implementation of the AML/CTF provisions but should also include scrutiny of internal procedures and adequate monitoring of the handling of confidential data. Given the conflicting competence within AUSTRAC, it would be appropriate that an independent body conduct such supervision.

6.3.3 *Erosion of Criminal Law Principles*

Anti-organised crime and anti-terrorism provisions have purposes other than punishing the offender. They trigger both proactive and post-crime measures. AML/CTF legislation play an important part in identifying the persons involved after the fact. However, the pro-active measures also impact on fundamental rights such as the presumption of innocence, the principles of legality and the right of an independent review. Post-crime provisions pave the way for the confiscation of assets, sometimes even without conviction, impacting on property rights and privacy rights.

6.3.3.1 The Presumption of Innocence

A traditional view in criminal law is that a person is presumed innocent until proved guilty. In AML/CTF and related legislation, the principle of the presumption of innocence is eroded in two ways: by the reversal of the burden of proof in forfeiture and confiscation provisions, which will be discussed in the context of the legality principle, and by the way the financial data are collected, processed and shared.

172 A defence is available but only in proceedings for an offence against the regulations or for a contravention of a civil penalty provision if the defendant proves that he or she took reasonable precautions and exercised due diligence, in other words when the defendant can prove he or she has not been reckless (s 236, AML/CTF Act 2006).

6.3.3.1.1 *The Collection of Data*

Traditionally, in criminal law, warrants are issued when there is evidence that a crime has been committed. House search and telecommunication interceptions for instance are ordered by a competent authority when strong suspicion have been presented that there is a connection between a certain person or group of persons and the crime being investigated. This is not the case in AML/CTF legislation: Financial data are largely being collected, processed, analysed and transmitted without any crime having been committed and without any strong suspicion or evidence of a connection between the person to whom the data belong and a crime. In addition, this systematic and continuous collection of data pertaining to financial transactions does not require a warrant. Furthermore, despite AML/CTF machinery recommending institutions and businesses develop policies aligned to the risk which their industry and particular clients represent, legislation does allow for exception in the collection of data pertaining to financial transactions according to a categorisation of individuals on the basis of their potential risk. The collection of private data has become the norm rather than an exception. In Australia, every transaction above a pre-determined threshold is collected and transmitted to supervising authorities for further analysis, without any suspicion of it being connected to money laundering or terrorism financing. The pro-active aspect of legislation has the adverse consequence of treating everyone with some degree of suspicion, as if he or she were a potential money launderer or terrorist financier. As Milaj and Kaiser explain:

> As a customer will be unable to prove that he is not a money launderer, and especially as nobody is able to establish that he or she will not commit a crime in the future, there can be no defence in order to free oneself from such suspicion. Therefore, there is no way for a customer to escape the constant monitoring of his financial transactions. There is no mechanism to object to this surveillance of one's bank account, and there is no possibility for any customer to be exempted from scrutiny.[173]

In short, the presumption of innocence has given way to the presumption of potential guilt.

6.3.3.1.2 *The Right of Privacy*

The continuous collection of data provides, once processed and analysed, detailed information about a person's daily life and habits. The monitoring of

173 Milaj, Kaiser (2017), p. 122.

expenses may for instance reveal health problems, interests, political affiliations (and therefore personal opinions), sexual habits and orientation. This wide-ranging breach in someone's' privacy is, according to the European Court of Justice, likely to generate in the minds of the persons concerned the feeling that their private lives are the subject of constant surveillance.[174] These data are kept for prolonged period of time. For instance, in Australia, the retention period is 7 years, exceeding the FATF requirements of 5 years. Further, there is no guarantee, once the retention period has expired, that all data will be destroyed, particularly when they have been transmitted to third parties or foreign agencies.

The current trend is towards extended cooperation and speedy flow of data between domestic agencies and international FIUs, whether spontaneously or on request. Taking this recommendation forward, the EU is working at making national registries accessible in real time. Australia also favours unrestricted data sharing mechanisms between law enforcement authorities and intelligence agencies. The internationalisation of data sharing poses a higher risk when the information is sent to foreign agencies where States have weak data protection legislation or show deficiency in protecting the data. In a time of interconnectivity, the risk of data being hacked, sold and processed for purposes other than for which they were collected, namely the investigation and prosecution of a serious crime, has never been higher. After the European Court of Justice declared the 2000 EU–USA agreement on the protection of trans-Atlantic data transfer (safe harbour agreement) invalid because the law and practice of the United States do not offer sufficient protection against surveillance by the public authorities of the data transferred to that country,[175] international cooperation agreements between the EU and non-member States have been called into question. For instance, in an preliminary ruling, the ECJ concluded that the draft agreement between Canada and the EU on the transfer and processing of Passenger Name Record (PNR) data was incompatible with the European Charter and required specific modifications.[176] In the light of the caselaw of the ECJ, the European Data Protection Supervisor (EDPS) has recommended revisiting the draft cooperation agreements allowing the exchange of data between Europol and eight third countries.[177] He pointed to

174 *Digital Rights Ireland Ltd* (2014), point 37.

175 *Maximillian Schrems v Data Protection Commissioner*, para.98; Court of Justice of the European Union (2015). The *Safe Habour Agreement* was replaced in 2016 by the *Privacy Shield Agreeement*, adopted on 12 July 2016 and entered into force 1 August 2016.

176 *Opinion 1/15* of the Court, 26 July 2017.

177 European Data Protection Supervisor (EDPS) (2018).

several deficiencies and in particular that these States are not even Parties to the Council of Europe *Convention for the Protection of Individuals with regard to Automatic Processing of Personal Data.*[178] This convention, which is open to non-member states, protects the individual against abuses which may accompany the collection and processing of personal data and regulates the transfrontier flow of personal data. Considering that Australia is not a party to this convention, further cooperation with the EU requiring the transmission of data may be prejudiced.

6.3.3.2 Principle of Legality

The principle of legality, which is considered as a fundamental principle of criminal law, is compromised by the breadth of the very legislation that seeks to protect this order. Furthermore, the extensive use of recklessness as a fault element constrains law enforcement agencies to invest their resources in too large an array of conduct, or in ineffective and counter-productive strategies.[179]

Risk avoidance is pronounced in Australia's legislation. It is manifest in AML legislation and in the extended use of inchoate offences and recklessness in organised crime and terrorist offences to a point where the connection with the harm and criminality is so remote that there may be no effective safeguards against arbitrary prosecution, conviction and punishment. For instance, the offence of financing can be committed recklessly as to whether another person will engage in terrorist act, and even if a terrorist act or terrorism offence does not occur. The extensive breadth of the security offences leads to uncertainty as to their scope, and therefore insecurity, hence reducing the expression of the freedoms previously enjoyed.

Over-flexible legislation puts law enforcement in an almost impossible situation, given that resources are limited. By criminalising conduct that is very remotely associated with the commission of a terrorist act, the legislation does not prevent individuals that have no criminal intent from being investigated and prosecuted. For instance, the intention of funding a humanitarian branch of a criminal organisation, even it if has been proscribed, should not be confused with the intention of financing an organisation's criminal activity; or, in a similar way, the intention to invest laundered assets in the activity of a criminal organisation should be distinguished from the mere concealment of the criminal origin of the assets. Such intentions should be reflected in the penalty.

178 ETS 108. The Convention entered into force on 01.10.1985, ETS 108.

179 Vlcek (2004), p. 234.

6.3.3.2.1 *A Punishment That Fits the Crime*

The rationale of CTF provisions is to prevent loss of life and considerable damage to infrastructure that impact on life and health. From that perspective, imposing more severe penalties on those who finance terrorism than on money launderers is justified. By contrast, in terrorism financing matters, the extent of the harm does not depend on the amount spent. Hence, CTF legislation does not include penalties proportionate to the amount. A source of concern is the harsh penalty incurred for conduct that includes recklessness or negligence as a fault element.

Australian federal AML provisions should be aligned to the core international definition and make the concealment of the criminal origin of the proceeds of crime the characteristic element of any type of money laundering offences. Less characteristic forms of dealing with money, such as possession of proceeds of crime, should be dealt with in a similar way as to possessing stolen goods. In that scenario, a person found guilty of intending to conceal the criminal origin of proceeds or intending to help conceal said origin would be liable for breaching AML laws. Such penalty would be increased if the offender has acted within or on behalf of a criminal organisation. The more severe penalty for money laundering should be imposed not on the predicate offender but on a third party involved in organised crime. Surprisingly, under the Code, there is no aggravated penalties mechanism for laundering assets on behalf of a criminal organisation.

Money laundering has been described as a "crime without victims".[180] The crime that violates the victim's right is the predicate offence, not the laundering of proceeds. The threat of laundered money to social order lies in the *potential risk* of investment in criminal activities such as corruption of public servants, state officials and politicians. It does not carry any direct threat to lives. It is the investment of monies to pursue criminal activities that is dangerous and should warrant stringent penalties, the severity of which should depend on the amount and the envisaged activities. Studies indicate that most illegally acquired monies are spent on lavish lifestyle rather than investment in further criminal activities.[181] It is surely immoral to enjoy the benefit of one's crime but laundered money used by criminals for their own enjoyment does not represent a danger. However, under the Code, money laundering may trigger higher penalties than the predicate offence. This is not justified. Money laundering gives law enforcement greater opportunity to recoup illegal assets than if they had been spent immediately. Because the proceeds of the crime

180 Stessens (2000), p. 160.

181 See Van Duyne (1997), p. 214; Bricknell, McCusker, Chadwick, Rees (2012), p. 18.

TABLE 23 Penalties for money laundering[a] and terrorism financing offences, Sections 400.3 – 400.8, the Code

		400.3	**400.4**	**400.5**	**400.6**	**400.7**	**400.8**
Value of money/ property		$1million or more	$100,000 or more	$50,000 or more	$10,000 or more	$1000 or more	Any value
Penalty	Ss (1) Intention	25 years	20 years	15 years	10 years	5 years	12 mths
	Ss (2) Reckless	12 years	10 years	7 years	5 years	2 years	6 mths
	Ss (3) Negligent	5 years	4 years	3 years	2 years	12 mths	10 p/units
				103.1 Financing terrorism	**103.2** Financing a terrorist	**102.6** Getting funds to/from/for a terrorist organisation	
Penalty	Ss (1) Intention			life	life	25 years	
	Ss (2) Reckless as to whether – the funds will be used to facilitate or engage in a terrorist act. – the organisation is a terrorist organisation.			life	life	15 years	

a https://www.cdpp.gov.au/crimes-we-prosecute/money-laundering.

have been laundered, AML agencies are able to follow the electronic trail left by bank transfers and eventually seize the proceeds.

The severity of the sanctions should be proportional to the harm that they cause, to the intention of the offender and to his or her involvement in a highly dangerous criminal organisation. Some present maximum penalties for offence of dealing with assets do not observe these principles. Even though the judiciary retains a large degree of discretion in imposing a sentence (there is no mandatory sentencing applicable here), the very high maximum penalties give a poor signal as to the nature of the offence and the values that Australia claims to uphold.

In addition, the purely administrative character of some sanctions makes them more akin to criminal penalties which should only be laid by an independent court following a fair trial, conditions that administrative authorities do not meet.

6.3.3.3 The Reversal of the Burden of Proof

Taking into account the punitive nature of the penalty, several scholars have argued that civil forfeiture regimes are criminal in nature.[182] Such provisions typically allow forfeiture of assets even when the person who owns them has not been proven at the criminal standard to have committed a crime by which the asset was directly or indirectly obtained. Hence, they allow the reduction of property rights through a non-criminal judicial process.

The harshness of these forfeitures is compounded by a reversal of the burden of proof. The Attorney-General's Department admits that it would be unjust to impose a burden of proof on the defendant if the said element of the offence is difficult for the prosecution to prove. Hence it recommends that the reversal of the burden of proof should only occur when the matter in question is not central to the question of culpability for the offence.[183] However, in the AML context, this reversal has been justified, mainly, because of the seriousness of the crime and the difficulty in proving beyond reasonable doubt the criminal origin of the assets. The argument of the seriousness of the crime has been criticised by Sachs J of the South African Constitutional Court in *State v Coetzee* who said:

182 Gray (2012); See also Parliamentary Joint Committee on Human Rights (2014). Senate Standing Committee for the Scrutiny of Bills (2009). Contra: Parliamentary Joint Committee on Law Enforcement (2012), p. 10.

183 AGD (2011), p. 50.

> There is a paradox at the heart of all criminal procedure in that the more serious the crime and the greater the public interest in securing convictions of the guilty, the more important do constitutional protections of the accused become... The perniciousness of the offence is one of the givens, against which the presumption of innocence is pitted from the beginning, not a new element to be put into the scales as part of a justificatory balancing exercise. If this were not so, the ubiquity and ugliness argument could be used in relation to murder, rape, car-jacking, housebreaking, drug-smuggling, corruption ... the list is unfortunately almost endless, and nothing would be left of the presumption of innocence, save, perhaps, for its relic status as a doughty defender of rights in the most trivial of cases.[184]

The Australian legal order does not place property rights, international recognised rights or the principle of proportionality above domestic law. This was clearly spelt out by Justice Kirby in *Leask v Commonwealth.* Stephen Leask was accused of contravening section 31(1) of the FTRA (Offence to conduct transactions so as to avoid reporting requirements). His principal criticism was that the removal of a requirement to establish *mens rea* under section 31(1) FTRA was a wholly disproportionate response to the problem being tackled and one which infringed the values traditionally protected by the common law.[185] To this Kirby J stated:

> Provided the law is within power, the means adopted will not ordinarily be a matter for the Court. In this regard McHugh J's remarks on an analogous problem are appropriate (225):
>
> > [T]he fact that the Parliament has chosen to make liability to forfeiture independent of the fault of the owner does not make [the section impugned] unreasonably disproportionate to the purpose which it seeks to achieve. The section is not invalid because, among a range of reasonable measures to combat breaches of the Act, the Parliament has chosen a particularly drastic one.
>
> Courts may, for good reason, be reluctant to construe legislation, especially criminal legislation, as reversing the onus of proof (226) or creating an offence without need to establish a guilty intention (227). However, such provisions certainly exist in legislation enacted by the Parliament and undoubtedly within power.

184 *State v Coetzee* [1997] 2 LRC 593 [220] at 677.

185 *Leask v Commonwealth* [1996] 187 CLR 579, 638.

> […]. If the Act be within power, this Court is not concerned, as such, with the merits of the legislation, with its wisdom, the need for it or the reasonableness of its provisions. Those questions are for the Parliament.[186]

A number of parliamentary committees responsible for scrutinising the bills have been established to assist the legislature in avoiding adopting legislation which may infringe on human rights. However, these committees are sometimes given little time to examine proposed legislation and bills are adopted before their reports are published. In other instances, little consideration is given to them. It has even been said that "there is little or no evidence that [the reports of the Committee] have had a significant impact in preventing or dissuading parliaments from enacting laws that infringe basic democratic rights".[187] This situation is likely to remain as long as a Bill of Rights is not adopted by the Federal Parliament.

6.3.3.4 Judicial Review of Administrative Decisions

In a democratic society, which is based on the separation of powers, the judiciary review legislation, including administrative decisions and, in some cases, executive decisions. Such judicial review is meant to secure freedoms and security. It is of concern that, parallel to the adoption of AML/CTF regulations, the scope of the judicial review of decisions has been significantly reduced. The running of security programmes, such as the TFTP, raises continued questions about oversight and democracy. The administrative decision process remains opaque and does not offer the guarantee of impartiality. The executive ministerial decisions in terrorism matters involve of a wide range of different considerations whose weight is often unknown, despite the statement of reasons that sometimes accompany them. It is submitted that when executive ministerial and senior police officers' decisions impact on fundamental rights, such as the freedom of movement and property rights, the opacity of the decision process should be lifted and a proper mechanism should be put into place so that they can be challenged and reviewed. The Administrative Review Council has recommended that the statement of reasons from administrative decisions-makers should accurately record the relevant basis for the decision so that it can effectively be appealed.[188]

Under UNSCR 1624, Member States are called to ensure that the anti-terrorism legislation measures they take "must comply with all of their

186 *Leask v Commonwealth* [1996] 187 CLR 579, 632.

187 ALRC (2015), pp. 71, 72.

188 See in particular Recommendation 11, Administrative Review Council (ARC) (2012).

obligations under international law, in particular international human rights law, refugee law, and humanitarian law". In Europe, when anti-terrorism and organised crime legislation has unduly affected persons and organisations, the ECJ and the ECtHR have re-stated the primacy of the rule of law and the respect of fundamental freedoms, requiring Member States to enact adequate judicial review, a requirement which is conspicuously absent under the Code and COTUNA. Therefore, it is suggested that the ECJ's rulings in *Kadi* and *OMPI/PMOI* could assist Australia to put in place effective judicial review and remedy of decisions that impact on individual or body corporate fundamental rights and freedoms. Given that the UN Security Council's authority rests on the UN Charter, which refers to the respect of human rights and freedoms, any proscription under the Code and COTUNA should not be envisaged without a proper assessment and without providing an independent review mechanism to ensure that these rights are respected. Guidelines should ensure that procedural fairness is guaranteed, and that an effective review of the listing is conducted at least before it is subject to renewal.

An explanation for the different treatment of the same issues between Australia and the EU may lie in their respective history. For centuries, human rights were negated in Europe, either by autocratic rulers, or because of civil or international wars. Europe had to fight to have these rights written in its various national constitutions and fight further to keep them. By contrast, modern Australia is a young State. The large majority of Australians, particularly lawmakers, has never known autocratic rule. It has never known occupation or the deprivation of freedom of speech, freedom of association and participation in democratic life whereas Europe has had first hand experience of totalitarian regimes and wars. This does not mean that Australia does not value these freedoms. It means that it may not realise how fragile they are. Unfortunately, there is presently, at federal level, no Bill of Rights in Australia and requirements under the ICCPR are not directly enforceable. Hence, notwithstanding the present caselaw, to strengthen the respect of fundamental rights that found democracies, and the provisions of the ICCPR that Australia has committed itself to implement, it is highly desirable that Australia adopt a federal Bill of Rights reflecting the principles laid down in the ICCPR thereby making them enforceable throughout all jurisdictions. This would ensure that the fight against terrorism and organised crime is not carried out at the expense of the values that Australia seeks to protect.

6.3.3.4.1 *Balance of Powers*

The objective of control mechanisms is to ensure that the democratic legal principles and legal provisions are properly implemented. Granting wide powers to Ministers, Head of Government Departments and other authorities can lead to abuse of power and serious miscarriage of justice. There are many examples in the past of governments and security agencies around the world seeking new powers in the pursuit of increased national security, only for those powers to infringe on the fundamental freedoms of their own citizens, thus compromising the security these laws were meant to bring. When considerable pressures are put on agencies to produce results quickly, granting exceptional powers without adequate independent supervision does not only create harder working conditions for those involved in the implementation of security legislation, it also endangers society as a whole by creating a breeding ground for illegitimate practices. Unsupervised powers are a potential corrupting factor in every echelon of authority. Naively assuming that certain agencies will not misuse their extraordinary powers opens the door to corruption. Petrus Van Duyne observed that "corruption", also by organised crime, is not a threat by "them" but a defect of "us".[189]

Even though the Independent National Security Legislation Monitor reported that he did not see anything to suggest that the anti-terrorism laws had been used during the period under his review for matters unrelated to terrorism and national security, and that scholars have described the manner in which the Australian courts have dealt with terrorism cases as exemplary,[190] the *Independent National Security Legislation Monitor Repeal Bill* 2014, discharged from Notice Paper in July 2014, sent a very worrying message.[191] Independent scrutiny of institutions is essential for the preservation of an effective democratic system.

If special and extensive powers are deemed necessary, they must be accompanied by adequate and on-going supervision. In its recent report, the Australian Law Reform Commission has stated that "[g]iven the quantity of delegated law in Australia, robust safeguards and on-going scrutiny appear to be suitable ways to limit inappropriate delegations of legislative power".[192] The greater the powers, the more effective the supervision must be. The way security legislation is implemented, be it proactively or after the fact, should be scrutinised by an independent body capable of reviewing special and extensive administrative decisions. It has been recommended that review boards be elected for one long term of service with no possibility of reappointment.[193] It would be a disservice to those bestowed with large powers, even at their request, if there

189 Van Duyne (1997), p. 234.

190 Lynch, McGarrity, Williams (2015), p. 124.

191 See Wright P (2012).

192 ALRC (2015), 17.54, p. 462.

193 Walker B (2014), pp. 2, 3.

were not comprehensive, independent and regular controls. Prime Minister Robert Menzies warned:

> Whatever may be the extent of the power that may be taken to govern, to direct and to control by regulation, there must be as little interference with individual rights as is consistent with concerted national effort ... the greatest tragedy that could overcome a country would be for it to fight a successful war in defence of liberty and to lose its own liberty in the process.[194]

6.4 What Democracy?

The AML/CTF regime has introduced a new form of international governance, built around the financial system. Although established by legislation enacted by democratically elected parliaments, some of its rules are set by non-democratically elected bodies. Although its laws are governed by well-established legal principles, parts of its way of governance (financial transaction monitoring, listing, exclusion, forfeiture without criminal conviction) infringe on fundamental principles. All this in the name of security and for the protection of democracy. It begs the question what democracy are these measures protecting?

This change, which initially started with the fight against money laundering, has been gaining momentum with the realisation that modern forms of terrorism require very little financial means. It follows that terrorist financial activities have become harder to detect. Monitoring suspicious transactions does not help to preventively identify terrorism supporters. The low-income value of funds evades detection by the first generation of the AML/CTF measures. As Emilie Oftedal points out, "few of the terrorist financial activities are in themselves suspicious or spectacular. Unless the individuals in such self-financed cells are already under surveillance for some other reason, their financial transactions are unlikely to raise red flags".[195] Second-generation of counter-terrorism measures were engineered to boost the AML/CTF apparatus. They aim at tightening the net and casting it wider. To achieve this, everyone's transactions are put under close monitoring, even when the person is not suspected of any wrongdoing. Each financial transaction must be transparent and every name and motive be laid bare in front of institutions, agencies and, as the case may arise, the public eye. Under this configuration, cash is viewed as a factor that facilitates

194 Menzies (1939).

195 Oftedal (2015), p. 45.

ML and TF, along with an underground economy which profits criminals and tax evaders. The FATF sanctions and exclusion regimes pursued initially, and banks' de-risking policies, are now widely considered as counter-productive. The present trend is towards inclusion and a cashless society so that every monetary transaction can be monitored. The best way to achieve this objective is to digitise payments.[196] According to the World Bank, in 2014, only 6% of adults in the high-income OECD countries were unbanked.[197] In 2018, it was estimated that 69% adults worldwide had a financial institution or mobile money account. The figure rises to 100% in Australia.[198] Steady efforts are being made to bring the 1.7 billion people who are unbanked into the global financial system.

The new technologies, such as Internet banking and crypto-currencies, previously blamed for facilitating money laundering and terrorism financing, are now prized for their ability to process data. However, the increasing monitoring of financial transactions, widely spread data collection and interconnectivity reduce the privacy of anyone using financial services. It raises the fear of mass surveillance and the spectre of authoritarianism. These considerations appear not to deter law enforcement agencies. In 2017, Europol advocated a broader access to suspicious transaction reports (STRS) for security agencies, beyond the limited use of money laundering or terrorist financing.[199] This rational is questionable considering that only around 10% of STRS lead to further investigation by competent authorities. If the information contained in the STRS has so little relevance in prosecuting money laundering for which they were designed, which reason would there be for them to be more effective to fight against other forms of criminal activities?

In Europe, Internet providers, telecommunication companies and members of the public have criticised the broad data collection and brought the issue of surveillance to the attention of the judiciary.[200] Holding "that the fight against serious crime, in particular against organised crime and terrorism, is indeed of the utmost importance in order to ensure public security and its effectiveness may depend to a great extent on the use of modern investigation techniques", the European Court of Justice (ECJ) found that such an objective of general interest, however fundamental it may be, does not, in itself, justify these wide-ranging interferences with privacy rights or deem them necessary for the

196 World Bank Group (2015).

197 Demirgüç-Kunt, Klapper, Singer, Van Oudheusden (2015).

198 Demirgüç-Kunt, Klapper, Singer, Ansar, Hess (2018).

199 EUROPOL (2017b), p. 40.

200 *Digital Rights Ireland* (2014), *Maximillian Schrems* (2015), *Tele2 Sverige AB* (2016), *Opinion 1/15* of the Court (2017).

purpose of the fight against serious crime. The Court stated that legislation needs to provide for minimum safeguards which effectively protect personal data against the risk of abuse and any unlawful access.[201] It views automatic processing and international transfer of data as presenting a particularly high risk of unlawful access. Following the judicial considerations, the European Data Protection Supervisor has recommended that the international negotiations towards exchange of data agreements between Europol and third countries should be put to on hold until "appropriate safeguards" be "adduced".[202]

To counter threats against our democratic way of life, the best way is to strengthen democracy, not to reduce it. This was strongly underlined by the Council of Europe Rapporteur for the Political Affairs Committee who recommended a wide popular consensus to support anti-terrorism policy and a consolidation of the public's confidence in democratic institutions.[203] However, Tzvetan Todorov observed that, since the end of the 20th century, there had been a multiplication of fora where democracy does not exist and where its control disappears. He noted that Western society looks more and more like a "banana republic" where the tendency is to reduce democracy to the electoral process, denying the importance of the quality of the public debate (pluralism), the activity of the institutions (separation of powers) and the activity of the society regarding these institutions.[204] Unfortunately, AML/CTF legislation offers some grounds for concern regarding a breakdown of democratic principles in particular when the national parliament is willing to follow the recommendations of non-elected bodies which offer poor accountability and whose procedures are often opaque, when it *de facto* delegates law enforcement tasks to companies for whom economic interests are paramount, when it agrees to reinforce the executive's prerogatives at the expense of fundamental rights and the separation of powers, or when personal data and other information is handed over without effective guarantee that their confidentiality will be maintained. The issue of privacy strikes at the heart of democracy. As Volker Boehme-Neßler explains:

> Personal autonomy is an essential condition for citizens' democratic competency. From a psychological perspective, privacy, and data protection are necessary conditions for autonomous thinking and acting. They are therefore basic principle of democracy that is indispensable.

201 *Digital Rights Ireland* (2014), point 54.

202 European Data Protection Supervisor (EDPS) (2018).

203 Calamandrei (1981), point 4.

204 Todorov (2012).

> This democracy syllogism means that the idea of post-privacy that aims to abolish privacy strikes at the roots of democracy. [...] Democratic constitutions do know this. They often guarantee privacy as a human right. [...] Totalitarian states purposely give their citizens as little privacy as possible.[205]

This issue of privacy was quickly dismissed by the Australian government. It claimed that "the public interest in allowing government agencies to use information, to prevent, detect, disrupt or investigate conduct that relates to a matter of security, outweighs the associated loss of privacy".[206] The former Director-General of Security heading ASIO, David Irvine, alleged in 2014 that "80% of Australians are prepared to accept at least current levels of infringement on their privacy and their civil liberties in order to gain the benefits of community protection".[207] In a democratic society, according to human rights treaties such as the ICCPR and the ECHR, such interference to privacy must be proproportionate and limited to what is strictly necessary. In other words, the human rights legislation does not prevent the adoption of legislation permitting, as a preventive measure, the targeted retention of traffic and location data, for the purpose of fighting serious crime, unless the retention of data is limited, with respect to the categories of data to be retained, the means of communication affected, the persons concerned and the retention period adopted, to what is strictly necessary.[208] Given the absence of a Bill of Rights in Australia, there is no independent assessment to challenge the view that the present infringements of privacy are indeed proportional to or curtailed within effective safeguards.[209]

The value of the AML/CTF scheme must be weighed against its costs to the democracy we want to protect. Considering that the AML/CTF machinery had not brought the expected success against organised crime or yielded any significant result to prevent terrorist attacks, that it is not faultless (it sparks false positives),[210] that a wrongly spelt name, an unwarranted addition on a matchlist can cause difficulties of enormous proportions for an individuals or small

---

205 Boehme-Neßler Volker (2016), p. 228.

206 Counter-Terrorism Legislation Amendment Bill (No.1) 2016_Explantory Memorandum, p. 41, para.234.

207 Grattan (2014).

208 *Tele2 Sverige AB*, p. 108.

209 Several academics have raised concerns regarding the inadequacy of the *Privacy Act* 1988 in age of data collection and interconnectivity: Daly (2017), Sarre (2017).

210 European Commission (2011), p. 4; Vlcek (2008), p. 27.

company, that it has devastating consequences on poor countries when financial institutions are excluded from financial services, and that it infringes on privacy and fundamental principles held in criminal law, do the benefits of the AML/CTF regime compensate its disadvantages? Financial data collection has been useful in tracking terrorist organisations after the fact, to identify other network members or their accomplices, and to understand their *modus operandi*, arguably allowing thus the disruption of existing groups and contributing to diminishing the threat of future terrorist events occurring. This justifies data collection, providing that effective safeguards are put in place against unlawful access. Given that AML measures have a different objective from CTF, it might be appropriate to distinguish between money laundering and terrorism financing data collection and accessibility.

Transparency International observed that "public scrutiny is essential for the accountability of the AML/CTF mechanisms".[211] However, data are often unavailable to assess the efficiency of the machinery, creating a major obstacle to any independent monitoring of the effectiveness of the AML/CTF apparatus by civil society and the media. Despite the looming threat of mass-surveillance, there has not been a public debate in Australia about the type of democracy that is aspired to in an age of interconnectivity, or if mass surveillance is the best way to tackle modern crimes. So far, only human right activists and some academics have expressed their concerns. The question that needs to be addressed is how far should the AML/CTF scheme go, and where should the line be drawn to guarantee the rights which are essential to the functioning of the democracy we want to retain? Bearing in mind that a surveillance apparatus set up to protect national security may undermine or even destroy democracy under the cloak of defending it, as the ECtHR puts it, we must be on guard against conventional and complaisant answers.

211 Kowalczyk-Hoyer, Heywood (2017), p. 3.

Bibliography

Articles, Books, Papers, Addresses, Reports, Reviews, Inquiries and Submissions

Abi-Saab, Georges (1993), *Eloge du droit assourdi, Quelque réflexions sur le rôle de la soft law en droit international contemporain*, in Nouveaux itinéraires en droit, Hommage à François Rigaux, Bruylant, Brussels, pp. 59–68.

Adams, James (1986), *The Financing of Terror*, New English Library, 1986.

Administrative Review Council (ARC) (2012), *Federal Judicial Review in Australia*, Attorney-General's Department, September.

AFP (Australian Federal Police) (2017), *Submission 9*, quoted in PJC-IS (2018), Review of police stop, search and seizure powers, the control order regime and the preventative detention order regime, pp. 4, 6.

AGD (2005), Attorney-General's Department, *Submission 7* to the Parliamentary Joint Committee on ASIO, ASIS and DSD, quoted in *Review of the listing of six terrorist organisations,* March, p. 14.

AGD (2011), *A Guide to Framing Commonwealth Offences, Infringement Notices and Enforcement Powers,* Attorney-General Department.

AGD (2016), *Report on the Statutory Review of Anti-Money Laundering and Counter-Terrorism Financing Act 2006 (AML/CTF Act) and the associated Rules and Regulations,* Attorney-General Department, April.

Aiolfi, Gemma; Bauer, Hans-Peter (2012), The Wolfsberg Group, in "*Collective Action: Innovative Strategies to Prevent Corruption*", Pieth, Mark (ed.), Dike Zurich/St. Gallen (http://www.dike.ch/Collective_Action_Pieth).

Allens, Arthur Robinson (2006), *Focus: A Summary of the key changes under the AML/CTF Legislation,* 17.11.2006, <www.allens.com.au/pubs/baf/foaml17nov06.htm> retrieved 28.05.2007.

Alvesalo, Anne; Tombs, Steve (2005), *Evaluating Economic Crime Control?*, Security Journal, Vol. 18(4), pp. 7–15.

Analytical Support and Sanctions Implementation Monitoring Team (2009), *Ninth Report submitted pursuant to resolution 1822 (2008) concerning Al-Qaida and the Taliban and associated individuals and entities*, S/2009/245, 13.05.2009.

Analytical Support and Sanctions Implementation Monitoring Team (2011), *Eleventh Report pursuant to Security Council resolutions 1267 (1999), 1988 (2011) and 1989 (2011) concerning linkages between Al-Qaida and the Taliban as well as other individuals, groups, undertakings and entities associated with the Taliban in constituting a threat to the peace, stability and security of Afghanistan*, S/2011/790, December.

Analytical Support and Sanctions Implementation Monitoring Team (2012), *Thirteenth Report pursuant to resolution 1989 (2011) concerning Al-Qaida and associated individuals and entities*, S/2012/968, December.

Andersson, Torbjörn; Cameron, Iain; Nordback, Kenneth (2003), *EU Blacklisting: The Renaissance of Imperial Power, but on a Global Scale*, European Business Law Review, Vol. 14, pp. 111–141.

Annan, Kofi (2006), *Uniting against terrorism: recommendations for a global counter-terrorism strategy*, Report of the Secretary-General, Point 113, A/60/825, 27.04.2006.

Arlacchi, Pino (2001), Under-Secretary-General Executive Director, United Nations Office on Drugs and Crime (UNODC), Keynote Speech to the International Conference on Strategies of the EU and the US in Combating Transnational Organized Crime Ghent (Belgium) 24 January, <www.unodc.org/unodc/en/about-unodc/speeches/speech_2001-01-24_1.html>, last viewed 30.03.2019.

Armitage, Laura (2014), *Westpac keeps Somali money transfers open until Federal Court hearing*, Herald Sun, 26.11.2014.

Armitage, Laura (2015), *Westpac to stop Somali money transfers on March 31*, Herald Sun, 29.03.2015, <www.heraldsun.com.au/leader/east/westpac-to-stop-somali-money-transfers-on-march-31/story-fngnvlxu-1227281376048>.

Ashworth, Andrew; Zedner, Lucia (2008), *Defending the Criminal Law: Reflections on the Changing Character of Crime, Procedure, and Sanctions*, Crim Law and Philos, Vol.2, pp. 21–51.

Ashworth, Andrew; Zedner, Lucia (2012), *Prevention and Criminalization: Justification and Limits*, New Criminal Law Review, Vol.15(4), pp. 542–571.

ASIO (2017), *Annual Report 2016–17*, October.

AUSTRAC (2011), *Annual report 2010–11*.

AUSTRAC (2014a), *Annual report 2013–14*.

AUSTRAC (2014b), *Terrorism financing in Australia*.

AUSTRAC (2014c), *Typologies and case studies report 2014*.

AUSTRAC (2014d), *Explanatory Statement – Anti-Money Laundering and Counter-Terrorism Financing Rules Amendment Instrument 2014 (No.3)* amending the *Anti-Money Laundering and Counter-Terrorism Financing Rules Instrument 2007 (No.1)*.

AUSTRAC (2015), *Annual Report 2014/5*.

AUSTRAC (2017), Annual Report 2016–17, p. 71.

AUSTRAC (undated), *Risk management – A tool for small-to-medium sized businesses*, <www.austrac.gov.au/files/risk_management_tool.pdf>, last viewed 14.03.2019.

AUSTRAC – ACNC (2017), *National risk assessment into the not-for-profit sector – money laundering / terrorism financing*, Commonwealth of Australia, <http://www.acnc.gov.au/nfprisk> (retrieved 15.04.2018).

Australian National Audit Office (2017), *Proceeds of crime*, ANAO Report N°43 2016–17.

ALRC (1999), Australian Law Reform Commission, *Confiscation that counts, a review of the Proceeds of Crime Act 1987*, Report N°87.

ALRC (2015), Australian Law Reform Commission, *Traditional Rights and Freedoms—Encroachments by Commonwealth Laws*, Final Report, December (ALRC Report 129, 2015).

Barone, Raffaella, Masciandaro Donato (2008), *Worldwide anti-money laundering regulation: estimating the costs and benefits*, Global Business and Economics Review, Vol.10, n°3, pp. 243–264.

Bartels, Lorana (2010), *The status of laws on outlaw motorcycle gangs in Australia*, Second edition, Research in Practice, Report No. 2 March 2010, Australia Institute of Criminology, Australian Government, Canberra.

Barwick, Garfield (1960), Attorney-General, House of Representatives Crimes Bill 1960, Second Reading Speech, Thursday, 8 September.

Bassiouni, M Cherif (1990), *Effective national and International Action against Organized Crime and Terrorist Criminal Activities*, Emory International Law Review, Vol. 4, pp. 9–42.

Bassiouni, M Cherif; Vetere, Eduardo (1998), *Organized Crime, a compilation of U.N. documents 1975–1998*, Transnational Publishers, New York.

Bernasconi, Paolo (1985), paper presented to the annual assembly of the Society of Swiss Lawyers, Basel, (ZSR NF 104, 2è sem, p.345s).

Bernasconi, Paolo (1988), *Finanzunterwelt: Gegen Wirtschaftskriminalität und organisiertes Verbrechen*, Orell Füssli, Zürich.

Biddington, Monica; Spooner, Diane; Scully, Sharon (2009), *Crimes Legislation Amendment (Serious and Organised Crime) Bill (N.2)*, Department of Parliamentary Services, Parliamentary Library, Bill Digest N° 68, 23 November 2009.

Black, Julia; Rouch, David (2008), *The development of the global markets as rule-makers: engagement and legitimacy*, Law and Financial Markets Review, May, Vol. 2(3), pp. 218–233.

Boehme-Neßler, Volker (2016), *Privacy: a matter of democracy. Why democracy needs privacy and data protection*, International Data Privacy Law, Vol.6, No.3, pp. 222–229.

Bottomley, Stephen; Bronitt, Simon (2012), *Law in context*, Federation Press.

Boutry, Timothée; Decugis, Jean-Michel (2018), *Lutte contre le financement de Daech : «L'argent permet d'identifier des terroristes»*, Le Parisien, 25.04.2018, <http://www.leparisien.fr/faits-divers/lutte-contre-le-financement-de-daech-l-argent-permet-d-identifier-des-terroristes-25-04-2018-7683828.php>, last viewed 17.05.2018.

Bowen, Lionel (1987a), Commonwealth Attorney-General, Second Reading Speech, *Proceeds of Crime Bill 1987*, *Parliamentary Debates* (HR Hansard), 30 April 1987.

Bowen, Lionel (1987b), Commonwealth Attorney-General, Second Reading Speech to the *Cash Transaction Reports Bill* 1987, Senate, *Parliamentary Debates* (Hansard), 25 November 1987.

Bozonnet, Jean-Jacques; Decamps, Marie-Claude (2007), *Pietro Grasso, "Nous avons décapité l'organe de direction de Cosa Nostra"* in Le Monde, 07.11.07.

Braithwaite, John (1993), *Following the Money Trail to What Destination ? An Introduction to the Symposium*, 44 Alabama Law Review, Vol. 44(3), pp. 657–668.

Bricknell, Samantha; Mccusker, Rob; Chadwick, Hannah; Rees, David (2012), *Money laundering and terrorism financing risks to Australian non-profit organisations*, Research and public policy series no.114, Australian Institute of Criminology, ISBN 978 1 921532 86 3 ISSN 1836-2079, Australian Government, Canberra.

Briggs, Gavin (2010), *The Cost of Laundering Dirty Money*, Strategic Analysis Paper, Published by Future Directions International Pty Ltd, Desborough House, Suite 2, 1161 Hay Street, West Perth, WA 6005, 2 February.

Bronitt, Simon (2003a), *Australia's Legal Response to Terrorism: Neither Novel nor Extraordinary?*, Paper presented at the Castan Centre for Human Rights Law Conference, *Human Rights 2003: The Year in Review*, Melbourne, 04.12.2003, <www.law.monash .edu.au/castancentre/events/2003/bronitt-paper.pdf> retrieved (17.05.2013).

Bronitt, Simon (2003b), *Constitutional Rhetoric versus Criminal Justice Realities: Unbalanced Responses To Terrorism?*, Public Law Review, Vol. 14, n°2, pp. 76–82.

Bronitt, Simon (2010), *Australia* in Heller, Kevin Jon; Dubber, Markus D, *Handbook of Comparative Criminal Law*, Stanford University Press, pp. 49–96, also published as ANU College of Law Research Paper N°09-25.

Bronitt, Simon; McSherry, Bernadette (2010), *Principles of Criminal Law*, Third Edition, Lawbook Co, Thomson Reuters, Sydney.

Brummer, Chris (2010), *Why Soft Law Dominates International Finance—and not Trade*, Journal of International Economic Law, Vol. 13(3), pp. 623–643.

Bures, Oldrich (2015), *Ten Years of EU's Fight against Terrorist Financing: A Critical Assessment*, Intelligence and National Security, Vol. 30 (2–3), pp. 207–233.

Cachia, Franklin (2017), *Aggressive Tax Planning: An Analysis from an EU Perspective*, EC Tax Review, pp. 257–273.

Calamandrei, Franco (1981), Rapporteur, *Defence of Democracy against Terrorism in Europe – Tasks and Problems*, Report, Political Affairs Committee, Parliamentary Assembly, Doc.4688, Strasbourg, 12–14 November 1980, 19.2.1981.

Caldini, Camille (2011), *Trio néonazi: l'échec des renseignements allemands*, Lexpress. fr 18/11/2011.

Camdessus, Michel (1998), *Money Laundering: the Importance of International Countermeasures*, address at the plenary meeting of the Financial Action Task Force on Money Laundering, Paris, 10 February 1998, in FATF (1998), *Annual Report 1997–1998*, June, pp. 40–41.

Cameron, Iain (2003a), *UN Targeted Sanctions, Legal Safeguards and the European Convention on Human Rights*, Nordic Journal of International Law, vol. 72, pp. 159–214.

Cameron, Iain (2003b), *European Union Anti-Terrorist Blacklisting*, Human rights law review, vol 3, pp. 225–256.

Cameron, Iain (2006a), *The European Convention on Human Rights, Due Process and United Nations Security Council Counter-Terrorism Sanctions*, Report, Council of Europe, 02.06.2006.

Cameron, Iain (2006b), *Terrorist Financing in International Law* in Bantekas Ilias, *International and European Financial*, Criminal Law, Butterworths, London, pp. 65–95.

Canellas, Claude (2009), *Un nouveau coup porté en France à la tête de l'ETA*, Reuters 11.04.09.

Caneppele, Stefano; Calderoni, Francesco; Martocchia, Sara (2009), *Not only banks: Criminological models on the infiltration of public contracts by Italian organized crime*, Journal of Money Laundering Control, Vol. 12 (2), pp. 151–172.

Canestri, Daniele (2015), *Fourth EU AML Directive: What is Missing? Section 319 Patriot Act and the New EU AML Directive*, European Journal of Crime, Criminal Law & Criminal Justice, Vol. 23, pp. 214–240.

Cassella, Stefan D (2003), *Forfeiture of Terrorist Assets under the USA Patriot Act of 2001*, Law and Policy in International Business, 34, 2002–2003, pp. 7–16.

CCBE – Council of Bars and Law Societies of Europe (2011), CCBE *response to FATF consultation paper "The review of the standards, preparation for the 4th round of mutual evaluations"*, 21,01.2011,<http://www.ccbe.eu/fileadmin/speciality_distribution/public/documents/ANTI_MONEY_LAUNDERING/AML_Position_papers/EN_AML_20110121_CCBE_response_to_FATF_consultation_paper_The_review_of_the_standards_-_preparation_for_the_4th_round_of_the_mutual_evaluation__October_2010_.pdf>, last viewed 03.05.2018.

CDPP (2014), *Money laundering – guidance for charging offences under Division 400 of the Code*, Australia's Federal Prosecution Service, Australian Government, September.

CDPP (2017), *Money laundering – guidance for charging offences under Division 400 of the Code*, National Legal Directions.

Chadwick, Elizabeth (1997), *Terrorism and the law: Historical contexts, contemporary dilemmas, and the end(s) of democracy*, Crime, Law & Social Change, Vol. 26, pp. 329–350.

Chaikin, David (2011), *Adapting the qualifications to the banker's common law duty of confidentiality to fight transnational crime*, Sydney Law Review, June, Vol. 33(2), pp. 265–294.

Chaliand, Gérard; Blin, Arnaud (2004), *Histoire du Terrorisme de l'Antiquité à Al Qaida*, Edition Bayard, Paris.

Chambraud, Cécile (2007), *Dix-sept dirigeants de Batasuna en détention provisoire*, in Le Monde, 08.10.07.

Champeyrache, Clotilde (2000), *L'analyse économique de la mafia: une revue de littérature*. In: Mélanges de l'Ecole française de Rome, Italie et Méditerranée, T.112, N°1, pp. 469–493.

Clarke, John QC (2008), *Report of the Inquiry into the Case of Dr Mohammed Haneef*, Vol. 1, November.

Commission of the European Communities (2004), *Communication from the Commission to the Council and the European Parliament on the prevention of and fight against organised crime in the financial sector*, COM(2004) 262 final, 16.4.2004.

Commonwealth Secretariat (2006), *Combating money laundering and terrorist financing: A model of best practice for the financial sector, the professions and other designated businesses* (2nd ed.), London.

Conference Internationale des Juristes (2004), *La liste des groupes terroristes: l'approche du droit européen et international – l'Organisation des Modjahedines du Peuple d'Iran (OMPI)*, L'Harmattan, Paris.

Cornall, Robert AO (2007), *The Effectiveness of Criminal Law on Terrorism*, in Lynch, Andrew; MacDonald, Edwina; Williams, George, *Law and Liberty in the War on Terror*, The Federation Press, Sydney, pp. 50–58.

Costa, Antonio Maria (2009), Director General, UNODC, *The global crime threat – we must stop it*, 18th Session of the Commission on Crime Prevention and Criminal Justice, Vienna, 16 April 2009, <www.unodc.org/unodc/en/about-unodc/speeches/2009-16-04.html>, last visited 16.03.2019.

Costigan, Frank QC (1982), *Royal Commission on the Activities of the Federated Ship Painters and Dockers Union*, Interim Report 4, Vol. 1, Australian Government Publishing Service, Canberra.

Costigan, Frank QC (1984), *Organized crime and a free society*, The Australian & New Zealand Journal of Criminology, Vol. 17, p. 7–19.

Costigan, Frank QC (1986), *International Money laundering*, Australian Banker, 100 (5), October, pp. 200–204.

Counter-Terrorism Coordinator (2008), *Revised Strategy on Terrorist Financing*, 11778/1/08 REV 1, Council of the European Union, 17 July 2008, <http://register.consilium.europa.eu/pdf/en/08/st11/st11778-re01.en08.pdf>, last viewed 30 May 2015.

Court of Justice of the European Union (2015), *Judgment in Case C-362/14 Press and Information Maximillian Schrems v Data Protection Commissioner*, Press Release N°117/15, Luxembourg, 06.10.2015.

Criminal Law Branch (2002), *National interest analysis document in support of the ratification of the 1999 Convention for the suppression of the financing of terrorism*, Attorney-General's Department, Criminal Justice Division, 18 June 2002.

Crimm, Nina J (2008) *Moral Hazard of Anti-Terrorism Financing Measures: A Potential to Compromise Civil Societies and National Interests*, Wake Forest Law Review, Vol. 43, pp. 577–626.

Daly, Angela (2017), *Privacy in automation: An appraisal of the emerging Australian approach*, computer law & security review, Vol. 33, pp. 836–846.

Dandurand, Yvon; Chin, Vivienne (2004), *Links Between Terrorism and Other Forms of Crime*, A report submitted to: Foreign Affairs Canada and The United Nations Office on Drugs and Crime, International Centre for Criminal Law Reform and Criminal Justice Policy, 1822 East Mall, Vancouver, British Columbia, Canada V6T 1Z1, April.

De Búrca, Grainne (2010), *The European Court of Justice and the International Legal Order after Kadi*, Howard International Law Journal, Vol. 51, n°1, Winter, pp. 1–49.

De Goede, Marieke; Wesseling, Mara (2017), *Secrecy and security in transatlantic terrorism finance tracking*, Journal of European Integration, 39:3, pp. 253–269.

De Kerchove, Gilles (2012), *L'Union européenne et le monde dans la lutte contre le terrorisme* in Dony, Marianne, *La dimension externe de l'espace de liberté, de sécurité et de justice au lendemain de Lisbonne et de Stockholm: un bilan à mi-parcours*, Éditions de l'Université de Bruxelles, Brussels, pp. 81–96.

De Koker, Louis; Singh, Supriya; Capal, Jonathan (2017), *Closure of bank accounts of remittance service providers: Global challenges and community perspectives in Australia*, University of Queensland Law Journal, Vol. 36(1), pp. 119–154.

De Schutter, Olivier (2002), *La Convention européenne des droits de l'homme à l'épreuve de la lutte contre le terrorisme*, in Bribosia, Emmanuelle and Weyembergh, Anne, *Lutte contre le terrorisme et droits fondamentaux*, Ed.Bruylant, pp. 85–152.

Delmas-Marty, Mireille (2010), *Libertés et sûretés dans un monde dangereux*, Edition du Seuil, Paris.

Deloitte Bedrijfsrevisoren (2011), *Final Study on the Application of the Anti-Money Laundering Directive*, European Commission DG Internal Market and Services – Budget, Belgium, 24.01.2011.

Demirgüç-Kunt, Asli; Klapper, Leora; Singer, Dorothe; Van Oudheusden, Peter (2015), *The Global Findex Database 2014: Measuring Financial Inclusion around the World*, Policy Research Working Paper 7255, World Bank, Washington, DC, <http://documents.worldbank.org/curated/en/187761468179367706/pdf/WPS7255.pdf>, last viewed 11.05.2018.

Demirgüç-Kunt, Asli; Klapper, Leora; Singer, Dorothe; Ansar, Saniy; Hess, Jake (2018), *The Global Findex Database 2017: Measuring Financial Inclusion and the Fintech Revolution*, International Bank for Reconstruction and Development/The World Bank, World Bank Group, 19.04.2018, <http://www.worldbank.org/en/programs/globalfindex>, last accessed 19.04.2018.

Douglas, Roger (2012), *The Judicial Review of Counter-terrorism Measures: a Comparative Study*, submission 18 to the Inquiry into the Independent Reviewer of Terrorism Laws Bill 2008 (n°2), 16.01.2012.

Doyle, Todd (2002), *Cleaning up anti-money laundering strategies: current FATF tactics needlessly violate international law*, Houston Journal of International Law, Winter, Vol. 24(2), pp. 279–313.

Dubuis, Etienne (2011), *Book review* of Bruckner, Pascal, *Le fanatisme de l'Apocalypse*, Grasset, Paris in Le Temps, 19 November.

Eckes, Christina (2009), *Test Case for the Resilience of the EU's Constitutional Foundations International Sanctions against Individuals*, European Public Law, Sept, Vol. 15(3), pp. 351–378.

Eckes, Christina (2011), *Controlling the Most Dangerous Branch From Afar: Multilayered Counter-Terrorist Policies and the European Judiciary*, Amsterdam Law School Legal Studies Research Paper N°2011-08.

ECOLEF (2013), *The Economic and Legal Effectiveness of Anti-Money Laundering and Combating Terrorist Financing Policy*, Final Report, Utrecht University, the Netherlands.

Eeckhout, Piet (2007), *Community Terrorism Listings, Fundamental Rights and UN Security Council Resolutions. In Search for the Right Fit.* European Constitutional Law Review, Vol. 3(2), pp. 183–206.

Emerton, Patrick (2007), Joint Committee on Intelligence And Security, Inquiry into the terrorist organisation listing provisions of the *Criminal Code Act 1995*, Wednesday, 4 April 2007, Hansard, pp. 24–37.

Emerton, Patrick (2009), Submission to the Australian Government on the National Security Legislation, Discussion Paper, 25 September.

European Central Bank (2005), *Opinion of 15 December 2005 on a proposal for an EC regulation on information on the payer accompanying transfers of funds* (CON/2005/56) (2005/C336/07), 31.12.2005, OJ C336, pp. 109–114.

European Commission (1995), *First report on the implementation of the Money Laundering Directive (91/308/EEC) to be submitted to the European Parliament and to the Council*, COM/95/54FINAL, 03.03.1995.

European Commission (2011), *Meeting with EU Private Stakeholders on Anti-Money Laundering and Counter Terrorist Financing Policy on 1st February 2011*, Directorate General Internal Market and Services, Brussels, 17.02.2011.

European Commission (2012), *Report from the Commission to the European Parliament and the Council on the application of Directive 2005/60/EC on the prevention of the use of the financial system for the purpose of money laundering and terrorist financing*, COM(2012) 168 final, 11.4.2012.

European Data Protection Supervisor (EDPS) (2018), *Opinion on eight negotiating mandates to conclude international agreements allowing the exchange of data between Europol and third countries*, Opinion 2/2018, <https://edps.europa.eu/sites/edp/files/publication/18-03-19_opinion_international_agreements_europol_en.pdf>, last viewed 02.04.2019.

European Economic and Social Committee (2006), *Opinion on the Proposal for a Regulation of the European Parliament and of the Council on information on the payer accompanying transfers of funds*, COM(2005)343 final – 2005/0138 (COD), (2006/C 185/16), OJ C185, 08.08.06.

Europol (2016), *TE-SAT 2016, European Union Terrorism Situation and Trend Report.*

Europol (2017a), *TE-SAT 2017, European Union Terrorism Situation and Trend Report.*

Europol (2017b), *From Suspicion to Action – Converting financial intelligence into greater operational impact,* Financial Intelligence Group report, 05.09.2017.

Europol (2017c), *Global anti-money laundering framework – Europol report reveals poor success rate and offers ways to improve*, Press release, 05.09.2017.

Evans, Chris (2008), Immigration Minister, Address to the 2008 National Members' Conference of the Migration Review Tribunal and Refugee Review Tribunal, The Windsor Hotel, Melbourne, 29.02.2008. <www.abc.net.au/news/2008-02-19/i-have-too-much-power-immigration-minister/1047184>.

Fassbender, Bardo (2006), *Targeted Sanctions and Due Process*, Study commissioned by the United Nations Office of Legal Affairs, Humboldt Universität zu Berlin, 20.03.2006. International Organizations Law Review (3), pp. 437–485, <https://www.eui.eu/Documents/DepartmentsCentres/AcademyofEuropeanLaw/CourseMaterialsHR/HR2009/Fassbender/FassbenderBackgroundReading4.pdf>, last viewed 02.04.2019.

FATF (1990), *Annual Report I*.

FATF (1991), *Annual Report II*, 13 May.

FATF (1993), *Annual Report IV*, 29 June.

FATF (1996), *Second Mutual Evaluation Report on Australia*, FATF-VIII, EVAL(96).3 REVI1, 11 December.

FATF (1998a), *Annual Report IX*, June.

FATF (1998b), *1997–1998 Report on Money Laundering Typologies*, 12 February.

FATF (1999), *Annual Report X*, 2 July.

FATF (2001a), *Annual Report XII – 2000–2001*, 22 June.

FATF (2001b), *Report on Money Laundering Typologies 2000–2001*, 1 February.

FATF (2002a), *Annual Report 2001–2002*, 21 June.

FATF (2002b), *Report on Money Laundering Typologies 2001–2002*.

FATF (2002c), *Guidance for Financial Institutions in Detection Terrorist Financing Activities*, 24 April.

FATF (2005a), *Annual Report 2004–05*, 10 June.

FATF (2005b), *Third Mutual Evaluation Report on Anti-Money Laundering and Combating the Financing of Terrorism – Australia*, 14 October.

FATF (2007), *The Implementation of Activity-Based Financial Prohibitions of UNSCR 1737*, October 2007.

FATF (2010), *Global Money Laundering and Terrorist Financing Threat Assessment*, July.

FATF (2015) *Anti-money laundering and counter-terrorist financing measures – Australia*, Mutual Evaluation Report (MER), April.

FATF (2016), *Guidance on the criminalisation of terrorist financing (Recommendation 5)*, October.

FATF (2017), *Anti-money laundering and terrorist financing measures and financial inclusion – With a supplement on customer due diligence*, November.

FATF (2018), *BCBS, CPMI, FATF and FSB Welcome Industry Initiative Facilitating Correspondent Banking*, 06.03.2018, <http://www.fsb.org/2018/03/bcbs-cpmi-fatf-and-fsb-welcome-industry-initiative-facilitating-correspondent-banking/>, last viewed 11.05.2018.

FATF – Lewis, David (2016), *Anti-money laundering and tax evasion – who sets the rule and how?*, public hearing, Committee of Inquiry into Money Laundering, Tax Avoidance and Tax Evasion, <http://www.europarl.europa.eu/cmsdata/112269/Replies_FATF_en.pdf>, last seen 08.03.2019.

Federation of Community Legal Centres (VIC) INC – FCLC (2006), Federation of Community Legal Centres, Submission to Security Legislation Review Committee, January.

FERWERDA, Joras (2009), *The Economics of Crime and Money Laundering: Does Anti-Money Laundering Policy Reduce Crime?*, Review of Law and Economics, 2009, Vol. 5(2), pp. 903–930.

FinCEN (2011), *Annual report*, 8 September 2011.

Fisse, Brent (1987), *Draconian Overreach in Organised Crime Control: The Real Dirt in Money-Laundering*, Law Society Journal (N.S.W.), 25 (9).

Fisse, Brent (1988), *The proceeds of Crime Act – the Rise of Money Laundering Offences and the Fall of Principle*, Criminal Law Journal, Feb, Vol. 13(1), pp. 5–23.

Fisse, Brent (1992), *Fraud and the Liability of Company Directors*, in Grabosky Peter, *Complex Commercial Fraud, Conference Proceedings*, Australian Institute of Criminology, Australian Government, Canberra, pp. 13–27.

Fisse, Brent (1994), *Money Laundering, Regulatory Srategy and Internal Corporate Controls*, Current Issues in Criminal Justice, Nov, pp. 177–195.

Fisse, Brent; Fraser, David (1992), *Smurfing: Rethinking the Structured Transaction Provisions of the Cash Transaction Reports Act* in Fisse, Brent; Fraser, David; Coss, Graeme, *The Money Trail. Confiscation of Proceeds of Crime, Money Laundering and Cash Transaction Reporting*, The Law Book Company Ltd.

Fisse, Brent; Fraser, David; Coss, Graeme (1992), *The Money Trail – Confiscation of Proceeds of Crime, Money Laundering and Cash Transaction Reporting*, The Law Book Company Ltd.

Fisse, Brent; Leonard, Peter (1997), *International Electronic Money Systems and Money Laundering*, Communications Law Bulletin, Vol. 16, Issue 2, Winter, pp. 22–25.

Fitzgerald, Peter L. (2007), *Smarter "smart" sanctions*, Penn State International Law Review, Summer, Vol. 26(1), p.37–56.

Flauss, Jean-François (2010), *« Les listes noires » de l'O.N.U. devant le Comité des droits de l'homme*, Revue trimestrielle des droits de l'homme, Vol. 82, pp. 371–382.

Flore, Daniel (2005), *La loi du 19 décembre 2003 relative aux infractions terroristes: Genèse, principes et conséquences* in *Questions d'actualité de droit pénal et de procédure pénale*, colloque organisé à Mons le 27 mai 2005, Bruxelles, Bruylant.

Fox, Richard (1998), *The Expansion of Federal Criminal Law in Combating Money Laundering*, in Weerasooria Wickrema , Jensen Neil , Visser John , *Money laundering in Australia, The Roles of the Financial Industry and Law Enforcement in Combating Money laundering: A Co-operative Approach*, Proceedings of a National Seminar Held in Melbourne on 31 March 1998, A Prospect Intelligence Report, Prospect Media Pty Ltd, St Leonards, NSW, pp. 11–14.

Freeman, Michael (2011), *The Sources of Terrorist Financing: Theory and Typology*, Studies in Conflict & Terrorism, Vol. 34, pp. 461–475.

Freiberg, Arie (1988), *Ripples from the Bottom of the Harbour: Some Social Ramifications of Taxation Fraud*, Criminal Law Journal, June, Vol. 12(3), pp. 136–192.

Freiberg, Arie (1992), *Criminal Confiscation, Profit and Liberty*, 25 ANZJ Crim, pp. 44–82.

Freiberg, Arie; Fox, Richard (2000), *Fighting Crime with Forfeiture: Lessons form History*, Vol. 6, Australian Journal of Legal History, pp. 1–50.

Galland, Jean-Pierre (2006), *Gestion des risques, lutte contre le terrorisme*, Canadian Journal of Criminology and Criminal Justice, June, 2006, Vol. 48(3), pp. 359–381.

Gani, Miriam; Mathew, Penelope (2008), *Fresh Perspectives on the "War on Terror"*, ANU E Press, Canberra, Australia.

Gani, Miriam; Urbas, Gregor (2004), *Alert or Alarmed? Recent Legislative Reforms Directed at Terrorist Organisations and Persons Supporting or Assisting Terrorist Acts*, Newcastle Law Review, Vol. 8(1), p. 23–50.

Garrigos-Kerjan, Mariel (2006), *La tendance sécuritaire de la lutte contre le terrorisme*, Archives de Politique criminelle, pp. 189–213.

Gautier, Marie (2008), *Lutte contre le terrorisme et droits fondamentaux: le droit international sous la surveillance de la CJCE*, La semaine juridique, édition générale n°45, 5 novembre, II 10186.

Geary, Joy (2009a), *Light is the best antidote*, Journal of Money Laundering Control, Vol. 12, n°3, pp. 215–220.

Geary, Joy (2009b), *The enforceable undertakings under the microscope*, Anti-Money Laundering Magazine, AFMA, Sydney, complimentary version, Sept, pp. 12–16.

Gillies, Peter (1997) *Criminal Law*, fourth edition, LBC Information Services, NSW.

Gilmore, William (2004), *Dirty money: the evolution of international measures to counter money laundering and the financing of terrorism*, Council of Europe Publishing, Strasbourg.

Giudicelli-Delage, Geneviève (2002), *La riposte pénale contre les organisations criminelles en droit français*, in Collective (2002), Manacorda Stephano, *L'infraction d'organisation criminelle en Europe (Allemagne-Espagne-France-Italie-Union Européenne)*,

Association de recherches pénales européennes, Programme Falcone 1998 de l'Union Européenne, Publication de la Faculté de Droit et des Sciences sociales de Poitiers, Tome 43, Presses Universitaires de France (PUF), pp. 111–190.

Golden, Tim (2002), *5 Months After Sanctions Against Somali Company, Scant Proof of Qaeda Tie*, A Nation Challenged: Money, New York Times, 13 April.

Gowlland-Debbas, Vera (2009), *Is the UN Security Council Bound by Human Rights Law?*, American Society of International Law Proceedings, Vol. 103, pp. 199–202.

Grabosky, Peter N (1989), *The Deputy Crown Solicitor and the bottom of the harbour scheme*, in Wayward governance: illegality and its control in the public sector, Australian studies in law, crime and justice series, Australian Institute of Criminology, Canberra, pp. 143–159.

Grabosky, Peter; Braithwaite, John (1986), *Of Manners Gentle – Enforcement Strategies of Australian Business Regulatory Agencies*, Oxford University Press, Melbourne.

Grabosky, Peter; Stohl, Michael (2010), *Crime and Terrorism*, Compact criminology, Sage, London.

Grattan, Michelle (2014), *Grattan on Friday: In Conversation with ASIO chief David Irvine*, 15.08.2014, <http://theconversation.com/grattan-on-friday-in-conversation-with-asio-chief-david-irvine-30536>, last viewed 25.04.2018.

Gray, Anthony (2012), The compatibility of unexplained wealth provisions and 'civil' forfeiture regimes with Kable, QUT Law & Justice Journal, Vol. 12, n°2, pp. 18–35.

Graycar, Adam; Grabosky, Peter; Tailby, Rebecca; Keelty, Mick; Deputy Assisted by Gordon, Sandy (2001), *Global and Regional Approaches to Fighting Transnational Crime*, International Policing Conference, Adelaide, Australian Institute of Criminology and Australian Federal Police, 6 March 2001.

Gurule, Jimmy (1995), *The Money Laundering Control Act of 1986: Creating a New Federal Offense or Merely Affording Federal Prosecutors an Alternative Means of Punishing Specified Unlawful Activity*, American Criminal Law Review, Spring, Vol. 32(3), p. 823–854.

Gurule, Jimmy (2008), *Unfunding Terror-the Legal Response to the Financing of Global Terrorism,* Edward Elgar Publ Ltd, Cheltenham, UK.

Hancock, Nathan (2002), *Terrorism and the law in Australia: legislation, commentary and constraints,* Law and Bills Digest Group, Information and Research Services, Department of the Parliamentary Library, Research Paper, No.12, 2001–02, 19 March.

Hanks, Peter; Keyzer, Patrick; Clarke, Jennifer (2004), *Australian Constitutional Law, Materials and Commentary*, 7th Edition, LexisNexis, Butterworths.

Hansch, Lindsay (1996), *Australia's National Anti-Terrorist Plan – Crisis and Response Arrangements*, in Thompson, Alan (ed.) *Terrorism and the 2000 Olympics*, Australia Defense Studies Centre, pp. 91–102.

Harris-Hogan, Shandon (2017), *Violent extremism in Australia: An overview*, Australian Institute of Criminology, No. 491 March, Australian Government, Canberra.

Harris Rimmer, Susan (2008), *The Dangers of Character Tests: Dr Haneef and other cautionary tales*, The Australia Institute, Discussion Paper Number 101, October 2008.

Harris Rimmer, Sue; Jaggers, Browen (2006), *Anti-Money Laundering and Counter-Terrorism Financing Bill 2006*, n°60, 2006–07, Law and Bills Digest Section, Department of Parliamentary Services, Parliament of Australia, 30 November, ISSN 1328-8091.

Harvey, Jackie (2005), *An evaluation of money laundering policies*, Journal of Money Laundering Control Vol. 8(4), pp. 339–345.

Harvey, Jackie (2008), *Just how effective is money laundering legislation?*, Security Journal 21, pp. 189–211.

Harvey, Jackie (2009), *The search for crime money – debunking the myth: facts versus imagery*, Journal of Money Laundering Control, Vol. 12(2), pp. 97–100.

HOME OFFICE (2006), *Report of the Official Account of the Bombings in London on 7th July 2005*, House of Commons, The Stationery Office.

Hooper, Hayley J. (2012), *Liberty before Security: Case T-85/09 Yassin Abdullah Kadi v. Commission (No.2) [2010] ECR 00000 (30 September 2010)*, European Public Law, Vol. 18, n°3, pp. 457–470.

Hope, J (1979), *Protective Security Review, Report (Unclassified Version)*, AGPS, Canberra.

Hosenball, Mark; Zengerle, Patricia (2013), *Cyber attacks are leading threat against US: spy agencies*, Reuters, 12 March.

Human Rights and Equal Opportunity Commission (1991), *Racist Violence*, Report of the National Inquiry into Racist Violence in Australia, Australian Government Publishing Service Canberra, <https://www.humanrights.gov.au/sites/default/files/document/publication/NIRV.pdf>, last viewed 18.03.2019.

IMF (2000a), *Offshore Financial Centres IMF, Background Paper*, Monetary and Exchange Affairs Department, 23 June.

IMF (2000b), *Issues surrounding Work on Offshore Financial Centres*, IMF Board reviews, 26 July.

Irwin, Angela S.M.; Milad, George (2016), *The use of crypto-currencies in funding violent jihad*, Journal of Money Laundering Control, Vol. 19(4), pp. 407–425.

Jack, R.B. (1993), in *International Efforts to Combat Money Laundering: the Role of the financial Action Task Force*, The Hume Papers On Public Policy, Vol. 1, n°2, Summer, Edinburgh University Press, pp. x, xi.

Jakobi, Anja P (2015), *Global networks against crime: Using the Financial Action Task Force as a model?*, International Journal, Vol. 70(3), pp. 391–407.

Jensen, Neil (2008), *Creating an Environment in Australia Hostile to Money Laundering and Terrorism Financing: A Changing Role for AUSTRAC*, MqBJL, Vol. 5, pp. 93–110.

Johnston, Angus; Nanopoulos, Eva (2010), *New UK Supreme Court, the Separation of Powers and Anti-Terrorism Measures*, The Cambridge Law Journal, Vol. 69 (2), July, pp 217–220.

Jonsson, Michael; Cornell, Svante (2007), *Counter Terrorist Financing, Lessons from Europe*, Conflict & Security, Winter/Spring, pp. 69–78.

Jull David (2006), Parliamentary Joint Committee on Intelligence and Security, Review *of Security and Counter Terrorism Legislation*, December, (JULL report 2006).

Kean, Thomas H, Chair; Hamilton, Lee H, Vice Chair (2004), *The 9/11 Commission Report: final Report of the National Commission on Terrorist Attacks upon the United States*, authorised edition, New York, <www.911commission.gov/report/911Report.pdf>.

Kersten, Armand (2002), *Financing of Terrorism – A Predicate Offence to Money Laundering*, European *Journal of Law Reform*, Vol. 4, Issue 2, pp. 299–306.

Kahdem, Nassim (2017), *Panama Papers 2 is coming: ICIJ could release Australian links to Bermuda law firm Appleby*, The Sydney Morning Herald, 30.10.17.

Kowalczyk-Hoyer, Barbara; Heywood, Max (2017), *Top Secret Countries Keep Financial Crime Fighting Data to Themselves*, Transparency International, Berlin, Germany.

KPMG (2011), *Global Anti-Money Laundering Survey 2011, How banks are facing up to the challenge*, <*https://www.kpmg.com/Global/en/IssuesAndInsights/ArticlesPublications/Documents/anti-money-launderingv2.pdf*>, last viewed 10.09.2016.

Kupperman, Robert H (1994), Project Coordinator, Center for Strategic and International Studies (CSIS), at the Global Organized Crime Conference for high-level American law enforcement and intelligence community personnel, 26 September, Washington in Raine, Linnea P and Cilluffo Frank, *Global Organized Crime, The New Empire of Evil*, CSIS, Washington DC.

Laurens, Henry; Delmas-Marty, Mireille (2010), *Terrorismes, Histoire et Droit*, CNRS Editions, Paris.

LCA (2011) Law Council of Australia, Submission, 27.05.2011.

Leader-Elliott Ian (2002) for the Commonwealth Attorney-General's Department in association with the Australian Institute of Judicial Administration, *The Commonwealth Criminal Code – A Guide for Practitioners*, March.

Legal and Constitutional Affairs Legislation Committee (LCALC) (2011), *Australian Transaction Reports and Analysis Centre Supervisory Cost Recovery Levy Bill 2011*, June 2011.

Legrand, Tim (2018), *"More Symbolic—More Political—Than Substantive": An Interview with James R. Clapper on the U.S. Designation of Foreign Terrorist Organizations*, Terrorism and Political Violence, Vol. 30(2), pp. 356–372.

Leighton-Daly, Mathew (2015), *Money laundering offences: out with certainty, in with discretion?* Revenue Law Journal, Vol. 24(1), pp. 1–16.

Le Monde.fr with AFP (2007), *L'Espagne et la France veulent renforcer leur coopération contre l'ETA*, in 09.12.07.

Le Monde.fr with AFP (2009), *Les Moudjahidine* [*sic*] *du peuple rayés de la liste terroriste de l'UE*, 26.01.09.

Le Monde.fr with AFP (2010), *Le chef militaire présumé de l'ETA arrêté en Normandie*, 28.02.10.

Le Monde.fr with AFP (2011a), *Vaste opération policière contre les soutiens de l'ETA en Navarre et au Pays basque espagnol* in 18.01.11.

Le Monde.fr with AFP (2011b), *L'appareil politique de l'ETA s'autodissout*, 01.10.11.

Le Monde.fr with AFP (2012), *Washington retire les Moudjahidines du peuple de la liste des mouvements terroristes*, 28.09.2012.

Le Monde.fr with AFP (2018), *Financement du terrorisme: 416 donateurs de l'organisation Etat islamique identifiés*, 26.04.2018.

Le Monde.fr with AFP & Reuters (2011), *La possible existence d'un gang de tueurs nazis choque l'Allemagne*, 13.11.11.

Le Monde.fr with Reuters (2011), *La meurtrière cellule néonazie allemande serait liée au NPD*, 01.12.11.

Letts, Stephen (2017), Commonwealth Bank hit with fresh terrorism financing allegations by AUSTRAC, ABC News, <http://www.abc.net.au/news/2017-12-14/money-laundering-things-just-got-a-lot-worse-for-cba/9259034>, last viewed 09.05.2018.

Levi, Michael (1997), *Taking the Profit Out of Crime: The UK Experience*, European Journal of Crime, Criminal Law and Criminal Justice, Vol. 5/5, pp. 228–239.

Levi, Michael (2010), *Combating the Financing of Terrorism, a History and Assessment of the Control of 'Threat Finance'*, Brit. J. Criminol, 50, pp. 650–669.

Levi, Michael; Gilmore, William (2002), *Terrorist Finance, Money Laundering and the Rise of Mutual Evaluation: A New Paradigm for Crime Control*, 4 Eur. J.L. Reform, pp. 337–364.

Levi, Michael; Reuter, Peter; Halliday, Terence (2018), *Can the AML system be evaluated without better data?*, Crime, Law and Social Change, Vol.69(2), pp. 307–328.

Lichtblau, Eric; Risen, James (2006), *Bank Data Is Sifted by U.S. in Secret to Block Terror*, The New York Times, 22.06.2006, <http://www.nytimes.com/2006/06/23/washington/23intel.html?hp&ex=1151121600&en=18f9ed2cf37511d5&ei=5094&partner=homepage>, last viewed 19.03.2019.

Liss, Carolin; Sharman, J.C. (2014), *Global corporate crime-fighters: Private transnational responses to piracy and money laundering*, Review of International Political Economy, pp. 1–26.

Lindsey, Lawrence (1999), *Invading financial privacy*, Financial Times, March 19.

Lloyd of Berwick Rt Hon Lord (1996), *Inquiry into Legislation Against Terrorism*, Vol. 2, October, CMD3420.

Lusty, David (2002), *Civil forfeiture of proceeds of crime in Australia*, Journal of Money Laundering Control. London, Spring, Vol. 5(4), pp. 345–359.

Lynch, Andrew; McGarrity, Nicola; Williams, George (2009), *The Proscription of Terrorist Organisations in Australia*, Federal Law Review, Vol. 37, pp. 1–40.

Lynch, Andrew; McGarrity, Nicola; Williams, George (2015), *Inside Australia's anti-terrorism laws and trials,* NewSouth Publishing, UNSW Press Ltd.

Magnusson, Dan (2009), *The costs of implementing the anti-money laundering regulations in Sweden,* Journal of Money Laundering Control, Vol. 12(2), pp. 101–112.

Makarenko, Tamara; Mesquita, Michael (2014), *Categorising the crime–terror nexus in the European Union,* Global Crime, Vol. 15(3–4), pp. 259–274.

Manacorda, Stephano (ed.) (2002), *L'infraction d'organisation criminelle en Europe (Allemagne-Espagne-France-Italie-Union Européenne),* Association de recherches pénales européennes, Programme Falcone 1998 de l'Union Européenne, Publication de la Faculté de Droit et des Sciences sociales de Poitiers, Tome 43, Presses Universitaires de France (PUF), pp. 231–321.

Mark, Steve (2008), *Implementing Anti-Money Laundering Legislation and the Professions,* Symposium on Money Laundering Tax Evasion and Tax Havens, Faculty of Economics and Business, University of Sydney, 7 November.

Marty, Dick (2007), Rapporteur, *United Nations Security Council and European Union blacklists,* Report, Committee on Legal Affairs and Human Rights, Parliamentary Assembly, Council of Europe, Doc. 11454, 16.11.2007.

Marty, Dick (2008), Rapporteur, *United Nations Security Council and European Union blacklists,* Addendum to the report, Committee on Legal Affairs and Human Rights, Parliamentary Assembly, Council of Europe, Doc. 11454 Addendum, 22.01.2008.

Masciandaro, Donato (2006), *Offshore centres post 9/11 economics and politics,* Journal of Money Laundering Control, Vol. 9, N°4, pp. 365–372.

Maspoli, Philippe (2012), *Un trafiquant a vendu 13 kilos de coke,* 24 Heures, 03.10.12.

McClelland, Robert (2009), Attorney-General, Second reading speech, *Crimes Legislation Amendment (Serious and Organised Crime) Bill 2009,* 24 June 2009, pp. 6964–6967.

MCCOC (1992), Criminal Law Officers Committee of the Standing Committee of Attorneys-General, *Model Criminal Code,* final report, December 1992.

McCulloch, Jude; Pickering, Sharon; Mcqueen, Rob; Tham, Joo-Cheong; Wright-neville, David P (2004), *Suppressing the financing of terrorism [Contemporary Comments.]* Current Issues in Criminal Justice, Vol. 16, n°1, July, pp. 71–78.

McGarrity, Nicola (2008), *Review of the proscription of terrorist organisations: What role for procedural fairness?,* AJ Admin Law, Vol. 16, pp. 45–66.

McGarrity, Nicola (2010), *"Testing" our counter-terrorism laws: The prosecution of individuals for terrorism offences in Australia,* Criminal Law Journal, Vol. 34, pp. 92–127.

McGarrity, Nicola; Williams, George (2018) *The Proscription of Terrorist Organisations in Australia,* Terrorism and Political Violence, Vol. 30(2), pp. 216–235.

McNeil, Chris (2007), *The Australian anti-money laundering reform in the international context,* Journal of International Banking Law and Regulation, June, Vol. 22(6), pp. 340–347.

McSherry, Bernadette (2004), *Terrorism offences in the Criminal Code: broadening the boundaries of Australian criminal laws*, University of New South Wales Law Journal, Spring, Vol. 27(2), p. 354–372.

Meagher, Douglas QC (1983), *Organised Crime*, Australian Government Publishing Service, Canberra.

Menzies, Robert (1939), Prime Minister, Speech introducing the National Security Bill 1939 (Cth), *Parliamentary Debates*, House of Representatives, 7 September 1939, p. 164.

Michaelsen, Christopher (2009), *Kadi and Al Barakaat v Council of the European Union and Commission of the European Communities: The Incompatibility of the United Nations Security Council's 1267 Sanctions Regime with European Due Process Guarantees*, Melbourne Journal of International Law, May 2009, Vol. 10(1), pp. 329–345.

Michaelsen, Christopher (2010a), The Security Council's A*l Qaeda and Taliban Sanctions Regime: "Essential Tool" or Increasing Liability for the UN's Counterterrorism Efforts?*, Studies in Conflict and Terrorism, May, Vol. 33(5), pp. 448–463.

Michaelsen, Christopher (2010b), *The Security Council's Practice of Blacklisting Alleged Terrorists and Associates: Rule of Law Concerns and Prospects for Reform*, NZJPIL, Vol 8, pp. 71–89.

Michaelsen, Christopher (2010c), *Australia and the Threat of Terrorism in the Decade after 9/11*, Asian Journal of Political Science, Vol. 18, n°3, December, pp. 248–268.

Milaj, Jonida; Kaiser, Carolin (2017), *Retention of data in the new Anti-money Laundering Directive – 'need to know' versus 'nice to know'*, International Data Privacy Law, Vol. 7, N°2, pp. 115–125.

Mitsilegas, Valsamis (2003), *Money Laundering Counter-measures in the European Union, A New Paradigm of Security Governance versus Fundamental Principles*, European Business Law & Practice Series, Kluwer Law International.

Moffitt, Athol (1985), *A Quarter to Midnight – The Australian Crisis: Organised Crime and the Decline of the Institutions of State*, Angus and Robertson, London.

Morris, Tim (2008), Assistant Commissioner, AFP, *Submission* to the Parliamentary Joint Committee on the Australian Crime Commission, *Inquiry into the legislative arrangements to outlaw serious and organised crime groups Committee Hansard*, 6 November.

Morrison, Shona (2002), *Approaching Organised Crime: Where Are We Now and Where Are We Going?*, n°231, Australian Institute of Criminology, Australian Government, Canberra.

National Counter-Terrorism Committee (2003), *National Counter-Terrorism Plan*, Australian Government, June.

Naylor, R T (2003a), *Predators, Parasites or Free Market Pioneers: Reflections on the nature and analysis of profit driven crime*, in Beare, *Critical reflections on Transnational*

Organized crime, Money Laundering and Corruption, University of Toronto Press, Canada, pp. 35–54.

Naylor, R T (2003b), *Towards a general theory of profit driven crimes*, The British Journal of Criminology, Vol. 43(1), pp. 81–101.

Neilsen, Mary Anne (2006), *Financial Transaction Reports Amendment Bill 2006*, n°21, 2006–07, ISSN 1328-8091, Law and Bills Digest Section, Department of Parliamentary Services, Parliament of Australia, 11 September.

NHRC (2009), *National Human Rights Consultation Report*, Commonwealth of Australia, ISBN 978-1-921241-89-5.

Oftedal Emilie (2015), *The financing of jihadi terrorist cells in Europe*, Norwegian Defence Research Establishment (FFI), FFI-rapport 2014/02234, January, <https://www.ffi.no/no/Rapporter/14-02234.pdf>, last viewed 27.04.2018.

O'sullivan, Paul (2007), ASIO's Director-General, address to the Australian National Security Conference 2007 – *National Security Intelligence and Counter-Terrorism*, 27.02.2007.

Odgers, Stephen (2010), *Principles of Federal Criminal Law*, Second Edition, Lawbook Co, Thomson Reuters Australia Ltd.

Öhlén, Mats (2009), *Al-Barakaat has been removed from terror list*, Stockholmnew.com, 16.10.2009.

Passas, Nikos (2006), *Setting global CFT standards: a critique and suggestions*, Journal of Money Laundering Control, Vol. 9, No.3, pp. 281–292.

Peretti-Watel, Patrick (2006), *L'expert, le profane et le terrorisme: quelques éléments de réflexion socioloque*, Canadian Journal of Criminology and Criminal Justice, Vol. 48(3), pp. 383–395.

Pieth, Mark (1998), *Prevention of Money Laundering: A Comparative Analysis*, 6 Eur. J. Crime Crim. L. & Crim. Justice, pp. 159–168.

Pieth, Mark (2002), *Financing of Terrorism: Following the Money*, European Journal of Law Reform, Vol. 4 (2), pp. 365–376.

Pieth, Mark; Aiolfi, Gemma (2003a), *Anti-Money Laundering: Levelling the Playing Field*, Basel Institute Governance.

Pieth, Mark; Aiolfi, Gemma (2003b), *The private sector become active: the Wolfsberg process*, Journal of Financial Crime, Vol. 10(4), pp. 359–365.

Pieth, Mark; Aiolfi, Gemma (2004), *A Comparative Guide to Anti-Money Laundering – A Critical Analysis of Systems in Singapore, Switzerland, the UK and the USA*, Edward Elgar, Cheltenham, UK.

Parliamentary Joint Committee on Human Rights (2014), *Offence Provisions, Civil Penalties and Human Rights*' (Guidance Note No 2).

Parliamentary Joint Committee on Law Enforcement (2012), *Inquiry into Commonwealth Unexplained Wealth Legislation and Arrangements* (March).

PJC-ACC (2007), Parliamentary Joint Committee on the Australian Crime Commission, *Inquiry into the future impact of serious and organised crime on Australian society*, September.

PJC-ACC (2009), Parliamentary Joint Committee on the Australian Crime Commission, *Inquiry into the legislative arrangements to outlaw serious and organised crime groups*, August.

PJC on ASIO, ASIS and DSD – Parliamentary Joint Committee on ASIO, ASIS and DSD (2005), *Review of the listing of six terrorist organisations*, March.

PJC-IS (2006), Parliamentary Joint Committee on Intelligence and Security, *Review of Security and Counter Terrorism Legislation,* December.

PJC-IS (2007a), Parliamentary Joint Committee on Intelligence and Security, *Inquiry into the proscription of "terrorism organisations" under the Australian Criminal Code,* September, (JULL report 2007).

PJC-IS (2007b), Parliamentary Joint Committee on Intelligence and Security, *Review of the re-listing of ASG, JuA, GIA and GSPC*, February.

PJC-IS (2008), Parliamentary Joint Committee on Intelligence and Security, *Review of the re-listing of the Kurdistan Workers' Party (PKK)*, the Parliament of the Commonwealth of Australia, Canberra, June.

PJC-IS (2018), *Review of police stop, search and seizure powers, the control order regime and the preventative detention order regime, Division 3A of Part IAA of the Crimes Act 1914; Divisions 104 and 105 of the Criminal Code,* February.

Pozen, David E (2005), *The Mosaic Theory, National Security and the Freedom of Information Act.* Yale Law Journal 115, pp. 628–679.

Pricewaterhouse Coopers LLP (2003), *Anti-money laundering current customer review cost benefit analysis,* The Financial Services Authority, London, ISBN: 0117047031, 23 May, <http://www.fsa.gov.uk/pubs/other/ml_cost-benefit.pdf>.

Quaedvlieg, Roman Alexander (2009), Acting Deputy Commissioner, Operations, Australian Federal Police, Official Committee Hansard, SLCLC, 29 October.

Real Assurance Risk Management Limited (2006), *Estimation of FSA Administrative Burdens,* June, <http://www.fsa.gov.uk/pubs/other/Admin_Burdens_Report_20060621.pdf>.

Redlich, Robert (1984), *Annual Report of the Office of Special Prosecutor 1983–4.*

Reuter, Peter (1996), *The Mismeasurement of Illegal Drug Markets*, in Pozo, Susan, pp. 63–80.

Reuter, Peter; Truman, Edwin M (2004), *Chasing Dirty Money: The Fight against Money Laundering*, Washington, DC: Institute for International Economics.

Reuter, Peter; Truman, Edwin M (2005), *Anti-money laundering overkill ? It's time to ask how well the system is working,* The International Economy, Wntr, Vol.19(1), pp. 56–60.

Ricketts, Aiden (2002), *Freedom of Association or Guilt by Association: Australia's New Anti-Terrorism Laws and the Retreat of Political Liberty,* Southern Cross University Law Review, Vol. 6, pp. 133–150.

Roberge, Ian (2007), *Misguided policies in the war on terror? The case for disentangling terrorist financing,* Politics, Vol. 27(3) Oct, pp. 196–203.

Robert, Emilie (2012), *L'Etat de droit et la lutte contre le terrorisme dans l'Union européenne – Mesures européennes de lutte contre le terrorisme suite aux attentats du 11 septembre 2001,* Thèse pour obtenir le grade de Docteur en droit, Université Lille 2 – Droit et Santé, Présentée et soutenue publiquement le 16 février 2012.

Roele, Isobel (2013), *Disciplinary Power and the UN Security Council Counter Terrorism Committee,* Journal of Conflict & Security Law, Vol. 19, pp. 49–84.

Romaniuk, Peter; Keatinge, Tom (2018), *Protecting charities from terrorists … and counterterrorists: FATF and the global effort to prevent terrorist financing through the non-profit sector,* Crime, Law and Social Change, Vol. 69(2), pp. 265–282.

Roos, Oscar; Hayward, Benjamin; Morss, John (2010–2011), *Beyond the Separation of Powers: Judicial Review and the Regulatory Proscription of Terrorist Organisations,* UWA Law Review, Vol. 35, pp. 81–118.

Rosand, Eric (2005), *Security Council as 'global legislator' – ultra vires or ultra innovative,* Fordham International Law Journal, Vol. 28, pp. 542–590.

Rose, Gregory L; Nestorovska, Diana (2007), *Australia counter-terrorism offences: necessity and clarity in federal criminal law reforms,* Criminal Law Journal, Feb 2007, Vol. 31(1), pp. 20–55.

Roy, Olivier (2004), *Al-Qaida, label ou organisation?,* Le Monde diplomatique, Septembre, pp. 24–25.

RSR.ch (2011), *Les envois de fonds des migrants vers les pays pauvres en hausse de 8% en 2011 à 351 milliards de dollars,* Broadcast of 02 December 2011, at 15:38.

Safi, Michael (2015), *The human cost of ending money transfers to war-torn countries,* The Guardian, 9 April.

Sarre, Rick (2017), *Metadata Retention as a Means of Combatting Terrorism and Organised Crime: A Perspective from Australia,* Asian Criminology, Vol. 12, pp. 167–179.

Sathye, Milind (2008), *Estimating the cost of compliance of AML/CTF for financial institutions in Australia,* Journal of Financial Crime, Vol. 15 n°4, pp. 347–363, <www.emeraldinsight.com/1359-0790.htm3>.

Saul, Ben (2007), *The curious Element of Motive in Definitions of Terrorism: Essential Ingredient or Criminalising Thought*? in Lynch, Andrew; Macdonald, Edwina; Williams George, *Law and Liberty in the War on Terror,* The Federation Press, Sydney, pp. 28–38.

Saul, Ben (2008), *Submission* to Parliamentary Joint Committee on the Australian Crime Commission, *Inquiry into the legislative arrangements to outlaw serious and organised crime groups,* 18 June.

Schloenhardt, Andreas (2009), *Palermo on the Pacific Rim, Organised Crime offences in the Asia-Pacific Region*, UNODC, Regional Centre for East Asia and the Pacific, Study Series n°1, August.

Sentas, Victoria (2011), *Terrorist Organisation Offences and the LTTE: R v Vinayagamoorthy*, 22 Current Issues Crim. Just. 159 (2010–2011), pp. 159–169.

Sheller, Simon (2006), *Report*, Security Legislation Review Committee (SLRC), Parliament of Australia, June.

Shelley, Louise I (1995), *Transnational Organized Crime: An Imminent Threat to the Nation-State ?*, Journal of International Affairs, Winter, Vol. 48(2), pp. 463–589.

Shelley, Louise I; Picarelli, John T (2005), *Methods Not Motives: Exploring Links Between Transnational Organized Crime and International Terrorism*, Trends in Organized Crime, Vol. 9(2), pp. 52–67.

Sherman, Tom AO (1991), *Taken to the Cleaners: Money Laundering in Australia*, Vol. 1, NCA.

Sherman, Tom AO (1993), in *International Efforts to Combat Money Laundering: the Role of the Financial Action Task Force*, The Hume Papers On Public Policy, Vol. 1, n°2, Summer, Edinburgh University Press.

Sherman, Tom AO (2006), *Report on the Independent Review of the Operation of the Proceeds of Crime Act 2002 (Cth)*, 20.07.2006.

Simonova, Anna (2011), *The risk-based approach to anti-money laundering: problems and solutions*, Journal of Money Laundering Control, Vol.14, n°4, pp. 346–358.

Senate Standing Committee for the Scrutiny of Bills (2009), *10th Report of 2009*, 09.09.2009.

SLC-ALC (2002), Senate Legal and Constitutional Affairs Legislation Committee, Proof Committee Hansard, Reference: Security Legislation Amendment (Terrorism) Bill 2002 and related bills.

SLC-ALC (2009), Senate Legal and Constitutional Affairs Legislation Committee, *Crimes Legislation Amendment (Serious and Organised Crime) Bill (No.2) 2009 [Provisions]*, Nov.

Smith, Russell G; Mccusker, Rob; Walters, Julie (2010), *Financing of terrorism: risks for Australia*, Trends & Issues in Crime and Criminal Justice, May 1, Australian Institute of Criminology, Australian Government, Canberra, pp. 1–6.

SSC-LCA (1988), Senate Standing Committee on Legal and Constitutional Affairs, *Report on the Cash Transaction Reports Bill 1987*.

SSC-LCA (1993), Senate Standing Committee on Legal and Constitutional Affairs *Checking the Cash – A Report on the Effectiveness of the Financial Transaction Reports Act 1988*.

Stessens, Guy (2000), *Money Laundering, a New International Law enforcement model*, academic dissertation, Cambridge University Press.

Stessens, Guy (2006), *Money Laundering*, International Review of Penal Law, Vol. 77, pp. 203–209.

Sullivan, Clare; Smith, Evan (2012), *Trade-based money laundering: Risks and regulatory responses*, Research and Public Policy Series n°115, Australian Institute of Criminology, Australian Government, Canberra.

Tapley, Mark (2002), *Suppression of the Financing of Terrorism Bill 2002*, Information and research services, Law and Bills Digest Group, Department of the Parliamentary Library, Bills Digest No.127, 2001–02,1 May.

Tavares, Cynthia; Thomas Geoffrey; Roudaut Mickaël (2011), *Money Laundering in Europe, Report of Work Carried Out by Eurostat and DG Home Affairs, Eurostat* Methodologies and Working Paper, November, ISSN 1977-037, <http://www.fi.ee/failid/Money_Laundering_in_Europe_Eurostat_and_DG_Home_Affairs_2010.pdf>, last viewed 20.03.2019.

Tham, Joo-Cheong (2007), *A Risk-Based Analysis of Australia's Counterterrorism Financing Regime*, Soc Justice 34, n°2, pp. 138–152.

The Canberra Times (1985), *Royal commission report Nugan Hand 'not into drugs, arms'*, 28.11.1985, <http://trove.nla.gov.au/newspaper/page/13764778?>, last viewed 20.03.2019.

Theguardian.com (2016), *Ten arrested in Netherlands over bitcoin money-laundering allegations*, 21.01.2016.

Theguardian.com (2017a), Commonwealth Bank accused of money laundering and terrorism-financing breaches, 03.08.17.

Theguardian.com (2017b), Commonwealth Bank accused of more anti-money laundering law breaches, 14.12.2017.

The Economist (2001), *Getting to Them Through Their Money*, 27.09.2001, <http://www.economist.com/node/798424>, last viewed 20.03.2019.

Thomson, Kevin (2010), *Afghanistan Speech*, Ministerial Statements, Main Committee, House of House of Representatives, Hansard 26 October 2010, pp. 1725–1727.

Thomson, Kevin (2012), *Iran Speech*, Private Members' Business, House of Representatives, Hansard 13 February 2012, p. 943.

Todorov, Tzvetan (2012), *Les ennemis intimes de la démocratie*, Robert Laffont, Paris.

Tully, Stephen (2010), *Implementing Targeted Sanctions in Australia: A Role for Procedural Fairness*, Australian Journal of Administrative Law, Vol.18 (1), pp. 44–58.

Tyre, Colin QC (2010), *Anti-money laundering legislation: implementation of the FATF forty recommendations in the European Union*, Journal of the Professional Lawyer, Annual, pp. 69–82.

Tzanakopoulos, Antonios (2010), *United Nations Sanctions in Domestic Courts: From Interpretation to Defiance in Abdelrazik v. Canada*, Journal of International Criminal Justice, 8, pp. 249–267.

Tzanakopoulos Antonios (2011), *Disobeying the Security Council – Countermeasures against Wrongful Sanctions*, Oxford University Press.

UN (2005), *Report of the Eleventh United Nations Congress on Crime Prevention and Criminal Justice*, Bangkok, 18–25 April 2005, A/CONF.203/18, 17.05.2005.

UN High Commissioner for Human Rights (2009), *Report on the protection of human rights and fundamental freedoms while countering terrorism*, A/HRC/12/22, 02.09.2009.

UN Press Release (2012), *Security Council Al-Qaida Sanctions Committee Deletes One Individual and 17 Entities from its List*, SC/10549, Department of Public Information, News and Media Division, New York, 21 February 2012, <www.un.org/News/Press/docs/2012/sc10549.doc.htm>.

Unger, Brigitte (2013), *Can Money Laundering Decrease?*, Public Finance Review, Vol. 41(5), pp. 658–676.

Unger, Brigitte; Van Waarden, Frans (2009), *How to Dodge Drowning in Data? Rule- and Risk-Based Anti Money Laundering Policies Compared*, Review of Law & Economics, Vol. 5(2), pp. 953–985.

UNODC (2003a), *Legislative Guide to the Universal Anti-Terrorism Conventions and Protocols*, New York.

UNODC (2003b) *Model Terrorist Financing Bill (for Common Law States)*.

UNODC (2010), *The Globalization of Crime, A Transnational Organized Crime Threat Assessment*, Vienna.

UNODC (2011), *Estimating illicit financial flows resulting from drug trafficking and other transnational organized crimes*, Research Report.

UNODC (2014), *Reported outcome of the expert group meeting on the management, use and disposal of frozen, seized and confiscated assets*, held in Reggio Calabria, Italy, from 2 to 4 April 2014, CAC/COSP/WG.2/2014/CRP, 08.08.2014.

UNODC (2015), *Annual Report*.

UNODC (2016), *Transnational organized crime – the globalized illegal economy*, retrieved from UNODC webpage, 10.09.2016.

US Department of State (2015), *Money Laundering and Financial Crimes*, International Narcotics Control Strategy Report (INCSR), Vol II, Bureau for International Narcotics and Law Enforcement Affairs, March.

Van Den Wijngaert, Christine (1980), *The political offence exception: The delicate problem of balancing rights of the individual and the international public order*, Kluwer.

Van Duyne, Petrus C (1997), *Organized crime, corruption and power*, Crime, Law and Social Change, Vol. 26(3), pp. 201–238.

Van Duyne, Petrus C (2003), *Money laundering policy: Fears and facts*, in Van Duyne Petrus , Von Lampe Klaus and Newell James (Eds), Crim*inal Finances and Organising Crime in Europe*, Nijmegen, The Netherlands: Wolf Legal Publishers, pp. 72–109.

Vidino, Lorenzo; Marone, Francesco; Entenmann, Eva (2017), *Fear thy neighbor – radicalization and jihadist attacks in the West*, edizioni LediPublishing, Milano, Italy, June.

Vlcek, William (2004), *The OECD and Offshore Financial Centres: Rearguard Action against Globalisation?*, Global Change, Peace & Security, Vol.16, n°3, October, pp. 227–242.

Vlcek, William (2007), *Surveillance to Combat Terrorist Financing in Europe: Whose Liberty, Whose Security?*, European Security, Vol. 16(1), pp. 99–119.

Vlcek, William (2008), A *Leviathan Rejuvenated: Surveillance, Money Laundering, and the War on Terror*, International Journal of Politics, Culture and Society, Sep, Vol. 20, pp. 21–40.

Vlcek, William (2018), *Global financial governance and the informal: limits to the regulation of money*, Crime, Law and Socical Change, March, Vol. 69(2), pp. 249–264.

Vogel, Joachim (1997), *Geldwäsche, ein europaweit harmonisierter Straftatbestand?*, Zeitschrift für die gesamte Strafrechtswissenschaft, Vol. 109, Issue 2, pp. 335–356.

Volk, Klaus (2002), *La riposte pénale contre les organisations criminelles en droit allemand*, in Collective (2002), Manacorda Stephano, coordinator, *L'infraction d'organisation criminelle en Europe (Allemagne-Espagne-France-Italie-Union Européenne)*, Association de recherches pénales européennes, Programme Falcone 1998 de l'Union Européenne, Publication de la Faculté de Droit et des Sciences sociales de Poitiers, Tome 43, Presses Universitaires de France (PUF), pp. 7–57.

Walker, Bret SC (2013), *Independent National Security Legislation Monitor Annual Report.*

Walker, Bret SC (2014), *Independent National Security Legislation Monitor Annual Report.*

Walker, John (1995), *Estimates of the Extent of Money Laundering in and through Australia*, prepared for Australian Transaction Reports and Analysts Center, John Walker Consulting Services, Queanbeyan, NSW, September.

Walker, John (2004), *Estimates of the Extent of Money Laundering in and through Australia in 2004*, AUSTRAC, RMIT University.

Walker, Clive (2018), *"They haven't gone away you know". The Persistence of Proscription and the Problems of Deproscription*, Terrorism and Political Violence, Vol. 30(2), pp. 236–258.

Walters, Julie; Smith, Russel G; Davis, Brent; Choo, Raymond Kim-Kwang; Chadwick, Hanna (2012), *The anti-money laundering and counter-terrorism financing regime in Australia: Perceptions of regulated businesses in Australia,* Research and Public Policy Series n°117, Australian Institute of Criminology, Australian Government, Canberra.

Warde, Ibrahim (2007), *The Price of Fear, Al-queada and the truth behind the financial war on terro*r, I B Tauris & Co Ltd, London & New York.

Watson, Graham (2003), European Parliament Debates, 03.12.2003.

Weigend, Thomas (1996), *The Criminal Justice Systems facing the Challenge of Organised Crime*, Section I, General Part, Preparatory for the XVIth International Congress of Penal Law, Theme Commentary, Questions Commentary, International Review of Penal Law, Vol. 67, n°3 + 4.

Weinberg, Mark QC (1989), *The Proceeds of Crime Act 1987 – New despotism or measured response?*, Monash University Law Review, Vol. 15 n°3 and 4, pp. 201–218.

Wesseling, Mara (2013), *The European fight against terrorism financing: Professional fields and new governing practices*, PhD thesis, Amsterdam Institute for Social Science Research (AISSR), <http://dare.uva.nl/document/2/126131>, last viewed 21.03.2019.

West, Michael (2015), *Tax avoidance as bad as bottom of the harbour schemes*, the Sydney Morning Herald, 10.02.2015, <http://www.smh.com.au/business/tax-avoidance-as-bad-as-bottom-of-the-harbour-schemes-20150209-13adf3.html>, last viewed 20 July 2016.

Wille, Paul (2009), Question écrite n° 4-5401 du 7 décembre 2009 au vice-premier ministre et ministre des Affaires étrangères et des Réformes institutionnelles, <www.senate.be/www/?MIval=/Vragen/SchriftelijkeVraag&LEG=4&NR=5401&LANG=fr>, last viewed 30 May 2015.

Williams, George (2002), *One Year On, Australia's legal response to September 11*, Alternative Law Journal, October, Vol. 27(5), pp. 212–232.

Williams, George (2003), *Australian Values and the War against Terrorism*, University of New South Wales Law Journal, Vol. 26, pp. 191–199.

Williams, George (2011), *A decade of Australian anti-terror laws*, Melbourne University Law Review, Vol. 35, pp. 1136–1176.

Woodiwiss, Michael (2003), *Transnational Organized crime: the strange career of an American concept,* in Beare, Margaret E, *Critical reflections on Transnational Organized crime, Money Laundering and Corruption*, University of Toronto Press, Canada, pp. 3–34.

Woodiwiss, Michael; Hobbs, Dick (2009), *Moral panics and the rhetoric of organized crime policing in America and Britain*, The British Journal of Criminology, Vol. 49(1), pp. 106–128.

World Bank Group (2015), *Bringing the 2 Billion Unbanked into the Financial System*, Findex Notes, April. <http://www.worldbank.org/en/programs/globalfindex>, last accessed 19.04.2018.

Wright, Penny (2012), Senator, Second Reading Speech, Independent National Security Legislation Monitor (Improved Oversight and Resourcing) Bill 2014, Hansard, 3 December 2014, pp. 10065–10069.

Court Cases and Legal Opinions

A Ansari v R, H Ansari v R [2007] NSWCCA 204.

A, K and M v HM Treasury [2010] UKSC 2.

A, K, M, Q & G v HM Treasury [2008] EWCA Civ 1187 (30 October 2008).

A, K, M, Q & G v HM Treasury [2008] EWHC 869 (Admin) (24 April 2008).

Abdelrazik v *Canada* (*Minister of Foreign Affairs*) 2009 FC 580; [2010] 1 FCR 267 (T-727-08), Judgment of 2009.

Ahmed Ali Yusuf and Al Barakaat International Foundation v *Council of the European Union and Commission of the European Communities*, Case T-306/01, Judgment of the Court of First Instance (Second Chamber, extended composition), 21 September 2005, ECR II-3533 (*Yusuf and Al Barakaat 2005*).

Alister Alister v R [1983] HCA 45, (1984) 154 CLR 404.

Ansari v R [2010] 241 CLR 299.

A. and Others v The United Kingdom, Application n°3455/05, Judgment of 19 February 2009.

Benbrika and Ors v The Queen (2010) 29 VR 593.

Burns v Ransley [1949] 79 CLR 101.

CMHV and Director-General of Security and Minister for Foreign Affairs [2017] AATA 1547 (22 September 2017).

Denlay v Commissioner of Taxation (2010) 276 ALR 675, [2010] FCA 1434.

Digital Rights Ireland Ltd, Joint Cases C-293/12 and C-594/12, Judgment of the Court (Grand Chamber), Preliminary ruling, 08.04.2014.

Director of Public Prosecutions (DPP) (Cth) – RE Section 19 of the Proceeds of Crime Act 2002; RE funds in a bank account; RE worldwide Holdings Ltd and South East Group Ltd, 01.03.2005, [2005] NSWSC 117, 400.

Drake v Minister for Immigration and Ethnic Affairs (1979) 46 FLR 409.

European Commission, United Kingdom of Great Britain and Northern Ireland, and the Council of the European Union v. Yassin Abdullah Kadi, Joined Cases C-584/10 P, C-593/10 P and C-595/10 P, Judgment of the Court (Grand Chamber), 18 July 2013 (*Kadi* – 4 or *Kadi CJEU II*).

European Parliament v Council of the European Union (Case C-130/10), Judgment of the Court (Grand Chamber), 19 July 2012.

French Republic v People's Mojahedin Organization of Iran, Case C-27/09 P, Judgment of the Court (Grand Chamber) of 21 December 2011, (*PMOI GC–3*).

Giorgianni v R [1985] 156 CLR 473.

Haneef v Minister for Immigration and Citizenship [2007] FCA 1273.

Hann v DPP (Cth) (2004) 144 A Crim R 534; [2004] SASC 86 16.

Hannes v The Director of Public Prosecutions (Cth) (No.2) [2006] NSWCCA 373.

Harmeet Singh v R [2016] VSCA 163.

Heng-Sheng Lin v R [2015] NSWCCA 204, (unreported).

HM Treasury v Mohammed Jabar Ahmed and others (FC); HM Treasury v Mohammed al-Ghabra (FC); R (Hani El Sayed Sabaei Youssef) v HM Treasury [2010] UKSC 2 (SC).

Home Secretary v AF (N°3) [2009] UKHL 28.

Leask v Commonwealth [1996] 187 CLR 579.

Lee v R [2007] NSWCCA 71 [14].

Leghaei v Director General of Security [2005] FCA 1576.

Lord Alton of Liverpool & Others (In the Matter of The People's Mojahadeen Organisation of Iran) v Secretary of State for the Home Department, Proscribed Organisations Appeal Commission (POAC), Appeal No: PC/02/2006, 30th November 2007 (PMOI POAC – 1).

Maximillian Schrems v Data Protection Commissioner, Case C-362/14, Jugement of the Court (Grand Chamber), Preliminary ruling, 06.10.2015.

Mansour Leghaei et al v Australia, Communication N°1937/2010, U.N. Doc. CCPR/C113/D/1937/2010, 28 April 2015.

Minister for Immigration & Citizenship v Haneef [2007] FCAFC 203.

Milne v R (2014) 305 ALR 477; [2014] HCA 4.

Nabil Sayadi and Patricia Vinck v Belgium, Communication N°1472/2006, U.N. Doc. CCPR/C/94/D/1472/2006, 22 October 2008.

Nada v Switzerland (Application 1059/08), Judgment of Grand Chamber, 12 September 2012.

Nahlous v R [2010] NSWCCA 58.

Opinion 1/15 of the Court (Grand Chamber) on the envisaged agreement between Canada and the European Union on the transfer and processing of Passenger Name Record data, 26 July 2017. <http://curia.europa.eu/juris/document/document_print.jsf;jsessionid=9ea7d0f130de30bb75260d194edea48db3901a52c95c.e34KaxiLc3eQc40LaxqMbN4Pb34Teo?doclang=EN&text=&pageIndex=0&docid=193216&cid=357344>, last viewed 03.04.2019.

Opinion of Avocate General BOT, Joined Cases C-584/10 P, C-593/10 P and C-595/10 P, European Commission Council of the European Union, United Kingdom of Great Britain and Northern Ireland v Yassin Abdullah Kadi, 19 March 2013.

Organisation des Modjahedines du peuple d'Iran v Council, Case T-228/ 02, Judgment of the Court of First Instance (Second Chamber), 12 December 2006 (*OMPI CFI – 1*).

People's Mojahedin Organization of Iran v *Council of the European Union,* Case T-256/07, Judgment of the Court of First Instance (Seventh Chamber), 23 October 2008, (*PMOI CFI – 2*).

R v Anderson (1991) 53 A Crim R 421.

R v Demirian [1989] VR 97.

R v Evan Dunstan Pederick [1996] NSWSC 623.

R v Benbrika (Ruling No 35) [2009] VSC 142.

R v Izhar Ul-Haque (unreported, NSW Supreme Court, 8 February 2006).

R v Khawaja [2006] O.J. N°4245; 2006 ON.C. LEXIS 4158, judgement of the Ontario Superior Court of Justice, 24 October 2006.

R v LK; R v RK [2010] 241 CLR 177.

R v Lodhi [2005] NSWSC 1377 (23 December 2005).

R v Lodhi [2006] NSWSC 584.

R (Cth) v Milne (No 1) [2010] NSWCCA; 259 FLR 42.

R v Van Loi Nguyen [2010] NSWCCA 226.

R v Vinayagamoorthy & Ors [2010] VSC 148.

R v Yi-Hua Jiao [2015] NSWCCA 95 (unreported).

Schembri v R [2010] NSWCCA 149.

Secretary of State for the Home Department v Lord Alton of Liverpool and Others, [2008] EWCA Civ 443, Case No: 2007/9516, Royal Courts of Justice, 7 May 2008, (*PMOI POAC – 2*).

Shi v R [2014] NSWCCA 276 [41, 42].

State of South Australia v Slipper (2004) 136 FCR 259.

State v Coetzee [1997] 2 LRC 593 [220] at 677.

Tan v R (2011) 35 VR 109; [2011] VSCA 427 [33].

Tele2 Sverige AB & Tom Watson, C-203/15 and C-698/15, Judgment of the Court (Grand Chamber), 21.12.2016.

Thomas v Mowbray [2007] 233 CLR 307.3.

Thorn v R [2009] NSWCCA 294.

Trandy v R [2009] VSCA 321.

Yassin Abdullah Kadi v Council of the European Union and Commission of the European Communities, Case T-315/01, Judgment of the Court of First Instance (Second Chamber, Extended Composition), 21 September 2005, ECR II-3649 (*Kadi* – 1 or *Kadi GC I*).

Yassin Abdullah Kadi v European Commission, Case T-85/09, Judgment of the General Court (Seventh Chamber), 30 September 2010, (*Kadi* – 3 or *Kadi GC II*).

Yassin Abdullah Kadi, Al Barakaat v Council of the European Union, Case C-415/05 P (Joined Cases C-402/05 P, C-415/05 P), Judgment of the Court (Grand Chamber) of 3 September 2008, (*Kadi* – 2 or *Kadi CJEU I*).

Index

www.ingramcontent.com/pod-product-compliance
Lightning Source LLC
Chambersburg PA
CBHW031321230926
51848CB00001B/45
9789004359093